Joseph Cook

Christ and Modern Thought

Joseph Cook

Christ and Modern Thought

ISBN/EAN: 9783337165420

Printed in Europe, USA, Canada, Australia, Japan

Cover: Foto ©Lupo / pixelio.de

More available books at **www.hansebooks.com**

Boston Monday Lectures, 1880-81.

CHRIST

AND

MODERN THOUGHT.

With a Preliminary Lecture,

ON THE METHODS OF MEETING MODERN UNBELIEF,

By JOSEPH COOK.

E. B. WALSWORTH, ALBION, N. Y.

BOSTON:
ROBERTS BROTHERS.
1881.

Copyright, 1881,
BY ROBERTS BROTHERS.

UNIVERSITY PRESS:
JOHN WILSON & SON, CAMBRIDGE.

WHILE these lectures were delivered by gentlemen invited by the committee in charge of the Monday Lectureship, yet, in publishing this volume, the committee do not wish to be understood as being responsible for the views expressed.

Executive Committee.

Prof. E. P. GOULD, D.D., Newton Theological Institution.
Rev. WILLIAM M. BAKER, D.D.
President WM. F. WARREN, D.D., LL.D., Boston University.
Prof. L. T. TOWNSEND, D.D., Boston University.
ROBERT GILCHRIST.
Rev. GEO. Z. GRAY, D.D., Episcopal Theol. School, Cambridge.
Right Rev. Bishop PADDOCK, D.D.
Prof. E. N. HORSFORD.
Prof. J. P. GULLIVER, Andover Theological Seminary.
Rev. L. B. BATES.
Rev. J. L. WITHROW, D.D.
Rev. Bishop FOSTER, D.D., LL.D.

REV. A. J. GORDON, *Chairman.*

B. W. WILLIAMS, *Secretary and Treasurer.*

CONTENTS.

	PAGE
PRELIMINARY LECTURE. — METHODS OF MEETING MODERN UNBELIEF. By Joseph Cook	ix
I. THE SEEN AND THE UNSEEN. By Rt. Rev. Thomas M. Clark, D.D., LL.D.	1
II. MORAL LAW IN ITS RELATIONS TO PHYSICAL SCIENCE AND TO POPULAR RELIGION. By President E. G. Robinson, D.D., LL.D.	31
III. CHRISTIANITY AND THE MENTAL ACTIVITY OF THE AGE. By Rev. Thomas Guard, D.D.	61
IV. THE PLACE OF CONSCIENCE. By Rev. Mark Hopkins, D.D.	85
V. DEVELOPMENT: ITS NATURE; WHAT IT CAN DO AND WHAT IT CANNOT DO. By Rev. James McCosh, D.D., LL.D.	113
VI. A CALM VIEW OF THE TEMPERANCE QUESTION. By Chancellor Howard Crosby, D.D., LL.D.	141
VII. OLD AND NEW THEOLOGIES. By Rev. George R. Crooks, D.D., LL.D.	175
VIII. FACTS AS TO DIVORCE IN NEW ENGLAND. By Rev. Samuel W. Dike	197
IX. SIGNIFICANCE OF THE HISTORIC ELEMENT IN SCRIPTURE. By Rev. J. B. Thomas, D.D.	229
X. THE THEISTIC BASIS OF EVOLUTION. By Rev. John Cotton Smith, D.D.	285

METHODS OF MEETING MODERN UNBELIEF.

By JOSEPH COOK.

PRELIMINARY LECTURE.

By JOSEPH COOK.

METHODS OF MEETING MODERN UNBELIEF.

A Lecture delivered in the Memorial Hall, Farringdon Street, London, November 2, 1880, in connection with the Half-yearly Meeting of the London Congregational Union. Henry Wright, Esq., J.P., in the Chair.

THE PERILS OF GREAT CITIES.

CÆSAR could not drive around the Roman Empire in less than one hundred days; we now send a letter around the globe in ninety-six. London reaches all the zones as easily as Rome reached the territories of Augustus. You remember there was a day when a traveller might start from Alexandria, in Egypt, and, passing over the substantial basaltic pavement of the old Roman highways, drive to Carthage, then to Gibraltar, and on through Spain and France. He could then cross the Channel, drive north to the Scottish Border, return and go to Cologne, then to Milan, then under the shadows of the Alps and the Balkans to Constantinople, and so to Antioch and back to Alexandria, — a distance which could not be traversed in less than a hundred days. But not long ago there came a collection of more than three hundred mail-bags from Melbourne and Sydney to San Francisco; and they were four days ahead of time. The American Government asked the directors of our trans-continental lines to put them on a special train. They reached New York in six days from San Francisco; and if the Arizona, the speediest steamship afloat, did her duty, and your officers did theirs, these mails arrived here from more than half around the globe in forty-one days. There are no foreign lands.

Sursum corda! May God lift up our hearts to the breadth and to the height of our theme, so that we may not take provincial, insular, or even national views only. We want a Christian enterprise that shall at least fill the arms of England and America as they stretch towards the sunrise and towards the sunset. Perhaps God means to keep in order great portions of the human race by the arms of England and America stretched east and west, and ultimately locking hands. Only in this way can we obtain a "scientific frontier."

It is in our great cities that we are attacked; and it is there that our political arrangements are receiving their greatest strain. We are more and more, in the United States, aware of the perils of great cities. When you spoke, sir, of the unmanageability of London, I felt that in America we have more cause for fear than you. New York is a village yet, I know. When the bell strikes at noon in New York City there are about a million and a half of people within municipal limits; and in greater London you have four millions and a half. But we have not annexed to the city everything within twelve miles of our centre, as you have; we shall do it ultimately. In two centuries there will be a London at the mouth of the Hudson, perhaps another where Chicago now stands, and possibly a third at San Francisco. When the Duke of Wellington was in this city of the Thames, he could rough-grind his sabres and ride down a mob. We cannot do that in New York. We must manage there by count of heads and clack of tongues. We must manage by ward meetings and a multiplicity of party influences, often so complex that the average citizen does not understand them, and abstains from voting out of disgust or despair. As the power of the people advances, it will be found out ultimately under universal suffrage that Christianity is the only safeguard of civil liberty on both sides the sea. In a State filled with great cities, the only safety for the government of the people by the people, and for the people in the State, is to be found in the government of the saints by the saints, and for the saints in the Church.

I hold that it has been demonstrated by the experience in the United States for a century that the separation of the Church from the State has not injured either. American experience proves that the separation of Church and State prevents the State from governing the Church, but does not prevent the Church from governing the State. It was the conscience of the North which held the nation up to its work in our civil war; and if of late we have been paying our national debt, if the American conscience revolts at any idea of repudiation, if the sober American people are to-day bearing taxes as perhaps no equal number of millions ever did on the globe before, — it is because of the conscientiousness and the sobriety taught by a free Church in a free State. We have fifty millions of people already in the United States; and when we have four times the present population of Great Britain we may easily have four Londons, and God knows that representative government, triumphant elsewhere, is sufficiently strained to-day in our large towns. There are in the United States fifty millions of people, and about five millions are church-members; but if we had not one in five making a public solemn profession of Christianity, I for one should not have what I have to-day, — a firm hope that the future of government of the people by the people and for the people is safe. You know that I do not recommend English institutions to America. The opinion has been expressed by your great statesman, Mr. Gladstone, who is as much revered in America as here, that neither nation prefers the institutions of the other. To this proposition I venture to add that neither would do well now to exchange its institutions for those of the other. It is better that we should try two great experiments. But, sir, I believe that if that statesman were here he would justify me in the further assertion that the hope of civil liberty in Great Britain, and in your empire throughout the world, rests, as surely as it does in the United States, on the (purity, the intelligence, and the activity of the Christian Church.) The nations to which we are admitted by the growth of all lines of international communication depend for the progress of their civil liberties, no less than for the progress of their religious and intellectual culture, on our success in these two great experiments. I thank God that England and America are not circumstanced alike; and that, if one fail, the other may keep up the hope of the race. Abraham Lincoln and Prince Albert are possibly now looking with equal interest on the two experiments. In the world above they are not national merely any more. The martyrs who perished on this spot are not denominationalists any more. To-night I would begin by casting aside utterly everything merely denominational, everything merely national; and I would consider myself a citizen of a world now no larger than the Roman Empire was under the Cæsars. Religious internationalism makes all members of Christendom fellow-citizens. The colossal tasks assigned by Providence to England and America can be performed only when the two nations lock hands.

· METHODS OF MEETING MODERN UNBELIEF.

It is, of course, no part of my purpose to-night to instruct this dignified assembly, in the presence of which I ought to be dumb; but it may be that a few facts concerning rationalism in the United States, and a few glimpses of the power of our free churches, may not be without their worth, as the testimony of a stranger to circumstances within his observation at home.

I believe that the trend of history is toward the enlargement of civil as well as religious liberty. We must learn how to manage men when they all think for themselves. The time has come when every man will exercise his judgment for himself, and when, unfortunately, not every man has judgment to exercise. Adolescent culture of the masses is at once a glory and a peril of our republican age. This is the chief origin, I believe, of the scepticism of adolescent culture, which in our time is the most notorious. We are, I think, troubled now less than we have been for many ages with the scepticism of experts. Mr. Cobden used to say that the number of trained infidels, of really reasoned sceptics in England among the working classes, especially among the skilled operatives, could be put into a drawing-room. I venture to say that the number of infidels in the United States among the working classes who can give a reason for their unbelief, that would bear examination under the microscope and scalpel of scholarship, could be put into any small cabin on an Atlantic steamer, and that in the rolling of the ship there would be very much danger of physical injury by the space left for them in which to toss to and fro. It is notorious that American infidelity of the popular species publishes very little that is worth reading. There is almost nothing in American or British infidel publications that has a name on both sides of the Atlantic. Our Theodore Parker, indeed, whose antislavery politics deserved all honor, has been much read in America and here; but he left no theological school behind him in Boston. Theodore Parker is now far less a power in Boston than he was ten years ago; he was then far less a power than ten previously. He represents no extensive or permanent movement of thought.

We have learned in the United States, by our experience in heterodoxy, to judge it not so much by the men who make it, as by the men it makes. We have had noble men revolting from Puritanism; we have had a Socinian secession from orthodoxy, — Boston has been the centre of it; but experience shows that the third generation of rationalistic negation, on the line of the Unitarian faith, usually becomes far more rationalistic than the first generation. The third generation of Socinian negation is usually rationalistic in the extreme, sometimes infidel. You drop from Channing to Theodore Parker, from Theodore Parker to Frothingham, from Frothingham to the incomprehensible and undescribable! You arrive at last at a state where lax teachers have no gospel to preach; they become simply literary men, and in that way end their career as defeated propagandists of a fallen faith.

I.

To run rapidly over some general considerations touching this immense theme of the methods of meeting modern unbelief, let me say, in the first place, *that there is no modern form of scepticism which may not be exploded by a fair use of its own concessions.*

AGNOSTICISM.

Take, for instance, agnosticism, and what are its concessions? Sir, I believe agnosticism to be about half of it chaff and half of it chaffing. But when you approach its more serious representatives, you find them claiming that they are a sort of theists; they affirm that they are not atheists. The character of God to the agnostic is as unknown as the back side of the moon; but I have a right to assert that, although unknown, that side exerts an attraction on every flashing wave of all the great oceans, and has its power as well as any part of the orb which we can behold. We are indebted, I think, to Mr. Herbert Spencer, in this country, and to Mr. John Fiske, the most brilliant Spencerian in the United States, for the best representation of agnosticism. I suppose I need not pause to justify the assertion that agnosticism itself admits that the Great First Cause is, and is a cause, and is omnipresent, and has existed from eternity. Thus there are four things known about this Cause, — its existence, its power or causal energy, its omnipresence, its eternity. But Mr. Herbert Spencer will tell you that the nature of things works well; he will tell you that the arrangement of this universe is such that the right has immense advantages in the struggle for existence. We are told by Mr. Arnold that there is, in the universe, "an eternal power, not ourselves, which makes for righteousness." Now, take these concessions, and what follows? Why, if there be no personal God, but simply an eternal power, not myself, that makes for righteousness, then I must learn to love what that power loves, and hate what that power hates, or it is ill with me.

The doctrine that we need to love what the Supreme Power of the universe loves, and hate what he hates, stands even under the little that agnosticism knows about the Primal Cause, omnipresent, eternal, and everywhere making for righteousness. If I make for unrighteousness, the wheels of the universe are against me. The very nature of things requires that I shall love what it loves, and hate what it hates. And so I would approach all agnostics on the basis of their own concessions, and affirm that of self-evident necessity men cannot have harmonization with their environment, without similarity of feeling with the Eternal Somewhat which makes for righteousness.

THE UNIVERSE REVEALS A THINKER.

Modern science has shown us more clearly in these last ages than any science or imagination of man ever showed us before, that the universe is full of thought. All nature bursts with fulness of evidence that it is arranged on a plan. But I believe it is a self-evident truth that there cannot be thought without a thinker. Wherever we find in the universe thought not our own, we may be sure that there is a Thinker not ourselves.

The universe is not only a thing, it is a thought. And it is one thought. The broadest and most vaunted doctrine of physical science is the universality and inviolability of law. The reign of law, omnipresent, eternal, — teach it as much as you please! The thought that is behind the reign of universal and unified natural law must be regarded as one; and that one thought I hold to be the outcome and proof of the existence of one Thinker, omnipresent, eternal, and personal as is the thought. A thinker is a person. That Supreme Somewhat which, as the blindest agnostic admits, makes for righteousness is thus demonstrably known to be an Eternal Some One who makes for righteousness, and from whom we cannot escape.

THE CHARACTER OF THIS THINKER IS ASCERTAINABLE.

You have been told, I suppose, that the absolute and infinite must contain everything, or else they are not absolute and infinite. "To define God," said Spinoza, "is to deny him." Now, I hold that it is certain that infinite space is space, that infinite time is time, that infinite power is power, that infinite knowledge is knowledge, that infinite goodness is goodness. What is affirmed in calling the Divine attributes of power, knowledge, and goodness infinite, is intelligible and involves no self-contradiction. Except in the elements of infinity, any given quality is the same in its infinite as in its finite development. We cannot adequately conceive of the quantity, but we may of the quality of infinity. What is inconsistent with goodness will be inconsistent with infinite goodness.

Mr. Mill was perfectly right in saying, except that his profaneness should have been omitted, that he would call no being good who is not what he means when he applies the epithet to his fellow-creatures. "If such a being," said Mr. Mill, "can sentence me to hell for not so calling him, to hell I will go." There was an earthquake rent, and into this chasm the whole really puerile philosophy of nescience, I believe, will be ultimately cast, in the name of logic, and with the acclamations of all thinking men.

This unscientific doctrine of agnosticism has very little hold on what calls itself culture in the United States. My friend Mr. Fiske is a brilliant man and an agnostic; I speak always with respect of his honesty; but he is to this hour plunging in the Serbonian bog of the Spencerian philosophy. Professor Bowen, a profound metaphysician and devout Christian believer, and not Mr. Fiske, represents Harvard University.[1] Professor Bowen, of Harvard, President Porter, of Yale, and President McCosh, of Princeton College, the foremost American authorities in philosophy, are all vigorous opponents of the agnosticism of the Spencerian school. That man in London whose opinion I believe to be worth more than that of any other living Englishman on the subject, told me not long ago that he believed that Spencer's books would not be bought in large numbers ten years after his death.

The attributes of knowledge, power, and goodness, each of them in an infinite degree, can be intelligibly and without self-contradiction attributed to one Thinker, and to but one, and that one He whose thought the origination and preservation of the universe exhibit. Immense distinctions exist between the Absolute defined as the unrelated, or that which exists out of all relations, and the Absolute defined as the independent, or that which exists out of *one set* of relations, that is, out of all relations of dependence. It is in the latter sense only that scientific theism asserts that the One Person whose existence is proved by the one thought of the universe is absolute. Great distinctions exist between the Absolute defined as that which is capable of existing out of relation to anything else, and defined as that which is incapable of existing in relation to anything else. It is in the former sense that scientific theism calls God absolute. It is in the latter that Herbert Spencer, Mansel, and others, who deny that we can prove intellectually that God is a person, call God absolute. This false definition overlooks the distinction between infinite and all, and leads Mansel to Hegel's conclusion,—that God's nature embraces everything, evil included. The definition which Mansel and Spencer hold is repudiated by scientific theism. With that repudiation, all the alleged difficulties that arise from asserting the personality of God vanish. Herbert Spencer and his school admit that the Eternal Power, not ourselves, which makes for righteousness in the universe, is omnipresent, self-existent, omnipotent, and in this sense infinite and absolute.

In a recent volume of most searching applications of the scientific method to philosophical thought, Thomas Hill, lately President of Harvard University, writes (The Natural Sources of Philosophy, p. 32): "Spencer says that our belief in an Omnipresent Eternal Cause of the universe has a higher warrant than any other belief, that is, that the existence of such a Cause is the most certain of all certainties; but asserts that we can assign to it no attributes whatever, and that it is absolutely unknown and unknowable. Yet, in his very statement of its existence, he assigns to the Ultimate Cause four attributes,— being, causal energy, omnipresence, and eternity. And afterwards he implicitly assigns to it two other attributes, repeatedly expressing his faith that the Cosmos is obedient to law, and that this law is of beneficent result, which is an implicit ascription of wisdom and love to the Ultimate Cause. All thinkers concede that human reason is competent to discover the existence of an Ultimate Cause, to form the inductions of its being, its causal energy or power, its omnipresence, and eternity."

The intelligence, the unity, and, in a correct sense, the infinity, of the Cause of the universe are, therefore, proved in entire harmony with the scientific method on the one hand, and Christian theism on the other.

It is the business of the Church to echo God. His voice is multiplex, the same and yet different from age to age, and unapologetic from eternity to eternity. He cannot be patronized; and if we are his servants, our first duty is to see to it that we do not take a craven and apologetic attitude before the pinched physicism which, in our age, arrogates the titles of both religion and science, and deserves neither, and attempts to patronize God himself, or to bow him out of the universe in the name of agnosticism and atheism.

This is a transitional age of adolescent culture for the masses, and with the progress of popular enlightenment much of our crude infidelity will pass away.

There is in our time a scepticism of the dull-eyed, and of course a scepticism of the wild-eyed, but the worst scepticism is that of the wall-eyed, or of physicists, and sometimes of philosophical specialists, who will see nothing outside their own particular ranges of investigation, who never have looked at religious truth scientifically, and who, indeed, refuse to apply to the truths of theology the common axioms and principles which they are constantly using in science itself. A specialist may be lynx-eyed and yet wall-eyed. We must force the wall-eyed to the conclusions which follow from self-evident premises; we must take the "cans" and "cannots" of the Bible, the great self-evident propositions of religious truth based upon axioms which all scientific methods revere, and show that those "cans" and "cannots" justify us in asserting the necessity of similarity of feeling between man and God as required by the new birth, and the necessity of the harmonization of man with his past as required by the atonement.

In all the great themes of our modern Christian theology, there is hardly a controverted question which might not be settled by an appeal to the self-evident truths lying behind the Biblical "cans" and "cannots." Christ's fears for man were that he would not be delivered from both the love of sin and the guilt of it. These two fears are precisely those of the very nature of things; for it is self-evident that without harmony with God and conscience and our record, we cannot be in peace with our unescapable environment. These two fears produced Christ's bloody sweat, and yet he conquered both fears without adopting any belief out of harmony with the nature of things. He attained peace; his yoke was easy, his burden was light. But only he, in the whole history of the race, and such as have followed his method, have done this. The method of Christ and the secret of Christ are historically proved to be the only sources of peace when all the faculties are aroused and harmonized with the law of the ascent of life. Christianity, therefore, and it only, is in harmony with the absolute religion or the self-evident truths of the nature of things.

It is the joy of my life to defend what I call axiomatic theology, that is, the cans and cannots of the nature of things as revealed by self-evident truth. Axiomatic theology shows that mind is not matter; it thus answers materialism. It demonstrates that death does not end all, even if it cannot prove literal immortality. It establishes the supremacy of conscience, and shows that we can have no harmony with ourselves until we acquire harmony with the moral law pointed out by the moral sense, and with the God who is behind that law, and with the record of our own sins, on which that law places greater and greater emphasis the more we love what God loves and hate what he hates. Axiomatic theology thus applied to philosophy is the uprooting of agnostic, atheistic, materialistic, and pessimistic speculations. As applied to religious truth, axiomatic theology demonstrates the necessity of similarity of feeling with God to peace in his presence. Applied to our record in the past, it proves the necessity of an atonement; and although it does not pretend, from the point or view of mere reason, to prove that an atonement has been made, it does establish the certainty that an atonement is needed, and therefore the shallowness of all schemes of thought which do not contain that multiplex, under-girding truth, encircling the entire universe of moral speculation. Axiomatic theology points out the law of the ascent of life. By applying that law to theology and ethics, it proves that the soul, with all its faculties allowed free growth and action, *cannot* have peace unless it is harmonized with the highest in itself, that is, with conscience, and with the highest in history, that is, with the Christ. There is thus established a philosophy concerning the conditions of man's peace, and its conclusions from self-evident truth are entirely harmonious with the Scriptures themselves. Axiomatic theology can be systematized. It begins with principles of common sense, taken for granted in legislation, and behind counters, and in juries, wherever men reason. Axiomatic theology can be preached to scholars; for the supreme principles of self-evident truth are those on which all scholarship depends in every science. Axiomatic theology can be preached to the people; for self-evident truth is that which underlies the proverbs of the nations, and is the basis of common sense everywhere.

I like to begin by planting my foot on axiomatic theology, on self-evident propositions, on intuitions, properly so called; but I do not like to end there.

Far be it from me, my friends, to undervalue forms of Christian effort to which I am not accustomed myself. The needs of the people are very diversified, and if we echo God, I am very sure our endeavor to supply those needs will also be diversified. Our Lord and Saviour Jesus Christ not only *was* but *is*. These martyrs of Smithfield who perhaps hover in the air above us have messages for us; and from all the fields which martyrs consecrated in the British Isles, from all quarters of the world where Christians have had their triumphs, souls seem to gather around us with messages for the present hour. But where is the Spirit which once on earth spoke as never man spake? Where is Jesus Christ now? Our Christology, of course, includes the organizing and redemptive doctrine that the Holy Spirit is shed forth by our Lord. It was said at Pentecost, "He hath shed forth this." Our Lord hath yet many things to say to us of London and of Boston. If we follow the mind of the Spirit, we shall utter to our age our secret convictions. If we follow the impulse of the finger of the Spirit upon our souls, as we are differently trained by God's providence and by this constant touch of Christ's pierced right hand, we shall utter messages so diversified as to meet the diversified wants of our age.

The small philosopher's rule is to guess at the half and multiply by two. He is a very great character in modern history, and is likely to be a greater one as democratic influences progress in the world for good or evil. We cannot avoid the dangers of the day of small things of popular knowledge. We, therefore, need to tell the people all we know. The time has come when all that anybody knows on great and vital themes, everybody should know. A small draught from the Pierian spring is undoubtedly a dangerous thing, but the remedy for it is a deeper draught. The danger of the diffusion of a little knowledge must be met by more knowledge. In the present day the need of the time is that the esoteric should become the exoteric, and the convictions of scholars a possession of the masses.

The truth I suppose to be, not that we cannot know

anything of God, but that we can know a little, and that this little is enough for practical purposes. I believe that the twentieth century will teach, not agnosticism, but what I love to call miognosticism, or the doctrine that we can know a little of God, and not that we can know nothing of him. My conviction is that it is our duty to lift up over against the hardy, arrogant agnosticism of our times the by no means arrogant or extravagant, but cool and scientific doctrine of miognosticism, which is likely to be the doctrine of enlightened future times.

NECESSITY OF AN ATONEMENT.

In the concession of agnosticism that there is an Omnipresent, Eternal Power which makes for righteousness, we find no release from the doctrine of the new birth. Had I time, I should endeavor to show also that while that power enswathes us, we can find no release from the doctrine of the necessity of an atonement. I believe if the nature of things makes for righteousness, and if I have a black record behind me in the past, that record which I must face while I continue to exist will be a source of dissonance between me and my environment. I believe as thoroughly as that I exist that my environment must be made up of my own faculties and of my record in the past, and of an Omnipresent First Cause which makes for righteousness. How am I to be harmonized with that environment? It is self-evident that without similarity of feeling with this Power I can have no harmonization with it, for two cannot walk together unless they are agreed. I hold also that without a screen let down between me and my black past, I can have no harmony with that portion of my environment. On all who admit that there is a Power, not ourselves, which makes for righteousness, a merciless necessity of thought forces the admission of necessity of similarity of feeling with that Power, and of some great arrangement by which we can be screened from a past which is irreversible and inerasable. There are more things in the nature of things than have ever been dreamt of in our philosophy.

On the basis of mere positivism and secularism, believing in nothing but the nature of things, I would assert that similarity of feeling with God is demonstrably necessary to peace in his presence; or, in the language of the positivists, to love what the nature of things loves and to hate what it hates, is demonstrably necessary to our harmonization with our environment. Let us, then, emphasize these concessions, and bring those who make them into such a mood of seriousness as will at last enable them to lift up their eyes to inferences far above their present low plane of intellectual attainment.

DOES DEATH END ALL?

If I were to approach a positivist who denies that there is any existence for the soul after death, I believe that I should find him unable to prove that organization begins everything in our human existence; but if he cannot prove that, how does he know that disorganization ends everything? Organization implies an organizing power, and that power must go before its own effects. We are "woven by something not ourselves," as Tyndall says. What is the cause of form in organisms? There must be a cause, and if organization does not begin all, but is itself begun, no positivist, no secularist, no man of merely great adeptness in the physicist's portions of investigation, — I will not call these portions science, I call them a pinched physicism, — no man of that department has a right to assert that disorganization ends all. The thing that goes before organization may live after disorganization, and that may prove that death does not end all. And so I would say to the sceptic, As you do not know that death ends all, make preparation for that unseen world in which no doubt the laws of the nature of things are to be what they are here; make preparation to walk, while you have your existence, with a Being or with a nature of things which you cannot be harmonized with unless you make for righteousness as it does.

These are plain, straightforward concessions of the worst school of reasoned sceptics, and I hold that it is very important for the Christian pulpit to seize upon these outlying portions of the fortress of rationalism, and show that whoever takes them can take the citadel at last. There are no outlying fortresses of rationalism well protected; we can enter the outlying forts almost without the loss of a man; indeed, our spies are talking to each other constantly on the borders between our two armies. Let the talk be sometimes courteous, sometimes friendly, never apologetic on our part, and when we get a hearing let us stand on the outposts and take the citadel.

II.

Another method of meeting modern infidelity *is to insist on distinctness and verifiableness of definitions.* The very worst disease in the blood and bones of what calls itself liberalistic thought in our time is vagueness of definition. Our vague literary rationalism rarely attempts to define its chief terms, but drifts from fog bank to fog bank across the seas of discussion, making its protection very often the vapor itself. This has been the difficulty of

Unitarianism in the United States; it was the difficulty of Theodore Parker; it was the difficulty of Mr. Emerson, who so lately was a pantheist, and who to-day, as I thank God for being able to affirm, is a theist. He allows his friends to call him a Christian theist. Mr. Emerson, who began his career as more or less pantheistic, has of late been assisting his neighbor, Mr. Alcott, in conducting a summer school of philosophy at Concord, which teaches theism, and carries its doctrines almost up to the verge of Christianity. That school is full of mistrust of positivism, of agnosticism, and of all those forms of speculation which do not take an integral view of the universe.

All fractional schemes of thought science itself will ultimately distrust, and it will be found that of all views of the universe the Biblical is the least fractional.

Mr. Emerson said lately to Mr. Alcott, and the latter reported the words before fifty ladies and gentlemen in my parlor in Boston: "If you wish to call me a Christian theist, you have my authority to do so, and you must not leave out the word 'Christian,' for to leave that out is to leave out everything." Mr. Emerson's is the only eminent name that was quoted in America in support of rationalism, and to-day it can be quoted in support of theism, although I do not dare yet call Emerson exactly a Christian theist, in spite of his calling himself so.

III.

Another method of meeting modern unbelief *is to point out the practical character of unsound schemes of thought, and what infidelity usually becomes in the third generation.*

Is there an infidel book in the world that any serious man wants for a dying pillow? I look north, south, east, and west for such a volume. I look to the thirty-two points of the compass for any infidel book a hundred years old, yet holding its own among scholars. I find no such volume. I do not want for my dying pillow any book of Strauss or Renan, any more than of Voltaire. I have seen the decadence of the negations of Strauss, and I believe that we shall live to see the decadence of some arrogant philosophies which to-day underlie infidelity. Who is there here, above fifty years of age, who does not remember the time when Hegel was the great authority in Germany, and was quoted in support of rationalism? Who does not remember when that great man, John Stuart Mill, was such an authority that to differ from him was almost as much as one's intellectual reputation was worth? But you know that to-day, since the publication of his Autobiography, that philosophic authority of his has waned; and now Professor Jevons is telling us we must look yet further before we find logical infallibility. As these men have waxed and waned, so some who now fill the ears of the world with rationalistic speculations will wax and wane. We shall ultimately, out of our wrecks in philosophy, come to a profounder reverence for the Biblical view of the world as itself the best philosophy. What works well, age after age, is likely to be the truth. There is no unsound scheme of thought which does work well when transmuted into life; and, therefore, the sternest judge of error is its reduction to practice.

IV.

Of all methods of meeting unbelief, the most efficient is, in my judgment, the famous scientific one, — *repeated and prolonged experiment.*

PRAYER.

Who here is willing to try, for example, the experiment of testing whether prayer really has an answer? It is written in the Book which is an authority in Christendom, that God is more willing to give his Holy Spirit to those who ask him for it than fathers are to give bread to their children. What is prayer? It has commonly been taught that prayer consists of four parts, — adoration, confession, thanksgiving, petition. I love to teach that it consists of five parts, — adoration, confession, thanksgiving, petition, and total self-surrender. Any prayer that has not in the petition, "Thy will be done," is mere vain repetition. Where is the sceptic that dares try the experiment of prayer in that sense, and see whether the Holy Spirit will be given to him or not? A man is not manly who vaunts that he believes in the scientific method and will not test it. You believe that experiment is the test of all truth, and that the scientific method must prevail. England, Germany, and the United States are very well agreed in their best cultured circles that inductive experiment must be applied to theology as well as to all other themes. Reverence for proof, clear ideas at any cost, obedience the organ of spiritual knowledge, are the great points in the creed of all true culture. Our century believes in making known to everybody all that is thoroughly known by anybody. The Church is anxious that even the truths of Christianity should be tested by merciless experiment. Take the doctrine of prayer in all its five parts, and try an experiment with it. I hold it to be a truth of experience, that whoever yields himself utterly to God receives at the instant of surrender an inner illumination unobtainable in any other way. I hold that this experiment, repeated age after age in innumerable personal careers, has never once been repeated without success.

IS THERE ANOTHER PROBATION AFTER DEATH?

I am willing to test modern latitudinarianism within the Church itself by experiment. We are told that there is to be opportunity for repentance after death. We are told that extinction is to overtake ultimately the incorrigibly wicked. Is any man, as a practical experiment, willing to be incorrigibly wicked, and take his chance as to extinction? Eternal hope, we are told, is before us, whatever we do. There will be opportunity of repentance after death, say some revered men; but are these men willing to trust their own chances of eternal peace to the opportunity of repentance after death? That is a practical experiment for you, and the application of the scientific method which you revere to this department of religious research.

Thomas Corwin, governor of Ohio, was renowned for his quick retorts. He once met a negro who had fled from Kentucky, and whom he had known in that slave State. The negro had left friends and a comfortable home, and in Ohio was dressed in rags. The governor said to the negro, "Were you not well treated in Kentucky by your master?" "Yes." "Did you not have other friends there, and clothing and food enough?" "Always." "Well, then," said the governor, "I must say you made a mistake in running away." "Governor Corwin," said the negro, "the situation in Kentucky is open with all its advantages, and, if you like it, you can go and occupy it." We are told by a few of the representatives of circles of society, of whose culture and seriousness I must speak with respect, that it is a barbaric doctrine to teach that character tends to a final permanence, good or bad, and that, in the very nature of things, a final permanence can come but once. Without using the scriptural argument at all, I beg leave to say to any man who teaches this doctrine of repentance after death, "The situation is open with all its advantages. Do you purpose to go and occupy it?" Not he, not I, not you, if we are in our senses. What I dare not, and will not, do for myself, I will not recommend to others.

Christianity includes all ethics; it is a philosophy, it is an art, it is a science, it is a revelation of the nature of things in which there is no variableness or shadow of turning. But it is more and better, — it is a life in God's love and strength. Permeated everywhere with the doctrine of the new birth and the atonement, and also by the truth that character tends to a final permanence, good or bad, and that a final permanence can come but once, Christianity has for its central thought the personal love of a holy infinite Personality revealed both in nature and in revelation as Redeemer and as Lord, and of love for that Person as the only possible means of purifying the world. Behold in him a Redeemer, and you become glad to take him as Lord. Look on the Cross, and it becomes no cross to bear the cross. God as an atoning God, God revealed in history as at once Saviour and King, God revealed in our Lord and now moving the world through the Holy Spirit and moving it as both Redeemer and Lord, the acceptance of that God first as Redeemer and then utter affectionate submission to him as Lord, the personal love of Infinite Perfection as a regenerating passion, — this is the beautiful and awful, which has triumphed, and will continue to triumph.

V.

It is high time that we should turn from the general to some of the special methods of meeting modern unbelief, and I hope you will bear with me if I suggest arrangements already well known on this side of the Atlantic.

A MODERN NECESSITY.

The first of these is *the foundation of professorships in our theological colleges on the relation of Christianity to science*. I believe this suggestion will not be a novel nor an unwelcome one to the scholars in this audience, and certainly not to theological teachers. I hope they will find it in the line of modern Christian development to found such professorships, some of which exist in England already, in the shape of lectureships, renowned throughout the world for the products which they have given from time to time to the nations for the strengthening of Christian faith. But we are resolved in the United States to meet the demands of our young men in theological schools for equipment in scientific armor. It is no purpose of a theological professor who teaches the relations of Christianity to science, to know the *materia medica*. He does not expect to be a practical chemist, biologist, astronomer, or geologist. His business is to study each vessel, so to speak, every ship in the fleet of the sciences along the line between wind and water. Where science and Christianity meet, he must understand them both, and so his task is not one out of all proportion to human powers. We have appointed in the oldest theological seminary of the United States a professor to discuss the relations of Christianity to science, and have put

$50,000 behind him. That has been done in Massachusetts, at Andover Theological Seminary, the most mossy and mediæval of all our theological institutions, as its enemies would say; but mediæval and mossy as it is, Andover dares to expend £10,000 to teach the relations of Christianity to science. Where is the rationalistic professorial chair that in any way compares for intellectual dignity in the United States with the chair thus founded at Andover? Princeton has a theological professorship of this kind; the Union Seminary in New York has a lectureship of similar character. It has been my fortune for five years to stand in Boston, or to move to and fro through the northern cities of the Union, and to discuss the relations of Christianity to science; and the demand for even poor discussion like mine shows what the demand would be for good discussion, if you had it. I do not magnify myself, but I do magnify this glorious office of discussing the relations of Christianity to science, and I affirm that if you had a dozen men in England, and if we had a dozen men in the United States, adapted to the work which I have been endeavoring to do, and have done so poorly, we could shake the foundations of rationalism on both sides the sea, within one generation. You cannot expect your pastors to make a specialty of this theme. You cannot expect the professors of dogmatic theology or ecclesiastical history to do this in your theological colleges. It is altogether too much to put upon one man, to make him a pastor, a preacher, and a lecturer on Christianity and science besides. We must subdivide our work and diversify it, and so meet the exigencies of the times. As there is now such a demand for knowledge concerning the relation of Christianity to science, why not develop the Church in response to a providential call as she has been developed again and again in her equipment in times past? Why not meet the demand of the hour by a measure for the hour?

THEOLOGICAL STUDENTS NEED MORE THOROUGH EQUIPMENT.

What would I have besides? Let me say that some of us who have had in our American theological colleges three years of instruction *have felt that we needed a fourth year.* I would not have a fourth year for all theological students, but only for some. The fourth year I would ask should be not for all theological students, but for those who elect it. Preaching by students should be allowed in the fourth year, but not in the first three years to students who enter for the fourth. The larger portion of the fourth year should be devoted to perfecting work on the most important topics of the doctrinal department. It should include space for larger attention to metaphysics, history, and physical science, and the current forms of infidelity. It should give enlarged instruction in respect to all practical religious effort.

It is not too much to say one reason why the Church is weak is, that it is often fed on guesses. Still worse, in certain departments where it needs most strength, the Church is not fed at all, or, if fed, is not exercised at all. The scepticism of the land fattens on the crudity of the pulpit and the inactivity of church-members.

The chief topics of theology are inherently so important that no mistake concerning them can be so small as not to be colossal. And yet, on such topics — the fact of a revelation, the Deity of Him from whom all the years of time are numbered, the mysteries of election, fate, and free-will — we, to whom a college course gives hardly a trace of theological instruction, and who now know that our knowledge of theology derived from other sources previous to our studies here was superficial and fragmentary to a sometimes ludicrous extreme, are asked to form opinions in the course of three years' investigation, one year of which is devoted to evangelical and one to historical and rhetorical branches, the third year broken by permitted absences for preaching, not absolutely excessive, indeed, since they are an important method of training adopted by one of the most important departments of the course, but which are relatively excessive, because, in a course of but three years, they are necessarily premature, since they are such as to reduce the whole term of study, in respect to the matter to be preached, practically to two years and a half; and, on the basis of this amount of attention to what are assuredly the most difficult and awful of the problems the human mind is permitted to reach, we are asked to commit ourselves, in effect, for life, to certain opinions, and go out and stand beside the pillows of the dying, and put beneath them those opinions, not as guesses but as proofs. An honest man recoils when so much is asked of him. It is by no means expected that in three years we can master the whole range of theology. But we are expected to have mastered its strategic points. On these we are officially asked, in wholly informal yet definite terms, to express before examining councils what we hold for ourselves, not what we have been taught. Upon these greatest points at least, which, however, cannot be explored to the bottom without an examination of very nearly all the rest, we, as educated men and future public teachers, are called to express independent opinions. We are expected to become so clear as to be in no sense uncandid. It is expected that we will do this in the training of nine months' special doctrinal study, and in the collateral reading of perhaps four months more. We do not do it. We cannot do it. And yet this is the most accredited entrance to the ministry. The greatness of the topics of theology ought to secure their thorough treatment. The greatness and difficulty of the topics of theology demand an extension of the term of professional theological study. I claim a fourth year of study in the courses of the theological seminaries, in order that we may have time to be honest.

The Christian evidences and ethics are, indeed, now taught in college, but so hurriedly as to make little impression upon any except those who have a peculiar taste for them, or anticipate study in a professional theological course. Once out of college, those students who pursue law, medicine, art, science, or literature, become absorbed in their special fields of investigation. Once in their professions, they are still more absorbed. It is sometimes loosely said that no lawyer in full practice ever reads a book.

Only those few who have a taste for theological study ever take it up. More than half of ordinary college classes understand metaphysics too poorly ever to be able to take up the severer forms of theological reading. The result is, that while in the days of Edwards all liberally educated men, as such, had some knowledge of theology, now no liberally educated man, as such, has necessarily any knowledge of it. The knowledge of theology as a system is confined to those who study theology professionally.

Some of the classes in society, best educated in every other respect, are the least well educated in regard to theological truth. I mean no disrespect to members of the honorable professions of law and medicine, when I say that these classes constitute the best materials society contains for the formation of crude parties in theology.

The information of the people in regard to theological and religious questions has not kept pace with its advance as to secular truths. Without this distinction of its two parts, the growth of knowledge among the people might seem to have utterly inexplicable relations to the religious phenomena of the times. The world is, indeed, becoming more enlightened, but not with equal rapidity in all respects. The disparity between the degrees of advance of secular and religious intelligence is a fearful gap in the joints of the harness of truth at which scepticism strikes.

The most disastrous criticism of the pulpit is that it skips difficulties. The skipping of difficulties brings swiftly the charge of disingenuousness; and that charge hangs invisible in the secret thought of men, over more pulpits to-day than we are aware, — a Damocles' sword.

Princeton Theological Seminary in the United States has already added a fourth year to its course of study; Andover is calling for one, and probably within a few years will have organized one. It is now regarded as the proper thing to do when a man would be fully equipped, to remain a fourth year in a theological college. There are no sceptics trained as thoroughly as our best ministerial candidates will be trained under these new arrangements. I hold that no one of the learned professions has as much training in philosophy as the ministerial profession now has in the best theological schools. If you add a fourth year for some, if you put these theological professorships on the relations of Christianity to science into all your theological colleges of the first rank, you will very soon be sending out men equipped, not with bows and arrows, but with modern armor, equal to that possessed by the enemy.

UTILIZE THE GREAT SPECIALISTS.

What further extension of ministerial culture would I have? Here is a theological school, with a professorship in it on the relations of Christianity to science. *I would invite into it great specialists in science from outside theological circles.* In this renowned centre of the world, two great physicists who are theists, Dr. Carpenter and Professor Lionel Beale, have as much authority on the other side the sea as Huxley or Tyndall. I assure you, much as we revere the physiological knowledge of the last two of these men, we revere yet more the physiological knowledge of the first two. Dr. Carpenter only the other evening said in public, "There are four things no machine can utter, — 'I am, I ought, I can, I will;' but man utters them, and therefore he is more than an automaton." Professor Lionel Beale has published the opinion that no science now in existence can bridge by merely mechanical causes the chasm between lifeless and living matter. When, not long ago, Professor Huxley was asked in private by one of his friends to whom he had declared his disbelief in spontaneous generation, whether he had not the right to say that into that chasm between lifeless and living matter God comes to create the forms of organisms, Huxley himself was candid enough to reply, "You have a right to say it, and I do not know that I can disprove it." If Dr. Carpenter, if Lionel Beale, were to come to the professorships lately organized in the United States for discussing the relations between Christianity and science, they would have the heartiest of welcomes.

It will, of course, take time to train men to discuss

theology on one side and physical science on the other in their double relations; but little by little we shall create a new set of professors, and little by little we shall equip young men with such clear ideas and spiritual purposes, that they will become deadly in the onslaught upon rationalism based upon the scientific arguments of our time. There is no way to meet rationalism of the scientific species except by rendered reasons.

CHRISTIAN EVIDENCE SOCIETIES.

I would have societies organized for promoting the study of the Christian evidences. You have in London the Victoria Institute and the Christian Evidence Society; and I notice with great interest that the latter is recommending the formation in our churches of classes in the Christian evidences. The issuing of text-books on the Christian evidences is to be undertaken by this society, and the writing of such books is a task worthy of the best genius in the Church. We have not outgrown Paley or Butler, but we need to readjust their arguments; and if any man wishes to benefit the future, let him prepare text-books on the Christian evidences that will be read, and that when read cannot be answered by the ordinary carping of even our brilliant periodical literature, — some of it given to agnosticism, some of it dipping into the edges of atheism.

Of course the utmost caution is needed to spiritualize all these intellectual efforts, and prevent classes in the Christian evidences from becoming places for mere debate. Whenever the Church has tried to move by her intellectual wing or by her spiritual wing alone, her flight has been a sorry spiral. I would have prayers joined to the lectures. I would have every youth taught to study on his knees, —

whether he studies four years, or three, or only an hour. I would have him taught everywhere that the earnest Christian on his knees sees further than the haughtiest ×
atheistic philosopher on tiptoe.

VI.

THE POWER OF CHRISTIAN WORK.

In this crowded assembly, and standing as I am told I do, here and now, in the presence of some of the most aggressive Christians in England, and of many of the men who know best what it is to carry Christianity into the slums of a great municipality, *let me thank God for the philanthropic aggressiveness of the Christian laity as the best of all answers to secularism.* Do not let secularists outwork you in their approaches to the poor. Lazarus, in our time, lies in the slums of great cities, and there will be the spot where, for many ages to come, he will be found stripped and naked and half-dead. It was the glorious example of the Prince Consort, assisted by the patriotic efforts and the genial Christian persistence of scores of unknown men and women, that opened here in Great Britain the fashion of studying models for lodging-houses, attending to the unsavory topics of hygiene as to drains, and looking into all the wants of the working-man's cottage. Your Tennyson praises the Prince Consort for that life of his in which he hovered over the cottages of the poor, and did what he could for the perishing and dangerous in your great municipal populations. God knows that I have reverence enough for philanthropy even when I find it conjoined with secularism. When infidelity goes down into the slums and endeavors to lift the degraded, I would not rail too much at its efforts. But I would counteract the poison it distributes under this sugar coat of philanthropy. I would outwork it in the philanthropic way. I would not let it hold the ears of the uneducated masses on Sundays without sometimes myself going out to address audiences in the open air. I would not let the secularist address vast populations from week to week in his newspapers, without myself shedding printer's ink mercilessly for the benefit of those who will not attend church. The spoken word and the printed word outside the church must be brought into the service of the gospel if we are to counteract the secularist propagandism of our day. History never saw infidelity organized for popular effect as it is at the present moment. I believe that there is no more infidelity now on the globe than in past ages, but it can speak out now as it could not in the days of the Star Chamber. It has the ear of the masses through the great and wise and costly liberty of unlicensed printing. But this liberty was largely bought with Christian blood. On this spot I cannot but pause, as an American, to thank God for the work of some martyrs of the Fleet Prison incarcerated here[1] for what they did for the liberty of the press. That was work for America, that was work for Germany, that was work for all the lands of all the zones as well as for the British Isles. Let us be grateful to Almighty Providence that we are reaping in joy what other men have sown in tears, but let us reap as Christians. Let us take the vast liberty of the press, and overcome the

---

[1] The Memorial Hall, erected to commemorate the fidelity to conscience of the Two Thousand Clergymen expelled from the Church of England in 1662, stands on the site of the old Fleet Prison, in which so many of the Protestant and Puritan martyrs were imprisoned and mutilated.

mischief of its license by the omnipresent use of it in defence of healthful opinions.

VII.

CHRISTIAN CONTACT WITH THE UNCONVERTED.

What else would I have church-members do? I am coming to the very heart of this theme, and you have thought perhaps that I have omitted heart entirely, and have been speaking of the head almost too exclusively. It is, I believe, quite popular in London, it ought to be in Boston, and is becoming so there, *to close devotional meetings of churches with conversations on personal religion between Christians present and any unconverted ones who are willing to remain.* There is nothing to awaken a dead man like setting him at work to awaken a dead man. Put a cold church-member at the work of awakening an unconverted man, and you quicken the Church-member immensely. There is no scheme for quickening the blood of the Church like exercising the limbs of the Church. For keeping the Church from going into flaccidity and torpidity and diseases of stagnation in the circulation, there is no preventive but exercise and strenuous work. The Church is fed to repletion, and it is exercised so little that it has all the diseases of an indolent aristocracy.

When you give out an invitation at the close of a devotional meeting to any unconverted persons who are present to remain, and some such persons do stay, there is no discourtesy in approaching such persons with the topic of personal religion. A manly Christian aggressiveness will not be unobservant of courtesy. Let us close our church devotional meetings with gatherings in which all who remain of the unconverted class are told that they are to be conversed with personally on religious themes. Here is a man whose bargains for the last week have run perhaps as near to lies as the eyelids to the eyeball; and he must converse with a man he has tried to cheat: will not shudders run up and down his frame? But his Christian duty masters his will at last. What ought to be one of the first questions in such conversation? I like to begin with this inquiry, "What is your chief religious difficulty?" You do not go into such conversations without secret prayer; you do not go into them without a great deal of study of the Scripture; you have the "leaves for the healing of the nations," the Biblical passages, at your finger-tips and on your lips. The person with whom you converse may not know what his chief difficulty is, but the question fairly stated is well on its way towards solution. You induce him to raise the inquiry what his difficulty is; and you endeavor to untie the knot. Then you ask that man or woman to kneel down with you in God's house, and you implore the Holy Spirit to untie the knot; and in order that your prayer may not be blasphemy, you begin it by an affectionate, irreversible, total surrender of your own soul to God, and of the inquiring soul to the best it knows. The contagion of your surrendered will is possibly caught by the will of this inquirer. He, too, surrenders, and in seven cases out of ten it will be found that true surrender of the will unties all knots of the sceptical mind.

Effort like this is, I believe, the thing we most need for the healing our sceptical populations. If preaching in the pulpit is built on rendered reasons, if by all the glorious aggressiveness of Christian intellectual effort we can draw the masses to their knees, they will be taught more on their knees than they can learn on the loftiest heights of rationalism. Until we have a lay membership in our churches ready to enter into this work, and fit to be trusted with it, the Church will remain scandalously unequipped for its duties in modern times. Possibly pastors on my right and on my left are saying that many church-members cannot be trusted to do this work. A pastor, however, who does his duty will be present at such devotional meetings; he will instruct his church-members in a general way what to say; he will watch the effect of the conversations, and will supplement it by his own efforts. Little by little he will bring his church to skill in this style of conversation, and so he will make a living out of a dead church; so he will make a glorious aggressive Christian manhood out of a torpid, evasive, placid laity that had no right to be called God's servants, because they were not doing his work.

VIII.

VISITATION OF THE NON-CHURCH-GOING MASSES.

Let us have in our churches not only these conversational meetings, but little by little what they lead to, *a visitation of all the degraded quarters in our cities.* Undoubtedly with the spirit of the Prince Consort there floats above us the soul of Thomas Chalmers. Let us recollect what he did for the poor in Edinburgh; and pardon me if I, as an American, take a moment in which to recall to your attention facts well known here, well known on the other side of the Atlantic, but worth more to Americans than to Englishmen or Scotchmen. You remember that Chalmers selected a desolate quarter called the West Port, in Edinburgh, divided it into sub-districts, and sent men and women visitors into every family. He organized Sunday schools and day schools, savings-banks and wash-houses, and in other ways made himself the friend of the perishing and degraded. I have myself been in the room where Burke and Hare committed their murders, and it was in a tan-loft near that room that Chalmers began his work. Its result was that in a very few months he had a respectable congregation, and in less than two years it became a self-supporting church. Before Chalmers died it could have been said he had washed the quarter not white, indeed, but gray; and it had been sooty black.

Now, that district visitation, that organization of a church on the territorial principle, so that it shall be responsible for every man, woman, or child within its district, we, in America, think is, after all, the only real solution of our difficulties in managing great cities. America has no baptized population, for we have no State Church, and we do not think it, as our Puritan fathers thought it, important to bring the whole population into merely formal connection with the church unless we speedily transform that loose connection into a close and vital one. We want district visitation; we want Christian men and women to go about from house to house after our Lord's fashion; we want our great cities supplied with the opportunities of Christian edification as thoroughly as any rural populations have been supplied with them. It was Chalmers's theory that if a great city were as abundantly supplied with churches as any rural district, it would be found no harder to manage, because human nature in a great city is much what it is in the country, in spite of temptations being increased by the massing of the population. But the notorious fact in America is, that our great cities are not as well supplied with church-sittings as the country-towns. It is a suggestive fact, ascertained by the laborious investigation of the secretary of this Union (Mr. Mearns), that you have in greater London a million less sittings than you ought to have. Greater London includes Middlesex and some parishes in Kent and Surrey, and one or two other counties within twelve miles of Charing Cross. You have here a population of four and a half millions. I understand that one third of your present sittings are not occupied, and that you have not more than half what you ought to have, to accommodate fifty-eight per cent of the population, or the proportion that might go to church.

Take Chalmers's scheme of district visitation, take the famous territorial plan of his, and put behind it the Establishment, if you please, put behind it Nonconformity, put behind it Christianity of the vital species anywhere, and this threatening problem of managing cities under free suffrages will begin to look soluble. I hold that there is nothing that will make government by large popular suffrage a safe arrangement in great cities, except district visitation, and the carrying down of the gospel to the perishing and degraded populations, to the last man, woman, and child, and to every cradle and death-bed.

IX.

SCEPTICISM IN GERMANY.

In Germany, which I suppose to-day is better equipped in her universities than any other land on the globe, we have seen the defeat of school after school of rationalistic speculation. It has been my fortune to examine the religious history of the European universities very carefully, and I undertake to affirm that there are to-day in Germany only three universities that deserve to be called predominantly rationalistic in their theological department. I do not claim that Germany has not in it rationalism enough in its philosophical, legal, and medical faculties; but fifty or eighty years ago Germany sent us rationalistic works out of her theological faculties, while to-day she is sending us the best commentaries on the globe of the evangelical kind. It is from Belgium, it is from Holland, it is from parts of Switzerland, it is from Professor Kuenen and one or two of his type of thought, that we get a style of comment reminding us of what was popular in the theological universities of Germany fifty or eighty years ago.

Histories of the rise, progress, and decline of German rationalism have been appearing during the last fifteen years; and nobody doubts that rationalism, especially as connected with the mythical theory, has seen its best day in Germany. Strauss's theory concerning the origin of the Gospels perished before his own death. I may say that it was buried before he was. Some of the British artisans, some of the skilled workingmen in America, are fed to-day by infidel lecturers on the crumbs swept out of German theological workshops, and they think the food good because it comes from a learned land.

In the German universities the incontrovertible fact is that the rationalistic lecture-rooms are now empty, and the evangelical crowded; while fifty or eighty years ago the rationalistic were crowded, and the evangelical empty. Lord Bacon says that the best materials for prophecy are the unforced tendencies of educated young men. Take up any German year-book, look at the statistics of the universities, ascertain which way the drift of educated youth is now setting in the most learned circles in the world, and you have before you no unimportant sign of the times. But, in looking for this, you come upon another sign no less important, namely, that the leading universities of Germany are now, and eighty years ago were not, under predominant evangelical influence. Berlin, beyond doubt the university of first importance, and hallowed by the great names of Schleiermacher, Neander, Trendelenburg, and Twesten, is theologically led by Dorner, Semisch, and Steinmeyer, — stanch defenders of evangelical faith. Leipzig, with Kahnis and Luthardt and Delitzsch — and lately with Tischendorf — among her professors, contests with Berlin for the first place, and in the opinion of many deserves that rank, and is the renowned traditional seat of an orthodoxy which at some points New England and Scotland — agreeing in the main with the present attitude of Berlin — might consider excessive. Halle, whose theology permeates Germany, both from the university and from Francke's famous Waisenhaus, had in it lately Tholuck and Julius Müller, known throughout the world as antagonists, and as successful antagonists, of the subtlest forms of scepticism. It was not uncommon to hear Julius Müller spoken of as the ablest theologian of Germany, and his successors at Halle inherit his spirit. Tübingen itself, where Strauss put forth one of his earliest works, and Baur founded a theological party, has had in it for years no Tübingen school, but through the professorships of Beck, Palmerer, and Landerer is permeated by vigorous evangelical influences. Heidelberg, under the theological leadership of Schenkel, Hitzig, Gass, and Holtzmann, is to-day the only prominent university of Germany given to views that can be called rationalistic.

Now, which of these institutions is most patronized by German theological students? Halle and Berlin may be compared, in a general way, as to their theology, with Andover and New Haven; Leipzig, with Princeton; and Heidelberg, with the Unitarian portion of Cambridge. I found Dorner's, Müller's, and Tholuck's lecture-rooms crowded, and Schenkel's empty. There are in 1880 but twenty-four German theological students at Heidelberg; and I have heard Schenkel often, and never saw more than nine, eight, or seven students in his lecture-room. Counting both the native and the foreign theological students in these institutions, the whole number at rationalistic Heidelberg is 24; at evangelical Halle, 304; at evangelical Berlin, 230; at hyper-evangelical Leipzig, 437 (*Universitätskalender*, 1880–81).

It must be remembered that German students often change universities, passing one period in one and another in another, according to the attractions of different professors. It is immaterial to the German student where he hears lectures, provided he is prepared to pass with credit the severe final examinations. When a professor is called from one university to another, a large number of his hearers often follow him. Thus it is a fair test of the direction of the drift of educated youth in Germany, to point to the fact that they give their patronage to evangelical, rather than to rationalistic professors, and this in the overwhelming proportion of ten to one.

"By far, by far," was Professor Tholuck's constant answer, when asked by foreign students if orthodoxy is not stronger in Prussia than fifty or eighty years ago.

In 1826, at Halle, all the students except five, who were the only ones that believed in the Deity of our Lord, and all the professors of the university, united in a petition to the Government against Tholuck's appointment to a professorship there, and the opposition rested solely on the ground of his evangelical belief. The students at Tübingen, not far from the same date, ceremoniously burned the Bible. "When I came to Halle," said Professor Tholuck to me once, as he walked up and down that famous, long, vine-clad arbor in his garden, where his personal interviews with German and foreign students have exerted an influence felt in two hemispheres, "I could go twenty miles across the country and not once find what, to use an English word, is called an 'experimental' Christian. I was very unpopular. I was subjected to annoyance, even in my lecture-room, on account of my evangelical belief." "His adversaries are bold and cunning. A baptism of fire awaits him at Halle," wrote Frederick Perthes of the young professor, in 1826.

Contrast these murky threats of Tholuck's morning with the clear sky of his westering sun. In December, 1870, he had completed so much of a half-century of work at the University of Halle that three days were given by his friends to the celebration of the event. There were social gatherings, and suppers, and speeches at the hotels. All the halls and staircases of Tholuck's residence were crowded with guests. The Emperor William sent to him the star of the Red Eagle. Courtpreacher Hoffman brought to him the salutations of the ecclesiastical council, as to a veritable church-father of the nineteenth century. The various universities of Germany were represented by their ablest professors.

liv CHRIST AND MODERN THOUGHT.

Pastors of different cities sent delegations. A letter to Tholuck was received, signed by theologians at that hour in the army before Paris. An immense torchlight procession of students filled a night with Luther's hymn:—

"Ein feste Burg ist unser Gott."

"No one can deny," Professor Tholuck would say to me repeatedly, "that since the death of Frederick the Great, or the French Revolution, or the opening of the century, or even since fifty or forty years ago, there has been a great reaction in Germany against infidelity and rationalism."

X.

THE OUTLOOK FOR THE FUTURE.

Why do I outline thus the large results of Christian conflict with unbelief? Because I believe in the law of the survival of the fittest. In the presence of men who are perpetually telling us that this law governs all human history, I take leave to remind you that in the beginning of this century only £250,000 were expended in all Christendom for missions; now there are expended about £1,250,000. At the opening of this century there were 50 translations of the Scriptures, now there are 226. There are now printed and distributed so many Bibles that there is one in circulation for every ten persons on the face of the earth. There are a million church-members now scattered through the dark lands of the world, and gathered out of heathendom itself. I was told by a secretary of the American Board of Commissioners for Foreign Missions that it is within the power of the Christian Church in all its branches to bring either the printed or the spoken gospel to the notice of every living being before the close of this century. We shall pass out of the world, but God will remain in it, and the plan on which he has been acting undoubtedly will be that on which he will continue to act. Unto us a Son was to be born, and he has been born. Unto us there was to be given One who was to be called Wonderful, Counsellor, the Mighty God, the Everlasting Father, the Prince of Peace, and unto us One has been given to whom those epithets apply. Of the increase of his government there was to be no end. It appears in the progress of missions, and in the way in which commerce has been made of God a propagandist of the faith, that there is to be an opening into every nation, and an emigration either of Christian ideas and institutions, or of infidel poisonous opinions, into those new lands within the next century. London ought to make herself the great colonizer of the globe in the new aspect of colonization, as she was in the old. But what if London and Edinburgh fail? what if Boston and New York fail? what if Paris and Berlin fail? God will not fail. What he does is successfully done.

Whoever ascertains the trend of the historic constellations through long periods obtains a glimpse of the hem of the garment of Almighty God. What Providence does, it from the first intends. A sifting of Christianity has taken place in this last age by a prolonged contest of unbelief with faith, each armed with the best Damascus blades the world furnishes either to-day; and the result has been a defeat of doubt on all central points. It is, therefore, now certain that it was divinely intended that there should be a sifting of Christianity in this last age, and that a defeat of doubt should be the result. Prolonged historic tendencies are allowing portions of his plan for the government of the world to become humanly comprehensible.

When the completion of a cycle of events reveals what the plan of the cycle was from the first, it behooves men, co-ordinating latest with earliest cycles, to ascertain the trend of the movements in the sky; and to gaze more solemnly than upon the stars themselves, upon that Form loftier than the stars, which passes by in the darkness behind them, its outlines not wholly visible, but the direction not unknown in which it is moving the constellations.

I commend the German, the English, and the American theological battle-field to the timid and the hopeful, who go out to walk and meditate in the world's eventide. Goethe could say that the only real and the deepest theme of the world's and of man's history, to which all other subjects are subordinate, is the conflict between faith and unbelief. We are the ancients, as Bacon said; but the inscription, written by history, which is God's finger, and no accident, before the sad eyes of the bruised and staggering ages, on the trophy erected after the severest intellectual battle of this oldest and newest of the centuries, is: *Via Crucis, Via Lucis!* — "The way of the Cross is the way of Light."

I do not respect any proposition merely because it is ancient, or in the mouths of majorities; but I do respect propositions that have seen honest and protracted battle, but not defeat. The test of the soundness of scholarship is that it should contend with scholarship, not once or twice, but century after century, and come out crowned. But the intellectual supremacy of Christianity in the nineteenth century is not a novelty. There are other battle-fields worth visiting by those who walk and meditate, on which Christian trophies stand, more important, as marks of the world's agonies and advances, than any that ever Greek erected for victory at Salamis or Marathon. I respect the law of the survival of the fittest. I lean on church history. I go to its battle-fields, and lie down on them. They are places of spiritual rest. Gazing on their horizon, I see no narrow prospect, but a breadth of nineteen hundred victorious years. Looking into the sky, as I lie there, I hear sometimes the anthem: "As it was in the beginning, is now, and ever shall be, world without end." I obtain glimpses of a heaven opened; and behold, a white horse, and he that sits on him is called the Word of God, King of kings, Lord of lords. He is clothed in a vesture dipped in blood; but his eyes are as a flame of fire, AND ON HIS HEAD ARE MANY CROWNS.

BOSTON MONDAY LECTURES.

I.

THE SEEN AND THE UNSEEN.

By RT. REV. THOMAS M. CLARK, D.D., LL.D.

I.

THE SEEN AND THE UNSEEN.

By RT. REV. THOMAS M. CLARK, D.D., LL.D.

THERE is not much that is essentially new in the fundamental postulates of our modern philosophies. The immutability of matter, the law of evolution, the persistence of force, and the principle of natural selection, are all recognized in some form by ancient authors; but a flood of light has been thrown upon these doctrines by the more recent discoveries of science. They have been enlivened by rare and varied styles of illustration, drawn from every department of nature, and brought into much closer contact with the popular mind than they ever were before. There is great apprehension on one side, and corresponding exultation on the other. The old-fashioned believer fears that the foundations will be destroyed; the unbeliever affirms that henceforth belief in the supernatural is impossible. Both the affirmation and the fear which it excites are exaggerated. At the present moment there is a decided reaction on the part of those who have been regarded as the enemies of spiritual truth; and, finding themselves suspended in mid-air between heaven and earth, with no sufficient hold upon either, even the substance of matter having evaporated in the process of eliminating the spirit which vivified it, obliged to choose between God and the atom, and finding the difficulties which encompass the existence of the former surpassed by those which pertain to the being and functions of the latter,—men of science are now beginning to revise their own record, and I believe that the wisest and most profound amongst them will soon be found on the spiritual and supernatural side.) Having already done a good work in overturning some of the idols of belief, in which we had trusted too fondly and too blindly, they will now furnish us with a true and rational basis of faith, which will be none the less *faith* because it rests upon *intelligent* conviction.

ARE MATTER AND SPIRIT IDENTICAL?

The question at issue to-day, and it involves all that is essential in the intellectual warfare that is now raging, is this,—are matter and spirit identical? and, if they are not, is the spiritual world a product of the physical, or is the original pattern of the material universe to be found in the spiritual?

Mr. Herbert Spencer says "that there is no *precise* line of demarcation between physiological and psychological facts, and that every *absolute* distinction is illusory. Sensations, sentiments, instincts, intelligence, all constitute a world apart; but which comes out of the animal world, in which it is rooted, of which it is, as it were, the efflorescence. Between the most humble practice and the most lofty thought there is no opposition of nature, but there is difference in degree, each being only one of the innumerable manifestations of life." If this is not the doctrine of pure, materialistic monism, it is a plain denial of "the existence of any *precise* line of demarcation between spirit and matter."

Dr. Carpenter, in his principles of mental physiology, quotes with approval from the late Charles Baxter as follows: "Irresistible, undeniable facts demonstrate that man is not a den, wherein two enemies are chained together, but *one being;* that soul and body are one,— one and indivisible. We had better face this great fact. 'T is no good to blink it. Our knowledge of physiology has come to a point where the old idea of man's constitution must be thrown aside. To struggle against the overwhelming force of science, under the notion of shielding religion, is mere play."

Dr. Priestley, who "thought that he had sufficiently proved that mind is nothing but a modification of matter," is a little more outspoken than some of our modern materialists; and so also is Mr. Hume, who says expressly: "Within myself I am conscious only of impressions and ideas. (The substance called mind is a mere fiction, imagined for the support of these, as the substance called matter is imagined for the support of sensible qualities.") This is the ultimatum of denial; unless, indeed, it is surpassed by the statement once made to me by a learned *savant*, to the effect that he could not honestly affirm his belief in anything "but the relation of mathematical quantities."

THE MATERIAL MONADIC THEORY.

Let us see what is involved in this material, monadic theory. In the first place, matter must be alive, and must have been so from eternity; just as much alive as it is to-day, for there could be no *accession* of life at any given period. This, according to the theorem of immutability and continuity, of which the materialists make so much, is impossible. There can have been no *first* monad, a germ of life, for the introduction of this would also violate the same theorem; and so every monad now in existence must have always existed, possessing always the same degree of potency. These monads must have not only been eternally alive, but they must also have always possessed the element of force, in virtue of which, acting in concert, they were able to organize everything in the universe that exists, or ever existed. Now force is not a *thing*, any more than sight or sound; it is a mere transference of energy, and can be exerted only on the condition of a change of state or position. If I wish to get mechanical force out of air or matter or any form of matter, I do it by altering the position of things, by making a vacuum in the air, or causing the water to fall from a height, or by withdrawing a portion of the electric fluid from one substance, in order to develop action by contact with another. But, whatever I do, I can neither increase nor diminish the actual amount of energy that exists in the universe, any more than I can increase or diminish the quantity of matter. So that whatever degree or amount of energy exists to-day must have always existed. Again, energy can be transmuted into force only by an influence coming upon it *ab extra*. Nothing moves unless it is impelled. Now the monad is matter; and force is not matter, but something analogous to the spiritual. The clearest conception that we have of force originates in the action of the will, which is not force in itself, but only a condition, upon the exercise of which energy is transmuted into force. There must, then, have always been something more than matter in the universe. Energy, which is not a thing, or an atom, or a compound of atoms, must have existed from eternity; and then there must also have been some sort of influence also not atomic, by means of which this energy is transmuted into force.

.THE THEORIES OF BAIN AND PALEY.

The eternal living monad must have had the power, not only to organize itself, but everything else that exists, or ever has existed. This supposes something more than life or force. Organization involves the idea of a *plan*, and therefore the monad, or atom, or molecule, must be intelligent. Professor Bain says: " This tendency on the part of matter to *organize itself*, to grow into shape, to assume definite forms in obedience to the definite action of *force*, is all-pervading. It is in the ground on which you tread, in the water you drink, in the air you breathe. *Incipient life*, as it were, manifests itself throughout the whole of what we call inorganic nature." When we speak of "the tendencies of matter," we merely describe the mode in which it acts, or the law under which it acts, but obviously *law is not force*. Paley puts the matter in his clear way as follows: "It is a perversion of language to assign any law as the efficient operative cause of anything. A law presupposes an agent; for it is the only mode according to which an agent proceeds. It implies a power; for it is the order according to which that power acts. Without this agent, without this power, which are both distinct from itself, the *law* does nothing, is nothing." And when Mr. Bain talks about "incipient life" as "manifesting itself throughout the whole of what we call inorganic nature," he virtually recognizes the presence of something that is not material. The principle of life in a seed, or an egg, or in any sort of embryo, is not inherent in the materials of which it is composed, or the mere result of juxtaposition, — no art of mechanics or chemistry could ever manufacture a seed that would grow.

Again, according to the theory of the monists, the atom must have in it an inherent æsthetic element, and be competent to organize in accordance with the laws of beauty, both of form and color. It is an architect, a sculptor, a painter. The splendors of the landscape, the glory of the flower, existed potentially in the monad, interminable ages before this tiny, invisible god saw fit to develop itself in the present forms of what (for want of a better word) we have been accustomed to call creation. But the greatest marvel remains to be noticed. The monad must have been endowed, not only with æsthetic intelligence, but also with a conscience; for in these latter days it has seen fit to take upon itself the form of a being who is competent to distinguish between right and wrong, and still further to become conscious of what is popularly known as the sentiment of reverence. All this must be so, because there can be nothing in an effect which did not already exist in its cause, and the effect can continue only so long as the cause continues to work in it. When the cause ceases, of course the effect must also cease; and to say that nature is both cause and effect is nonsense. It is equally absurd to say that nature and life are identical. In.the words of Swedenborg: "Nature, in respect to life, is dead. If nature lived it would live either from itself or from some other being, or by some other being. If it lived from itself, then that would live which we clearly see does not live, and nature would destroy itself whenever it destroys its forms, in which and according to which life exists. So, also, it would not only be the principle of its own causes and effects, but also the principle of its principle; or else this principle would convert itself into nature, in order that it might be enabled to be what it is not; which every one sees to be opposite to common sense."

But, we are told that no one ever heard, or saw, or tasted, or smelt a spiritual substance, and that the term itself conveys no intelligible meaning. No one ever heard, or saw, or tasted, or smelt a molecule, and the whole atomic theory is only a working hypothesis, plausible enough and provable perhaps, but still resting upon no testimony of the senses.

RELATIONS OF MIND AND MATTER.

Again, it is said to be inconceivable that a particle of matter should come into being or pass out of being, while what is called spirit is supposed to come and go, and the act of consciousness may be temporarily suspended. This point has been satisfactorily met by a very striking analogy in the kingdom of nature, where "energy of visible motion often disappears by transformation into the dormant or latent energy of position." The *capacity* of consciousness does not cease when we stop thinking. It is urged still further that every act of thought is attended by some corresponding change in the tissue of the body, and cannot be exercised except upon this condition; so that, even if there were an inherent distinction between mind and matter, the former is dependent upon the latter, and cannot exist separate from the structure which excites its activity. It is assumed that "a definite thought and a definite molecular action in the brain occur simultaneously;" but, as the Rev. Mr. Gorman (to whose elaborate and very able treatise on Christian Psychology I am much indebted) has well said: "All simultaneous action in a living organism necessarily presupposes successive action. For example, thought precedes speech, and will precedes act. When the mind is excited from without, molecular movement of the brain must actually precede sensation. When the brain is set in motion from within, mental activity must actually precede cerebral movement." That the mind is capable of acting, without being moved or prompted by external stimulus, our consciousness affirms, and this is enough to determine the question of its independent or absolute existence.

THE CONNECTION BETWEEN THE BODY AND THE SOUL.

But, while we deny that mind or thought is a mere function of the body, we cannot help allowing the necessity of some intermediate link between the body and the soul, in order to explain their mutual reaction; or the existence of an intermediate substance of almost inconceivable tenuity, constituting a link or bond between the gross *corporeal body* and the spiritual substance commonly called the *soul*. I must here be allowed to quote a very striking passage from a sermon preached by Dean Mansell in the pulpit of the University Church: "All action, whether free or constrained, and all passion implies and rests upon another great mystery of philosophy,— the commerce between mind and matter. The properties and operations of matter are known only by the external senses; the faculties and acts of the mind are known only by the internal apprehension. The energy of the one is motion, the energy of the other is consciousness. What is the middle term which unites these two, and how can their reciprocal action, unquestionable as it is in fact, be conceived as possible in theory? How can a contact between body and body produce consciousness in the immaterial soul? How can a mental self-determination produce the motion of material organs? How can mind, which is neither extended nor figured, nor colored in itself, represent, by its ideas, the extension and figure and color of bodies? How can the mind be determined to a new position in space by an act of thought, to which space has no relation? How can thought itself be carried on by bodily instruments and yet itself have nothing in common with bodily affections? What is the relation between the last pulsation of the material brain and the first awakening of the mental perception? How does the spoken word, a merely material vibration of the atmosphere, become echoed, as it were, in the silent voice of thought, and take its part in an operation wholly spiritual?" These are tough questions, and, in the opinion of the Dean, they have not yet been answered. The attempt has been made by theories of Pre-established Harmony, a Plastic Medium, and so on, all of which he regards as so many confessions of an unresolved mystery. And yet one of the ablest modern psychologists says that "the battle-ground of a rational psychology lies here. Now, more than at any previous time, it behooves all who desire to contribute to the real and solid advance of psychological science, to endeavor, by adequate analysis of the phenomena, to penetrate the mysterious middle region occupied by what has been called the 'animal spirits.' There is the 'passage,' 'gulf,' 'film,' *limbus*, or by whatsoever name called — alleged, without an attempt at proof, to be impassable — which divides the two distinct but closely correlated spheres of soul and body." It would be useless, within the limited space allowed me, to attempt to give an outline of the theories propounded by Christian Wolf, Raymond Vieussens, Unzer, Prof. Bain, Drs. Maudsley and Beale, Claude Bernard, Dr. Richardson, and Dr. George Moore, which have relation to this subject. I will, however, cite a passage from the last-named writer, which seems to me to be very suggestive: " We possess evidence that there exists an all-pervading something, not to be defined as matter, but which may be regarded as the substantial medium of those actions known as light, heat, electricity, gravitation, and magnetism. That the mind operates on this medium in our visible bodies we find in the fact that a man, by the mere act of his will in contracting the muscles, say of his arm, causes a current of influence which sensibly deflects the needle of the galvanometer, the currents being opposite in the opposite arms. Moreover, it appears that the nerves of sensation are positive, the nerves of motion negative, so that every act of impression and of will seems to operate through an agency similar to that of an electric telegraph. The will being capable of moving this agency and of being moved through it, may we not reasonably imagine it possible that the soul is to be forever associated with it in some specific and identical form? This agency is probably one with the all-penetrating medium of the universe, called, for lack of a name sufficiently definite, ether. It is calculated to serve as a spiritual body, which, taking direction and impression as the vehicle of the soul, might be capable of influence and action in sympathy with all the changes, mental and physical, of the universe."

I have room, in the present connection, to cite only one further extract, and that is taken from Unzer's Principles of Physiology, a work of no inconsiderable authority: "All the phenomena of motion and sensation, manifested through the nerves, render probable the existence of a remarkably subtle fluid essence, which is present invisibly in the medulla of the brain and nerves, and is the means whereby all the functions of both are performed. It is termed the *vital spirits* or nervous fluid, but it is not known how and when it contributes to the animal actions. It is not that fluid matter which is seen in the medulla of the brain and nerves, but a much more subtle fluid imperceptible to the senses. It is inferred from the phenomena which betray its existence, that this nervous fluid is a remarkably mobile fluid, a spirituous vapor, which can be neither aqueous, nor glutinous, nor elastic, nor ethereal, nor electrical. The *brain is the laboratory of the vital spirits.* It appears certain that there is such a fluid essence secreted from the vessels of the gray matter of the brain into the hollow tubes of the medullary matter, which is carried by the tubes of the nerves to their termination, and supplies the principle whereby the nerves are rendered capable of being the agents of the senses and of movements."

MAN A THREEFOLD BEING.

It would appear, then, that man, in his present stage of existence, is a threefold being, consisting of a material body, a vital principle, and a mind. By the first he stands connected with all material forms; by the second, with all vitalized forms; and by the third, with all beings of his own particular species and all above him in rank. The first is transient, always in a state of flux; the second gives form to this transient body, and directs all its special functions; the third gives man the consciousness of being what he is, and enables him to know and perceive what is going on around him. In his present state the three are inseparable, and have mutual relations.

The body, or the atomic part of man, cannot create vitality; the vital or organizing principle cannot be a result of the mere collocation of atoms. The vital principle affects the spiritual or mental, but does not absolutely control it, and certainly does not create it. The spiritual, after all, is supreme. The power of perception, the consciousness of thought, the will, and the moral sense constitute the soul, and the soul is the man.

And now, coming back to the main question, which may be thus stated, Is the original pattern of things material, and does what appears to be spirit flow out from that, as a result and effect; or is the universe, man of course included, the simple reduction of a spiritual conception to form? I will illustrate the point at issue by the simple analogy of what is called music. We become conscious of musical sounds through the medium of atmospheric waves striking upon a mechanical instrument in the ear, the vibrations thus caused being then carried by certain strings or cords to the brain, where the material process is translated into the perception which we call sound. We then go back a little farther and we find that these waves in the air were produced by certain mechanical movements in the throat, or through the agency of instruments made of parchment or wire, or wood or brass, or some other physical substance, so that, thus far, until we come to the last factor of the problem, which is the transmutation of these vibrations into the act of perception or sound, everything seems to lie on the material plane. And now, going back one step farther, we find that the special action of the throat or the brass instrument, which gave character to the musical sounds, was determined by certain written or printed lines and dots and figures, known as the score; and where did this score come from? Out of the mind of the composer; and in the realms of his spiritual being all these harmonies and melodies existed as a fact before he ever put pen to paper. In his apprehension the music exists, and it is capable of being enjoyed by him, independent of any material pulsations; although, indeed, his sense of gratification is greatly enhanced when he hears the thought of his mind reproduced in actual song. Now observe that at both ends of the process we need to have a spiritual being, in order to the existence of music, — a mind to compose it, and a mind to perceive it. The universe is constructed upon the same principles of harmony which constitute music. There is a singular analogy between the laws of sight and the laws of sound: there are seven primary colors and seven primary sounds,— thirds, fifths, and octaves make harmony in both; there are complementary colors and complementary sounds; there are discords of color and discords of sound, occasioned by the same general law, and as the eye is offended by one, so is the ear offended by the other. There is a law of rhythm which pervades the universe, and if the spiritual ear were quickened, we might actually hear the music of the spheres.

Is it possible for a human being to believe that all this can be, without also believing that there is a divine, spiritual, preconceived plan, of which the material universe is only the manifestation?

OUR PERSONAL IMMORTALITY.

The bearing of all this upon the question of our own personal immortality gives to the subject a most profound and solemn interest. It is hardly conceivable that man should have been endowed with immortality, and yet so constituted as to be unable to arrive at any satisfactory proof of the fact. To those who receive the records of the New Testament as authentic and true, no further demonstration is needed; for those records not only declare the fact of eternal life, but also give a tangible assurance of the same in the reappearance of Christ after his death. In these days of sharp and ruthless historical criticism it is, however, very desirable, if we can, to supplement and confirm the doctrine of that Book by argument drawn from other sources; and the most implicit believer will surely not object to our drawing upon the resources of science and philosophy to establish a truth which science and philosophy have done so much to discredit. A work, entitled "The Unseen Universe," by B. Stewart and P. G. Tait, published last year in London, attempts to construct upon a scientific basis the doctrine of man's continued existence after death. The book has been assailed on one side by those who regard it as teaching only a "dangerously subtle materialism," and on the other as "orthodoxly credulous and superstitious," as being, in fact, "the most hardened and impenitent nonsense that ever called itself original speculation." The intervention of one who aims to reconcile science with religion seems to operate like a *red rag* in stirring up to hot strife both the orthodox bull, who does not believe in science at all, and the heterodox bear, who does not believe that there is a God, or that man ever had any soul.

There is, perhaps, no grosser form of materialism than that of the theological school which teaches the doctrine of a final reconstruction of the animal body; a recomposition of the physical atoms disintegrated by the act of death; the man thus raised to become a resident in some sort of physical heaven, — a dogma which destroys the basis upon which the only satisfactory philosophical or scientific argument for immortality can be constructed, namely, *the law of continuity*. This is the universal law of nature, and all our calculations rest upon it. Now, scientifically speaking, what is the effect of death? It certainly does not wipe out of being an atom of the substance by which our material organism was built up. It simply precipitates a process which had always been going on by gradual degrees,— the return of our primordial substance to its normal or original condition. Neither is it conceivable that the energy which actuated the body while it lived is annihilated at death; for energy, as we have before seen, is just as much a fixed quantity as matter. The demonstration of *force*, resultant from that energy, may cease to be manifested, just as all indications of force cease when opposite persons become equalized. When I discharge a Leyden jar, I neither add to nor diminish the *amount* of electricity. Once more, unless the soul is a mere function of the body, and the brain secretes consciousness as the liver secretes bile, the principle of continuity demands that it should continue to be, after the machine or framework which it shaped and inspired has fallen to pieces.

Everything, then, depends upon the question whether or not there is such a thing as a spiritual universe,— anything, anywhere, beside atomic matter, or what the philosophers now call *stuff*. There are not many wise men in our day who are ready to remit everything to non-existence that is of the nature of spirit, and, if there was anything antecedent to the visible universe, there may be something which will survive it.

One thing is quite certain; this visible universe

must, sooner or later, have an end, just as truly as the body of man wears out and ceases to be. There is no immortality for that. All motion in that universe must cease, whenever everything is brought into equilibrium, which the constant dissipation of energy that is going on makes inevitable. The energy thus dissipated, and the force thus destroyed, may be restored if we suppose it to originate in a spiritual universe, but not otherwise.

Is it, however, possible for us to apprehend the nature of that spiritual existence which is involved in our personal immortality? The existence of finite beings, unconditioned by time and space, is inconceivable. The old idea of the soul, as passing off into space like a puff of empty nothingness, without form or substance, without any kind of organ or function, still existing, but nowhere in particular, is about equivalent to annihilation. St. Paul tells us that when his earthly tabernacle, or tent, is removed, there is another dwelling-place awaiting him, — a new vesture, after the old one is worn out. Thomas Aquinas argues "to the effect that it is not repugnant to the nature of a spiritual substance to be the form of the body; since this only means that, in relation to the body, it is the principle of these perfections through the instrumentality of which the body has some resemblance to the spirit, and is a being at once actual, subsistent, corporeal, living, and sensitive." It has been well said "that we are logically constrained to admit the existence of some form or organ which is not of this earth, and which survives dissolution, if we regard the principle of continuity and the doctrine of a future state as both true." "There *is*," says the Apostle Paul (not there shall be), "a spiritual body." "We *have* a building of God, an house not made with hands, eternal in the heavens."

The next stage of existence is, then, a conditioned life, otherwise we could not retain our individuality. And now I remark that the law of continuity demands that this life should be subject to an endless process of development. What may finally come to us as the result of this development we are probably as unable to conjecture as the infant is to forecast the experiences of his maturity. It is much easier to grasp the conception of a future life than it is to apprehend the *endlessness* of that life. Having once begun to be, shall I never cease to be? Will this conscious soul of mine continue to exist and assert itself after the visible universe upon which I now look has burnt out its last spark and vanished? Shall I live as long as God lives? We read that Christ, in bringing life and immortality to light, has "*abolished* death." If, then, death is abolished, I must live forever. My powers give way in the attempt to grapple with this stupendous fact; but I accept it as revealed by One who knew whereof He spake, — I accept it, because existence would be intolerable on any other condition.

CHARACTERISTICS OF SPIRITUAL BEING.

I next observe that spiritual being, however it may be developed in the future, must always retain the same characteristics of identity. In this primary stage of being it has relations to a physical universe which in a certain sense are temporary, but there must also be certain inseparable relations between this life and the next, in order to the continuance of our personal individuality. The consciousness of the *Ego* must be eternal, and in order to this, the power of memory must continue, and the same essential activities of the mind remain intact. Although it is not to be believed that our future life is to be on another and a higher plane of the physical, I am not certain that there may not be something in it analogous to the physical. Why may there not be something there corresponding to what we here call natural science, and art, and all those occupations which are neither menial nor sensual? Why may there not be a field for the exercise of those peculiar gifts with which different men are endowed, and to which they have here, in a measure, devoted their lives? The laws of art and science are as immutable and eternal as the law of morals. They proceed from the same divine source, and have their seat in the bosom of God. It is a very dreary prospect, if we are to anticipate an immortal existence with no variety of employment, and with nothing to interest us there corresponding to the best and noblest things which concern us here. The eternal life may be one perpetual act of worship, but that worship will not be in a monotone. God will be adored in the study of his manifold works, and in the exercise of the manifold powers which he has given us. I believe that everything seen and temporal, which is not of the nature of sin, is a type and symbol and prophecy of something unseen and eternal, only purer and more glorious. Altogether too much is said about the rest of heaven, delightful as the rest from carking cares and spiritual contentions and corroding anxieties must be; but some people seem to think that to die is only "to lie down to pleasant and everlasting dreams." If we are to live forever, I presume that there will be something for us to *do* forever, — something beside enjoyment.

The light that is thrown upon the next stage of existence in the Scriptures is designedly somewhat general and limited. All the direct information on the subject which they give could be condensed into a very small space. The eschatology of the Old Testament could all be written on a single page, and very much in the New Testament which has been supposed to relate to the subject is now referred to the setting up of the kingdom of truth and righteousness here on earth. "The kingdom to come" in many cases means simply the kingdom of Christ among men. Revelation was not intended to gratify our curiosity, and it would not be well to make the veil which hangs between us and the future too translucent. Our work is here, and if that work is properly done, we can afford to wait until an actual entrance into the next world reveals its mysteries. The time is not most profitably employed which is spent in speculating about these mysteries.

But we do want to be at rest so far as the fact that

there is such a world is concerned, and it is most desirable that we should know enough about it for the proper regulation of the present life. With this knowledge we may be content. And let us be thankful for any help, let it come from whatever quarter it may, which may be of service in determining the great fact that there is a spiritual as well as a natural life, and that the power abides after the latter is over. Theologians ought to be careful lest they encumber the truth of our immortality with notions and theories which the man of science finds it impossible to receive, and the philosopher should be on his guard against any such prejudgment of the point at issue as will prevent him from giving due consideration to the proof by which that point is established. There can be no collision between science and faith so long as science confines itself to its legitimate sphere, and faith does not allow itself to degenerate into a superstition. Science cannot take a single firm step, unless it has faith in something that is unseen and spiritual; and faith is a blind guide, unless it has eyes to see what lies around. I do not think that the two parties will reach the final goal of absolute and certain truth by separating and going different ways; let them travel together, the one as the interpreter of the seen, and the other as the interpreter of the unseen. The material will help to explain the spiritual, and the spiritual will disclose the end for which the material exists.

THE HOW OF THE UNIVERSE AND THE WHY.

"A division as old as Aristotle separates speculators into two great classes, — those who study the How of the universe, and those who study the Why. All men of science are embraced in the former of these, all men of religion in the latter." I would like to understand both, if this is possible; but if I must choose between the two, I would rather know the reason for which I exist than the mode by which I exist. The one is an end, the other only a means. If it is impossible to discover the end, or if that end, when it is supposed to be discovered, does not seem to be such as justifies the elaborate process by which it is reached; if all the magnificent discoveries of science land us in the conclusion that the universe is only a great clock, put together and weighted and wound up to run for a certain period, and then, when it has struck the last hour, to fall to pieces and become resolved into the materials of which it was originally made, — the clock having marked the passage of time, faithfully and truly, as long as the flow of events continued, but the time itself leaving behind no permanent results which abide after the clock has ceased to strike, — if the end of existence is exhausted in the process by which that existence is registered and terminates with the process; or, again, if the universe is only a huge electric wheel, throwing out sparks of life which glisten for an instant in the darkness and vanish forever; or, again, if man is only the efflorescence of a physical compound, that buds and blossoms, and then dies as soon as the soil furnishes no further sustenance, — why, then the universe is a sham and man an impertinence. All comes to nothing in the end; consciousness ceases when the phosphorus in the brain ceases to burn, and, with the end of consciousness, the material world might as well shrivel and die and come to nothing also.

This is the teaching of a school of science, "falsely so called," which mad materialistic diviners, with many high-sounding words, now offer to our acceptance.

It is not easy to keep within the limits of a frigid logic, in dealing with matters in which all our highest aspirations and all our profoundest feelings are concerned. There is a spiritual department of our nature which is as real as the monad, and as vital as the physical affinities of the body or the working of the reason and understanding. All that is beautiful and all that is frightful, all that appeals to the imagination and the emotions and the sense of rectitude, centres here. This is mere cloudland to the materialist, — like that superb display which sometimes appears in the western horizon as the day is drawing to a close, when the azure and vermilion and green and golden hues shape themselves into forms more beautiful than anything ever seen on the plane of earth; but all which, he tells us, would prove to be a sad delusion, if we should be suddenly transported to the very region of those gorgeous clouds, for then they would be resolved into a dull, chill, leaden mist, obscuring the sun and the stars and the earth.

It is very true that what a man sees depends upon the place where he stands, and it is very possible for one to take such a position as must, of necessity, rule out all the beauty and glory from the universe. But is the splendor of the autumnal sunset any the less a reality because it is painted with drops of dew,— the same material which the machinist uses to start his engine?

Which is the more real, if potency be the measure of reality,— the solid shaft of granite, or the imponderable lightning which shivers it to fragments? Do we not approach the region of power just in proportion as we pass from the material to the spiritual, from the solid to the fluid? The water grinds the rock, the heated air dissipates the water, the electric influence decomposes the air, and the will of man excites and directs the electric force. The granite pile on Bunker Hill oscillates every day, as the warm rays of the sun play upon its eastern and its western side.

THE SEEN AND THE UNSEEN.

This is the conclusion of the whole matter,— "Nature represents things spiritual." The Seen is the type and symbol of the Unseen, and that which is seen is temporal, while the things which are unseen are eternal. Nothing can be seen but forms, and these are in their very nature transient and changeable. The substance of these forms is indestructible. We live in two worlds, one temporal and the other eternal,— the world of forms and the world of realities. With the one we come into communication by our senses, with the other we come into communication by the soul. Material things are the symbols of spiritual things, and we are able to express the latter only through the medium of the former. The next stage of existence will be simply the unfolding or development of this primary stage of being. There is no arbitrary line separating the temporal from the eternal; the one passes over into the other by natural, orderly law. The change induced by death cannot in any way affect our personal identity. We must retain a memory of the past and the consciousness of possessing the same mental and moral qualities by which we are individualized here on earth. The time has been when you might hear the great congregation sing such strains as these:—

> "The living know that they must die,
> But all the dead forgotten lie;
> Their memory and their sense is gone,
> Alike unknowing and unknown."

The words had a solemn sound, and it was not noticed that they taught the doctrine of annihilation.

Neither is there any propriety in speaking of the unseen world as a "final state," as if we had entered upon a fixed, unchangeable, and completed condition of being. There is no point of finality in human existence. However high we may climb, there will always be a higher summit left unscaled, something new to be learned, some loftier attainment to be reached.

And, if we are to retain our personal identity, —
without which immortality would not be a gift worth
taking, — those whom we have known and loved here
we must know and love hereafter. It would be a
dreary thing if we thought that we were going to
a land of strangers. Is it to be supposed that the
emotional part of our nature will be extinguished, or
so modified, that we shall cease forever to love that,
which, here on earth, was the centre of our most earnest
and tender affection? Shall we be so overwhelmed
by the glory of consorting with angels that we shall
cease any longer to care for the poor fellow-creatures
with whom we wept and toiled when we were pilgrims
together on earth? Will Raphael and Gabriel and
Michael be nearer and dearer to us than the child we
once lost, or the father and mother who taught us
how to pray? Those who have gone before cannot
forget those whom they have left behind; and is it to
be supposed that their cup of happiness can be full
if they never expect to welcome their friends in

"The bright and blessed country, — the home of God's elect"?

I feel that I am forbidden, by the nature of the
occasion, from trespassing any further upon the do-
main of feeling, and I therefore close by saying, that,
as I understand the matter, the distinction which
separates the Seen from the Unseen is not determined
by any supposed differentiation of spirit from matter.
I do not know that any distinct line, dividing the
two, exists, and if it does exist, I do not know where
it runs; but the distinction is best defined by the

words *phenomenal* and *actual*, — the forms and the realities. The things which are seen are passing by like a swift panorama, ever changing, ever fading, ever decaying; but the things which are not seen abide forever. Which do you care for most? Are you mistaking shadows for realities, and realities for shadows?

II.

MORAL LAW IN ITS RELATIONS TO PHYSICAL SCIENCE AND TO POPULAR RELIGION.

By PRESIDENT E. G. ROBINSON, D.D., LL.D.

II.

MORAL LAW IN ITS RELATIONS TO PHYSICAL SCIENCE AND TO POPULAR RELIGION.

By PRESIDENT E. G. ROBINSON, D.D., LL.D.

NO word plays a more conspicuous part in modern thought, and none is more loosely used, than the word "law." Originally used in a single sense, its meaning was unambiguous and universally recognized. It is now employed in many senses, some of which are plain and have become necessary, others are obscure and doubtful, and others still it is difficult, if not impossible to justify. Its primary meaning undoubtedly was, "a rule of conduct prescribed and enforced by some kind of authority." In this sense of the word, law was essential to the continuance of individual life, as well as to the formation of individual character. It was equally necessary for the organization and conservation of society.

Natural science, borrowing the term "law," has given it a wide range of application. Observers of the phenomena of nature, noticing that these always occurred in an orderly sequence, declared their occurrence to be by law. Physical laws, therefore, in the sense of rules according to which physical phenomena of given classes always occur, became a needed and a familiar expression. Out of this signification in the progress of science have grown other meanings, to which it is not necessary here to advert.

But whatever may be said of the new senses which science has attached to the word "law," it must be admitted to have thrown new light on the original meaning of the phrase "moral law." It has sent back to ethics its borrowed term endowed with a widened and deepened significance; the metaphorical use of it has enabled us to get a deeper insight into the fulness of its literal sense. How this has been accomplished forms the first half of our present discussion.

PROPERTIES OF MATTER.

Natural law always implies and reveals some kind of force, denoting a rule according to which the force always acts. But the rule is not an arbitrary decree; it represents no mere imposed order of sequence, but expresses that which makes the sequence orderly. Its origin, so far as matter itself is concerned, must be in the properties of matter, or in the conditions under which matter is found uniformly to exist. These remaining ever the same, the modes or laws of their manifestation must continue unchangeably the same.

Modern science has made us familiar with the phrases, "mechanical laws" and "chemical laws." Whatever the explanation that may be given of the difference between these, that explanation will be found in the last analysis to rest on the account given of the subtile properties of matter. Matter being found to be what it is, the laws which determine the order of its phenomena are necessarily what they are. Two classes of properties may be set to work in one and the same substance at one and the same instant. Thus, an explosive substance enclosed in a retort with a reagent may be set to work chemically, and ·its bulk so expanded as mechanically to blow the retort into fragments. Our respiration is mechanical, and the accompanying oxygenation of our blood is chemical; and the two sets of laws, the mechanical and the chemical, that rule conjointly in these phenomena, so rule because the properties of matter of which our bodies are composed necessarily so reveal themselves. Whatever may be the distinctions, therefore, in our conceptions of physical law, the law necessarily exists because necessitated by the properties of matter. To know and understand the modes or laws of physical phenomena is to know and understand all that is knowable of the nature of matter.

PROPERTIES OF THE PERSONAL BEING.

Corresponding to the properties of matter are also the properties of the personal being. Nothing exists which does not exist in a given mode and with a given constitution. That in us which thinks and feels and wills, has its own constitution, and acts under its own unvarying laws, as well as the bodily

organism which executes our volitions. Some of
these laws of the personality are distinctively moral;
and moral laws are just as much a revelation of the
moral properties of the personal being as physical
laws are a revelation of the properties of matter.
The properties of the one do not more immediately
necessitate its laws than do the properties of the
other. Personal existence is only in given modes
and under fixed conditions; any description which
can be given of these modes as moral will be found
to be equivalent to a description or statement of
the moral laws under which all personal beings are
found to exist. To know and understand moral laws
is to know and understand all that is knowable of
the moral nature of man; and it is so because the
phrases "original moral nature" and "moral law" are
descriptive of one and the same thing.

LAW AS FORMULA AND AS CONSTITUTIVE PRINCIPLE.

Thus, there are two senses in which the phrase
"moral law" may be used, and which should be carefully distinguished. The one conceives it as a constitutive principle of personality; the other conceives
it as a precept, a command, a statute which formu-
lates the principle into an authoritative rule of action.
There is necessarily recognized, therefore, in the use
of the word "law" what in technical language we
may call the objective precept and the subjective
principle. The subjective principle, as a property
of the personal being, always underlies the idea of
moral law, just as the properties regulative of physi-

cal force underlie the idea of physical law. As the constitutive properties of matter manifest themselves in physical laws, so the constitutive properties or principles of the personal being manifest themselves in given modes or according to moral laws. No conception of moral law, therefore, is complete which does not regard it as a principle of being as well as a formal command.

But just here there are two points of distinction between physical law and moral law which should be made and remembered. The first of these is, that while all statutory law is declaratory, physical law formulated is simply declaratory of what is necessarily true, of what always has been and always must be true of all material phenomena; moral law as precept, on the contrary, is the declaration of what ought to be, and what from the very nature of a rational intelligence must be, if the typical idea of the personal being is ever to be realized. — The other point is, that while moral law may be broken, physical law never can be broken. You may arrest one physical force by the application of another, but you never can violate the law according to which the force acts. You can, by appliances, arrest the force of gravitation; you cannot, by any possibility, violate the law of gravitation. I know that in popular language gravitation is oftentimes spoken of as itself a law; but gravitation is the expression or action of a given force; its law is that the force always acts "directly as the mass and inversely as the square of the distance." That law you can in no sense break or violate; and the force which acts in accordance with it, whatever else you can do with it, you never can suspend. But in moral law there is always implied a force of will which is to be regulated; it is to the will that moral precepts are always addressed. The precepts can be voluntarily complied with, or they can be voluntarily over-ridden. We can break the objective rule because we can suppress or suspend the subjective principle. The constitutive properties of a finite moral being might prompt him instinctively to worship the supremely best Being; by force of will he may bring himself to worship the supremely worst being. The self-acting nature of an unperverted man might prompt always and spontaneously to tell the truth, but he can will habitually to falsify and mislead. But if the external precept be true to the internal principle, if it command only what that exacts; then, if broken, its penalty can no more be escaped than personal identity can be changed.

IMMEDIATE OR SECONDARY SOURCE OF LAW.

Here we see the immediate or secondary source of moral law. All law has its immediate origin in whatever is ruled by it, — the physical in matter, the moral in the human soul. As statutes, the moral simply formulate what is eternally true of the human personality as such.

But here let us not mistake. Moral law is not derived from every, or from any, personal being now found in life. Human nature is exceedingly diverse, is an extremely variable quantity; and the actions of every man, when understood, are sure to reveal the moral qualities of his innermost nature, and that nature may be radically perverse. But his acts will be in accordance with the ruling principles of his existing nature. He will, by necessity, obey the ruling law of his being as it now is. And it is in this explanation that we see the meaning of the language of the Apostle Paul when he says, "I find another law in my members warring against the law of my mind." He saw the law of a superinduced and perverse nature; and he saw the law of his original and deeper nature. A superinduced nature may manifest itself in acts of uniform perversity; but they are acts whose uniformity shows them to be according to law, — a "law in the members," it may be, and yet a law from within the person acting. There is also the profounder and original or ideal nature with its deeper law, of which conscience takes cognizance, and that law is what the Apostle calls the law of his "mind."

But what we are now dealing with is the formulated duties of man: the laws which declare the unalterable obligations of all men; the moral laws which were codified by Moses, which were expounded and illustrated by Jesus of Nazareth, which are now incorporated into the moral code of Christendom; and these simply represent man as he was intended to be, as he is intended to become. They constitute collectively a word-picture of the ideal man. They describe what will always be true of the perfect man. They tell what was actualized in the perfect man of Nazareth. The outlines of a perfect manhood had been drawn by Moses; Jesus filled up the picture with the color and warmth of real life. The Sermon on the Mount was simply an exposition of the law of Moses; that exposition irradiated and made it luminous for all time. And what the Expounder said and did was only the spontaneous expression of what he was. He was the moral law incarnate. In him and his life it was made legible to all eyes and articulate to all ears. His teachings were not reasoned conclusions, but intuited truths. What he enjoined on others he was; and he was all that the law, as instituted by Moses, required, and all that the boundless fulness of his own exposition has laid open to the wondering gaze of men. He was at once the Archetypal Being in whose likeness our nature was originally fashioned; and he was the typical man after whose example every clear-sighted man has felt that his own life ought to be regulated.

RESPONSE OF THE MORAL CONSCIOUSNESS.

But here you may ask for the evidence that such was the secondary source of moral law. Take the ethical teachings of Jesus; address them to men; and where is the man, whatever his pride, whatever his culture, whatever his philosophy, or whatever his vices, who, if you can but secure his attention long enough for the teachings to flash their light into his consciousness, will not be humbled and startled by a power which he cannot resist. The ethical truth, which is but another name for law, if he submit to it, will slay him, and in slaying will renew and transform him, awakening him to obedience and quickening him into a new life. Armed with the power of this truth, even the unlettered are more than a match for prejudice and error, however these may be intrenched. It is this immediateness of response of the moral consciousness of every living man to the authority of moral truth which shows at once its power and the proof of its origin.

The origin of all other laws than moral, that succeed in getting themselves enforced and obeyed, will throw some light on the point in hand. The common law of England, of this country, of Christendom, the most authoritative and permanent of all civil law, changes not, because the facts of society which it represents are immutable; it is simply the formulated recognition of some of the deepest realities of society; so long as the realities remain, common law cannot change.

So of all positive laws; to secure observance of them they must represent the wants and condition of those to be controlled by them. Many a man has prescribed for himself a rule which he soon found it impossible to keep. He had misunderstood himself, his needs and his possibilities, and had attempted the impracticable. Legislative enactments are often found to be inoperative. The legislators of every State in our Union are perpetually enacting and repealing laws. And still the law-books are encumbered with dead-letter statutes. And why these endless changes and the laws which cannot be executed? Simply because legislators fail to understand the real and underlying facts of society. When the facts are comprehended, and society continues stable, to enact a just law is to insure its fulfilment; it may almost be said to fulfil itself. So long as our legislators continue to grope in the dark, guessing at the realities of society, or aiming at imaginary or Utopian results, so long will our statutes continue to involve the people in uncertainty and vexation.

The evident origin of the Constitutional laws of a State is specially instructive at this point. Written Constitutions, unless they represent the actual constitution of society, can never supply a permanent government. The Articles of Confederation, under which the government of the United States was for twelve years administered, gave a weak, uncertain, and incapable government, and they were abandoned. The Constitution under which we now live, adopted by the States in 1789, has given us a stable, strong, and beneficent government, simply because that Constitution recognizes the great facts of American society. As the facts have successively changed, the Constitution has been amended, and if the facts of American society can remain as they are, or change but slightly and gradually, and the Constitution be wisely changed to meet the changing wants and realities of the national life, then may we have a long-continued and beneficent government; but let the great heart of the American people change, let the wants of American society cease to be what they now are, let a new and strange national spirit spring up, and the Constitution of the United States will soon be among the things of the past.

When the Abbé Siéyès had concentrated all the force of his genius, all the resources of his learning, all the subtlety of his philosophy, in constructing a constitution for the French Republic, he offered it to the National Assembly. They smiled, and rejected it. Written as it was in the closet, it did not represent the existing facts of French society. The Assembly saw its impracticability. It was worth so much waste-paper. When John Locke, aided by the first Earl of Shaftesbury, drew up his "Fundamental Constitutions" of the Colony of Carolina, the colonists attempted a government under them. The constitutions were amended; they were re-amended; the government was found impracticable. The instrument had been drawn up by two philosophers, and drawn up for an imaginary state of society; when the government provided by it was attempted to be enforced upon the colony, it was found impracticable. It speedily gave place to a constitution that grew and formulated itself into law in accordance with the wants and real condition of the colonists.

Thus the immediate source of all positive laws is in the constitutive natures of those upon whom the laws are to be enforced; and so also the source of all real moral laws is in the nature of those who are to be ruled by them. They are derived not from the accidental conditions of man, not from the surface of human nature despoiled and corrupted, but from the constitutive principles of man as man.

PRIMAL SOURCE OF MORAL LAW.

So much for the immediate or secondary source of moral law. But what shall we say of its primary and original source? Where shall we look for this? In utility, in the theory of evolution, or in the archetypal nature of a Supreme Being?

The ethical principles now regarded as authoritative among the foremost nations of the world are found substantially, as we have before said, in the ten commandments of Moses. A statement of the principles, final and exhaustive, is given in the teachings of Jesus. Out of these teachings has sprung all that is ethically distinctive in the leading civilizations of the world. The moral law of Moses has now for some thirty-five centuries been on trial. The ethics of Jesus for eighteen centuries and a half have been subjected to every species of criticism which the progress of learning and science has made available. And yet the foundations of morality throughout Christendom, notwithstanding the boasts of assailants and the alarm of the timid, still abide.

Suppose now that Moses borrowed from the wisdom of Egypt, that by observation and induction the Egyptians had arrived at the conclusions which he appropriated; then the Egyptians saw what was useful because they saw what the human soul required. That Moses himself could have been accurate and wide enough in his observations to have reached generalizations in morals which no people has yet been able to improve upon, is incredible. That the Egyptians had reached them is conjectured, but not proved. That they could have been forged in the name of Moses, at a much later period of Jewish history, there is nothing in that history to warrant us in believing. Men who could have committed such a forgery would have been incapable of the requisite moral elevation. The statement of Moses that he received the commands from Jehovah is not yet shown to be false; and assuredly there was nothing either in the character or in the times of Jesus to warrant the notion that he could have appropriated the inductions of his day.

Turn we now to the modified utilitarianism of the theory of evolution. The great apostle of that theory, Mr. Spencer, tells us that the race has now evolved to a stage where, with fewest possible exceptions, the best we can do in our moral choices is to choose the least wrong. And, singularly enough, "among the best examples of absolutely right" he mentions one which, he says, existed "before social evolution began." But in his discussion "of absolute morality" he dwells upon a state of society, yet future, but sure to come, in which every one will always do only what is absolutely right. On what grounds, with his theory of evolution, he can venture to conceive such a condition of society, he has not stated; certainly on his theory the first vertebrate could form no conception of the life and advanced condition of an anthropoid ape, nor could the anthropoid conjecture even the lowest stage of rational existence, nor the first rational being the advanced civilization now existing ; and how, on this theory, any one can now assume to know what in the final stage and goal of evolution the condition of human society will be, is assuredly a puzzle, unless indeed moral laws as commands to absolute right already lurk in the human soul, and have a source, both secondary and primary, with which evolution cannot intermeddle. The truth is, that the evolution theory, after granting all that it can claim, can explain at its best only the origin and development of the moral sentiment, and never in any sense the origin of those great moral laws which, when enunciated, carry their own self-witnessing authority home to the heart of every one that hears them. And it is extremely doubtful whether even the moral sentiment could be developed except through some kind of apprehension of moral law as it shines out, dimly it may be, through the social environments which Mr. Spencer regards as so efficient in evolving the moral nature.

But if the primal origin of moral laws can be found neither in utility nor in evolution, can they be found in the infinitely perfect nature of a supreme and archetypal Being? We say not, in a supreme will, for will might be suspected of arbitrariness or caprice, but in a nature which is absolutely perfect.

In support of a Divine origin, let us look for a moment at the argument from the unimprovableness of moral law. Our knowledge of physical laws is perpetually advancing. New disclosures of the secrets of nature which require new formulas are being continually announced. To our progress in the discovery of these secrets, and in the formulation of laws to represent them, there are no apparent limits. As old theories and conjectured laws have in the past given place to new ones, and these to still newer, so may the progress be still onward indefinitely.

But moral laws — whatever has been our progress in the knowledge of mind, of human physiology, of climatic influences, of social reactions — have made no progress since they were laid down by the Author of Christianity. Human philosophies, many and able, have been propounded — new ones are still propounded — as substitutes for the ethics of Christianity; and yet not one of its principles has been invalidated, not a new one has been added to them. The moral law was long ago completed; its statutes have been established forever. The largest intellects have found amplest use for all their powers in simply explaining and applying them.

What the combined ingenuity of man has thus been unable to improve, we may justly conclude the combined ingenuity of man was incapable of originating or of discovering. And that any man, or that all men, could so read the human soul as to map out in completeness for the race, and for all time, the whole duty of man, is simply incredible. A more than human eye was needed to so read the human heart as to tell once for all the sum of its wants and of its obligations. The Omniscient Mind that could thus read and reveal the human heart must have been the mind of which ours is but a copy, — the mind that knew the "substance" of man while as yet it was "imperfect." No explanation of the origin of the moral nature of man is more reasonable than that which recognizes it as wrought, through whatever series of second causes, after the likeness of a Divine original. To that original, then, we may look as the real source of all moral law. It is a "transcript of the Divine nature" in a profounder sense than the popular use of that language implies. It is with the utmost fulness of meaning the "law of God." He has not made it for certain ends, but has simply revealed it. The Almighty *made* no moral laws, but created man in his own image. The moral laws of the Divine nature were incorporated in the nature of man. To tell what God and man are, and what are their mutual relations, is to tell whence moral law came. And just so long as God and man shall continue to be, just so long this law will remain as unchangeable as the eternal throne.

When Jesus proclaimed himself the Light of the world he illumined only the horizon of the distant East. To-day he irradiates the central and controlling nations of the globe. And physical science, which, it has been prophesied, will extinguish his light, is now adding to its transparency and its vivifying warmth. Thanks to science for its service. If moral law be grounded as we have stated, the time will yet come when from the Sun of righteousness there will go forth light, and warmth, and purity, and peace, and abiding joy to the remotest corner of the earth.

The unwillingness of sceptics to assail the moral teachings of Christianity is a curious but unintentional recognition of the impregnable basis on which they rest. You will observe that attacks on the Christian religion are directed almost exclusively against either its history, its creeds and theological systems, or its ecclesiastical organizations. The history of its beginnings pertains to the remote; it is easy to assail it. Creeds, which have too often been mere compromises between conflicting statements, and its theological systems, are mostly the productions of philosophies applied to the facts of revelation and of the moral consciousness. The philosophies have changed; the creeds and theological systems have been discredited, and so have become assailable. In like manner ecclesiastical organizations, which are essential to the conservation of the Christian life, have been either the product of circumstances or the contrivances of men. Organization began to exist only as the wants of the new life made necessary. When anything was to be done, some one was appointed to do it. To do an "office" for the Church speedily prepared the way for regarding office as a place into which some one must be put as an officer. Ecclesiasticism has been a natural growth; it has been open to attack on many sides, and the enemies of Christianity have not been slow to improve their opportunities. But moral law, which it is the one great office of Christianity to explain, to enforce, and to help mankind to fulfil, the enemies of Christianity are not eager to attack.

MORAL LAW AND POPULAR RELIGION.

Let us turn now to the other side of our subject,— the relation of moral law to popular religion. What is this relation? We could easily answer in the words of Jesus: "Think not that I am come to destroy the law, or the prophets; I am not come to destroy, but to fulfil. For verily I say unto you, Till heaven and earth pass, one jot or one tittle shall in no wise pass from the law, till all be fulfilled." The true meaning of the law had been concealed by false glosses. The Sermon on the Mount was distinctively and wellnigh exclusively an exposition of the law. The exposition made it seem like a new revelation; like an overthrow of the old to make room for the new. The assurance was necessary, therefore, that the purpose of Christianity was not the abrogation, but the strictest fulfilment of all moral law. That assurance is reiterated on every page of the four Gospels. Any conception, then, of Christianity which supposes it to be a scheme to evade law, to escape its penalties, or to avoid the fulfilment of it, is an unwarrantably narrow conception, and just so far as it is narrow, is false.

No error has crept into Christian teaching more radically mischievous than that which affirms all law to have been abolished by Jesus Christ. Out of it have come some of the darkest blots that have rested on the Christian name. The origin of the error is easily traced. In Judaism, out of which Christianity sprang, every conceivable relation in life was covered by a statute. A complete network of legal requirements enveloped the whole man every moment of his being. The state was a theocracy; the religion was a ritual; and the whole social and domestic life of the people was regulated by a system of ceremonials that descended to minutest particulars. The civil, the ritual, and the ceremonial being each and all subservient to the moral, each and all were included under the one generic term, the Law. Upon his compliance with the Law depended, without appeal, the whole fate of the Jew. But the civil law was overridden by the conquering Roman; the ceremonial and ritual were abolished by Christianity. To suppose moral law, however, to have been abolished, is to suppose man to have been transformed into something else than man; is to suppose the nature of God to have been changed, and the moral order of the universe to have been subverted.

REWARDS AND PENALTIES.

If the explanation we have given of the origin of moral law be correct, we may see the mistake of ascribing all moral sanctions to direct Divine agency. Rewards and penalties are certainly not arbitrarily distributed. The results of physical law are not more immediate, natural, and inevitable than are those of moral law. Rewards come by natural reaction from obedience to law. Glow of cheek, sparkle of eye, and flow of spirits are not more naturally and immediately the product of locomotion and respiration amid the crisp air of a New England winter day than are

the glow of soul and peace and joy of heart which
flow from vigilant obedience to moral law amid the
stir and strife of the world.

So of moral penalties. These are natural reactions
from disobedience to moral law. Bodily disease and
death do not more immediately and necessarily follow
the violation of physical laws than do mental diseases
and moral death the violation of moral obligations.
The penal sanctions of one set of laws are just as
natural and invariable as are those of another. Vice
in the vicious man leers out of his eye, sensualizes his
lip, riots in his blood, fouls his imagination, corrupts
his whole being. And then those subtler sins with
which it is so difficult to deal, — envy, jealousy, pride,
covetousness, those vices of the soul, — do they not
write their penalties on the moral nature of man?
Do they not blunt the moral sensibilities? Do they
not, by their natural sequences, corrupt through and
through every fibre of the soul?

Nor will it here suffice for any one to interpose the
objection that he recognizes a supreme will in nature;
that he regards the so-called forces of nature as "God
acting," and physical laws as rules according to which
he has chosen to act; and that he believes the
rewards and penalties of moral law are directly distributed by the hand of a Supreme Being; let us look
at this for a moment. Does the universal confidence
which is always reposed in a man of well-tried integrity result as a natural sequence of his integrity, or is
it a supernatural bestowal? Is the public distrust
of the liar and the forger by natural sequence, or by

Divine interposition? Does virtue naturally refine the soul, or is refinement bestowed from without? And are the rewards and penalties any less the expressions of the Divine will, because coming naturally by law, than they would be if proved to come directly by Divine interposition?

And here we see how gratuitous is the noisy indignation of those sentimental souls who wax so eloquent in their denunciations of the idea of a Divine punishment of evil-doers, especially of the idea that punishment should run into another life; and, most horrible of all, should for a moment be thought of as possibly unending. Has it never occurred to these tender-hearted people to rail against Nature for her cruelty in leaving the man with crushed limbs to writhe in pain, and, if he survive his first agony, to linger through a long life of suffering and helplessness? Has it never occurred to them that possibly the pangs of remorse are just as natural and enduring as the anguish of lacerated or disordered nerves? And why distinguish between penalties in the body and penalties in the soul? On their own theory, is Nature less cunning in repairing the material organism than in healing the wounds of the soul? Should the soul survive the body, why may not the vitiated tastes, the wounds, the dwarfed powers, the crippled energies, which have come to it in life, continue so long as it endures, just as pain and deformity and enfeeblement of body continue with it so long as it lasts?

There was a time within the memory of living men when Boston resounded with the doctrine that every man at the last would be judged and awarded to his final destiny in strict accordance with his obedience or disobedience to moral law. That doctrine was a great truth, however severed from others that qualified it; and it has left its marks on the Boston character. The descendants of the prophets of that great truth, building their sepulchres, too often inscribe on them: "God is too merciful to punish the wayward and the weak."

REMISSION OF PENALTY.

To rescue man from the doom of moral penalty is one of the first and most distinctively announced purposes of the Christian religion. And what it announced as its purpose, it proposes to accomplish not in mere form but in reality; not only accounting a man to be righteous, but making him so; imparting to him what it imputes to him; not so much throwing around him a cloak of righteousness as putting within him a righteous spirit. But the method by which it thus accomplishes its purpose of releasing from moral penalty is one of the disputed questions in popular theology. Yet it is a question to which every one who would teach Christianity to the people must give to himself some kind of an answer. He may answer it doctrinally, and if his doctrine is to have any meaning and power with him he must answer it to himself as a question of practical religious philosophy. We shall here content ourselves with the briefest possible glance at the latter side of the question.

Penalty may be contemplated under three aspects:

as the natural sequence of wrong-doing which stamps itself on the soul and penetrates into the inner being; as the inflictions of an accusing conscience, the self-judgment which every one pronounces on himself in view of neglected duties or of forbidden deeds; as punitive judgments immediately inflicted or held in reserve by the Supreme Ruler of all. But these are only different aspects of one and the same thing. The judgments of God can become effective as moral penalties only as they reach the soul through the conscience; and the upbraidings of conscience become penal only as they accord with the judgments of God and with the natural results of moral evil in the soul. The penalty, therefore, which the Gospel is to remove is in the soul of man. And it is a penalty which reduplicates its own cause. The sorest punishment of moral evil is an ever-increasing disposition to continue in it. There may be great and just judgments for wrong-doing which hang suspended in the hands of Omnipotence, and which in due time fall like thunderbolts on the iniquitous. But the sin and its penalty, from which the Gospel proposes to save man, are found in man himself. They are said to be written in a book; the imagery is admirable, but the real book is the human soul. It is from it that the penalty must be removed. But what is the method of its removal? Certainly not by fiat. God is always and everywhere consistent with himself. He will not violate one of his moral laws to save even a human soul. And we may be assured there will be no act in the process of saving him which will be arbitrary.

The one great fact of Christianity is, that a Being of infinite resources has appeared on the earth and announced himself as a Deliverer of man. His interposition in our behalf was the turning-point in the history of our race. And the one principle which makes available and effectual all that he wrought for us in his life and by his death, and all that he is for us in himself, is the principle of faith. And the object of our trust is not alone what he said or what he did or what he suffered, but also what he himself was and ever is. The source of our strength in the struggle for release, the ground of our hope for final deliverance, is not so much in a something which has been done for us as it is in the infinite Being who has done it. Our victory is alone through trust in Him who had no penalty of his own to bear, and has proved himself able to bear those of all others.

The one principle which exists among all peoples, and at the same time is the most efficient in the construction of human character, is faith. Neither social nor individual life is possible without some degree of it. The more completely the members of society are swayed by it, the more nearly perfect will be the social and the individual life. This principle Christianity adopts as its most efficient agency in working out its intent in man. And nothing could make more evident the effectiveness of faith in working out the purpose of Christianity than the certainty with which every one becomes like the object of his trust. These are the invariable and inevitable sequences of the law of faith. If the object of one's trust be personal and superior, it is impossible that his defects of character should remain uncorrected; if perfect, the correction may be continuous and endless. So in eradicating moral evil and in erasing its penalties from the soul; in the beneficent results of faith the penal sanctions of previous disobedience are overborne and carried away. Even the old spirit of disobedience is absorbed in the desire to be in harmony with the new object of trust. The beneficent working of the new law obeyed more than counteracts, it takes away, the penal results of the old laws violated. But the moral scars will remain with us, and humble us, and they never will exalt us. No doctrine was ever more pernicious than that which teaches that the greater the sinner the greater the saint.

THE TRUE AIM OF RELIGION.

What now in conclusion and in review of this discussion should be regarded as the one great aim of all true religion? Should it be anything else than to help every one to rise as near as possible towards a realization of the highest ideal of life? Can that man be said to be saved who has not already put himself upon a course of training in which the ruling purpose of his life shall be the fulfilment of every law of his being? The greatest defect and gravest peril of the popular religion of our day is its disposition to rest in mere negations as regards personal conduct and character, and in mere contributions of money as regards public activities. But to save a man in the true Christian sense of salvation is to round him out into the completest fulness of being of which he is capable,— is to make him pure in heart, exalted in purpose, unimpeachable in his integrity, keenly sensitive to every moral obligation, and supremely loyal to the will of God, whether expressed in command or in promise.

Man is a compound being. He is both animal and angel,— the tangential point between the two worlds of matter and of spirit. Every power and capacity of his being has its root and its ground in this twofold nature. And he is capable of three planes of life,— the animal, the intellectual, the moral and religious. But the three are indivisibly connected. As you can have no soil without rock, and no plant without soil, and no animal without plant, and no man without both plant and animal, so you can have no intellect without body, and no morality without intellect, and no real religion without both intellect and morality. Every law of his personal being to which man is subject is more or less immediately the expression of the possibilities of his twofold nature; and every moral law is a revelation of the capacities, the needs, and the deeper aspirations of his complex being. No one of these laws can receive attention to the neglect of others, that the neglected ones will not avenge their neglect. Merely seeking to save man from sinking into the animal will not insure his becoming an angel; nor in alone aiming to make of him an angel shall we save him from sinking into the animal. A true religion, which is to perform all its offices for man, must take account of, and provide for, the whole of his indivisible nature; and for the whole, because the whole is subservient to the moral. The one comprehensive and all-inclusive aim of a true religion is, and ever must be, to secure in man the unqualified and unfailing fulfilment of the moral laws of his being, which are as eternal as the soul and as immutable as the throne of the Almighty.

III.

CHRISTIANITY AND THE MENTAL ACTIVITY OF THE AGE.

By REV. THOMAS GUARD.

III.

CHRISTIANITY AND THE MENTAL ACTIVITY OF THE AGE.

BY REV. THOMAS GUARD.

A GLANCE over the vacant vastness of this audience-chamber suffices to remind me of the absence, beyond the water, of the gifted founder of your "Monday Lectureship." May he be preserved from all perils while he travels, and return from his wanderings, laurelled with fresh honors, to the scene of his frequent triumphs!

I am not here, I assure you, to attempt the task for which he proved himself so signally equipped. Who but himself could wield Ulysses's bow? Nevertheless, the task assigned me is no light one. I have asked myself, once and again, Why was I not requested to compress the globe into an ultimate atom, ensphere the sun in a dew-drop, or find for the most ancient ocean a home within the compass of a scallop-shell? For I am expected to discuss the relations of Christianity to the mental activities of our age, within the limits of an hour! It is impossible! I shrink from it. I cannot exhaust such a theme. I may be permitted to hope, however, that I shall prove suggestive.

Made in the image of the ever-living One, the human mind "faints not, neither is weary," by reason of activity; and to think, is to act. Our age is peerless in the *quantity* of intellectual activity, whatever may be said of the *quality* of that activity, or of its issues. Never so much free thought, never so much freedom of thought, as to-day. The schoolmaster is abroad. The press is in untiring operation. The spirit of inquiry is ubiquitous. History pores over coins, cipher correspondence, antique customs, hoary constitutions, dry-as-dust scrolls, acts of parliament, alabaster slabs, street ballads, fugitive tracts, diaries of lettered princesses and journals of court favorites; from such incongruous material extracting the substance wherewith to fashion those imperishable piles of wisdom with which our grateful and instructed hearts associate the names of Grote, Mommsen, Merivale, Prescott, Motley, Macaulay, Bancroft, and Carlyle.

Travellers haste o'er land and ocean without rest: now plunging into the wonders of Central Africa, now looking down upon the cradle of the Nile, now tracking the footsteps of the pre-Adamite progenitors of our race; to-day resting beneath the columns of Luxor, or two weeks hence within the shadows of the ruined temples, tombs, and theatres of Petra; then treading the sacred soil and climbing the sacred slopes on which redemption's truths were uttered and redemption's price was paid; then off and away to the land where every dell enshrined a deity, every fountain leaped to song, — whose breezes floated the melodies of Plato, or trembled to the thunder of Demosthenes.

Scientists are heaving the lead in deep-sea soundings; foretelling the birth of the tornado; weighing the earth in scales; interpreting the hieroglyphs carved on mountain summit and on sandstone stratum; pursuing the comet o'er the plains of ether; analyzing the elements of the light-wave propelled by Sirius across the amplitudes of space; solving the mysteries that lurk in frond and cell, in tinted sea-shells and in coral bowers; reckoning up the ages of the sun; defining the orbit of Neptune or ever its mass had crossed the disk of aided or unaided eye; in every motion finding an idea, in every form a purpose, and in every event the token of a plan and system; changing chaos and confusion into order and cosmos; and, in the unity impressed upon and interwoven through the vast and varied whole, beholding the reflected Unity of him "*by whom are all things, and for whom are all things, — God over all, blessed forever.*"

And the results of such activities are within the reach of every one desirous of copious and accurate information. With the sage most profound, with the scholar most erudite, with the scientist most accomplished, with the poet most subtle-minded, with the products of pen and pencil, of microscope and telescope, of scalpel and prism, the youth of eager longing and quenchless thirst for truth may hold communion, by reason of the prodigious triumphs of the printing-press.

What has Christianity to say to all this intellectual movement? What emotions heave her bosom? Is it with sentiments of envy, jealousy, and fear, or of favoring sympathy that she gazes on the scene of seething, surging, struggling spirit-life?

The study of her inspired records and of her historic chapters affords an answer; and in that answer we read amplest assurance of her friendship and aid.

1. To the *understanding* of man she ever appealed. "By manifestation of *the truth*" she proposes to conquer. With a sublime audacity she ignores physical force as an instrument of victory. "Ye shall know *the truth*, and *the truth* shall make you free," were the clarion tones which fell upon the ears of the inthralled victims of ignorance, superstition, priestcraft. Above her hosts, as they marched to further triumphs, her banner floated, and on its folds men read the strange device, "Prove all things, hold fast that which is good." Whenever permitted, she grappled with the Jew, and "*reasoned* out of his Scripture;" with the Greek, and argued out of his sacred writings of nature, conscience, history. Upon her converts she urged the noble duty, "Be always ready to give a reason of the hope that is in you." The divine Founder of our faith gave no uncertain sound when he said, "For this cause came I into the world, that I should bear witness unto the Truth. Every one that is of the Truth heareth my voice." To Christianity there is nothing ignoble and nothing insignificant in aught that touches or appertains to man. In her estimate he is of more value than many sparrows. His return to moral sanity, we are

assured, moves the ranks of seraphim with strange joy. For his eternal weal the counsels of the Infinite planned, when as yet nor light-ray travelled, nor force electric thrilled, nor mountain soared, nor ocean tossed, nor tempest marched, nor forest waved, nor landscape spread, all dewy and all fragrant, beneath the cloudless sun. To nothing human can Christianity be indifferent. Body, soul, and spirit have been redeemed and provided for by this divine system. As the Sabbath, so Christianity, "is made for man;" and such is man's relation thereto, that we may say, as of the sun in relation to our planet, "There is nothing hid from the heat thereof." *To* all that is profoundest in man the influence pierces; *over* all that is amplest in man the influence diffuses; and *on* all that is loftiest in man her inspiration breathes a benediction. Nor this alone: there are depths of our nature reached but by Christianity; chords of our hearts that refuse their harmonies to any touch but hers; and magnanimities, heroisms, martyrdoms, in life and in death, developed but by her plenipotence of holy love and blessed hope.

2. *Christianity provokes thought.* That the power of our holy faith may be experienced to the uttermost, *faith* is essential. Faith demands *reason* for its exercise. And to meet this demand of our nature Christianity presents *credentials.* Belief is impossible, unless *sufficient reason for belief* be furnished. Here, then, the scope for *intellectual action* appears. What are the credentials accompanying Christianity? Are they such in quality and in number as to warrant

our faith? The replies to those queries are given in the sumless writings called "The Evidences of Christianity." Certainly these are products of thought, scholarship, logic, philosophic investigation and discussion. Certainly these demonstrate the thought-compelling might of the Christian faith.

To a man possessed of an honest heart and quickened conscience, a system of truth and of religion *professing to come from the Supreme One*, with whom *we have to do*, cannot be treated with the slightest approach towards indifference. It *may be true*. If so, there is a duty corresponding to the bare probability of truthfulness,—that duty, *attention, audience, investigation*. At once the mind assumes an attitude of earnest wakefulness. The *substance* of the message shall be weighed, compared, judged. The *evidences* attendant upon the message and messenger shall win sober, courteous, brave, and honest investigation. And so, and only so, shall the *conscience* of the man approve of his *conduct*. But in all this see we not the tremendous stimulus imparted to the *intellectual* as well as the moral forces of the soul? Name a mental faculty not called into play by such a professedly divine communication. Memory, comparison, judgment, imagination, reason, all mental instincts, intuitions, affinities, and proclivities, are in succession, or combinedly, in utmost vigor of action. A *crisis* in the *intellectual life has arisen*. The man dates a new birth, *as a thinker*, from the advent-hour of such a system as our faith. Whether Christianity made him a saint, or by reason of his perverse will failed in that great work, she made him a thinker. He became a foe of that which extorted from him the exclamation, "Hast thou found me, O mine enemy?" And because a foe, a *thinker,— irritated into thinking* through *hatred of Christianity.* Therefore, compose the treatise and the essay to prove it a myth; visit Orient lands to demonstrate it an imposture; compile a comparative theology to minify its rank in the presence of other systems! Therefore, see but its difficulties and ignore the possible explanations of its seeming contradictions with history or science! Yet in all this, what see we but immense intellectual outgoing and energy, scholarship, science, philosophic subtlety and lore, æsthetic culture, literary creativeness? And inasmuch as for this intellectual action Christianity is responsible, both as cause and occasion, do we behold evidence of her power to arouse and develop thought.

3. There is *antagonism* to Christianity in much of the *intellectual* life of our age. This does not surprise us. It was to have been anticipated. No student of the mission of Christianity, at all familiar with the moral condition of our race, should feel "as though some strange thing happened," if Christianity developed hostility most bitter in the very ranks of those whom it came to woo and to save.

For it was in this very antagonism to its Author that the need for such a system obtained. But that man was a sinner, and that his depravity expressed itself in enmity to God, Christianity had been a superfluity of appliances and agencies. Its existence implies strife, and its career hitherto has been one of aggrandizement through struggle. Early in the history of man as the object of redeeming mercy, it was announced, "I will put enmity between Thy seed and her seed." Subsequent ages but illustrated the truth of the announcement. The Founder himself gave utterance to the same great verity: "Think not that I am come to send peace upon earth: I am not come to send peace, but a sword." The last prophet of inspiration depicts in symbols the most sublime and suggestive the process of the struggle.

And to-day the battle waxes in vehemence of purpose and of passion; nor is there prospect of speedy termination of the conflict. Possibly, ay, probably, the future shall witness scenes of combat, compared with which the fiercest of the past shall seem but gala-day sports. Not with sound of clarion, or tramp of war-horse, or rush of scythed chariot, or thunder of ordnance, or with garments rolled in blood, shall the battle rage or the fight be fought. The weapons shall be of spiritual and ethereal temper and substance; of ore drawn from the mines of spirit and forged in the white heat of passion fires; wielded by the Titans of error, or dexterous and death-dealing by reason of arms nerved with divine strength and fingers taught to fight by none other than the great Captain of the hosts of light himself.

Nor shall the struggle close until all *the foes' resources* shall *have been drawn upon, applied, tested*. Not until the last form and method of resistance to good shall have had scope for their endeavors and time for their display of skill and might, and shall have proved as impotent as are the birds of night to hinder the return of the daybreak and the noontide splendor of the regal sun,—not until then, shall discomfiture cover the emissaries of falsehood, and a ransomed world enter into "quietness and assurance forever." And, fear not, ye who read the times, and whose hearts sometimes fail! For He must reign until He hath put down all that exalteth itself against Him. "And when He *shall have put down all rule and all authority, then cometh the end.*"

We confess our delight in this aspect of the age. Nothing is more to be deprecated than intellectual stolidity, than uninquiring acceptance of the Christian faith. This is a state not to be permitted, not to be tolerated. Better strife than stupor. Christianity can never win her way but as she compels or constrains men into moods of investigation. She courts this. It is essential to her very existence. She is willing to take all the risks arising from the awakening of thought and the scrutiny of thinkers. Doubt may challenge her, scepticism may assail her. She welcomes the *honest* doubter; she disdains not to debate with him who, fearlessly searching after the true, sees not as yet evidence sufficient to warrant his assent and affiance. With tenderest solicitude she waits upon and ministers to such. Priests may scowl upon them, and churches threaten them with terror; but not so Christianity. Over the tortured toiler after truth she bends, with infinite compassion in her eye and solace on her lip; bares her ample bosom, and invites to shelter and repose there: "Come unto me, all — all ye that labor and are heavy laden, and I will give you rest." To the Master's treatment of Thomas Christianity points the bewildered, wondering doubters of all ages, as to Simon Peter and his Lord's treatment of the recreant Apostle she points the penitent though desponding gaze of all who under dreadful pressure proved traitors to their divine Master's name and cause; and in his treatment of both proves that "Wisdom is justified *of her children.*"

4. The action of Christianity through the *Laws of Heredity* deserves recognition and appreciation. Those laws have their expounders and illustrators in Galton and Ribot, in Herbert Spencer, Darwin, and Bain. Darwin's "Descent of Man" is almost altogether dependent upon the factor of heredity. It is no less potent in the philosophy of Spencer. By this "heredity" principle, "like produces like;" sometimes, indeed, "like" seems capable of producing very "unlike;" but it is only seemingly so. The new-born immortal is therefore "the very image of his father," be the fact flattering to the parent or otherwise. Physical characteristics are thus transmissible. The past can be reproduced. Nothing is lost that can serve the interests of the organization. Tendencies are "fixed," vicious proclivities descend, and disease becomes a legacy. Should "variety," by some inscrutable law, be introduced, and should that variety tend to secure the survival of the fittest, heredity seizes it, incorporates it, and secures its perpetuity

CHRISTIANITY AND MENTAL ACTIVITY. 73

through successive generations. The law of continuity sways it. To it, we are told, species owe their origin; and through it, we are assured, man has derived his finest sensibilities and his loftiest sentiments. From the dull oyster through the stupid donkey, up, still up, the germ of the coming man has never failed persistently to press, until the all but unbeginning past culminates in the creature whose *initial* condition proclaims him a little higher than the missing-linked one, and whose *perfectional* condition shall proclaim him "a little lower than the angels." Well, no doubt *according* to the laws of heredity the Eternal One has seen fit to act. The presence of the principle was not discovered yesterday. Jacob, in the days of his service between the rivers, caught sight of it and utilized it. To-day we have multiplied proof in its favor, and are not in any extreme danger of depreciating its potency as an element in our civilization.

Has not Christianity availed herself of this subtile force? Are we not justified in attributing to her, incalculable influence upon the mental capacity of our age, *along the lines of this authenticated principle* of our complex being? For eighteen hundred years has Christianity been working on, working with, working through, humanity. The physical nature of the race has thus been improved, and the moral has participated in the ennobling effects; why not the mental? Why not the mental aptitudes, — why not the affinities with, the capacity for, intellectual pursuits and attainments, ameliorated, strengthened, refined, by reason of the action and interaction of the manifold appliances of Christianity?

The greatest thinkers of our day (even when far other than the friends of our faith) are her legitimate *intellectual* offspring. John Stuart Mill came of Scottish Presbyterian ancestry. George Eliot descended from Christian parents and grew up amidst Christian influences. Christianity flowered in the genius of Walter Scott, and fruitens in the products of George Macdonald and William Black; permeated the being of Macaulay, and possessed the soul of Thomas Carlyle; inspired the splendid intellect of Sir William Hamilton, glowed in the poetic fires of Hugh Miller, and adorns the sanctified learning of our President McCosh. Professor J. W. Draper is the son of an English Wesleyan minister, and probably shared in the thorough training of a Wesleyan college, either as a "Woodhouse Grove," or "Kingswood" boy. Your own Channing, — calm, clear, comprehensive; the philosopher, the humanitarian; gentle as he was strong, and steeped both in "sweetness and light," — owed not he his intellectual manhood to Christianity? Theodore Parker, the vehement iconoclast, the intense hater of injustice; masculine in thought as poetic in sympathy and in imagination; he who speaks of the "Iris that scarfs the shoulder of the thunder-cloud," — did not he inherit the vigor of his mind and the energy of his athletic spiritual nature from Puritan forefathers? And so of that other, upon whose head the snows of time are gathering, but all impotent to quench the fires of his transcendent genius; the old man eloquent; the clairvoyant of Concord; the high dreamer whose thoughts live, move, and have their being in the world of men around you; whose weird skill oft wove for him webs of gossamer, and of these fashioned chariots in which to float away and away into realms ethereal, whither the tempests of life had not wing to follow, — is not he the intellectual culmination of generations of ancestors in the Christian faith and in the Christian ministry? The roots of these men's mental being are all in Christian soil, and thence drew nourishment and flavor. The tree-like life of these thinkers expanded in atmosphere surcharged with Christian ideas. Their ample and loaded branches ripened into tropic fulness in the solar floods of Christian culture and civilization; and I am not extravagant or unjust in pointing to them as splendid evidences of the power of our faith as the generator of intellectual life and activity.

Science tells me that all terrestrial light is from the sun, and that, though absent, the sun is still our light by night, be that night brief as midsummer's or prolonged as the six months' gloom of Arctic zones, — light of pine torch and of fire-fly, light of waxen taper and of oil and gas lamp, light upon ocean's phosphorescent wave, and light of moonbeams braiding Niagara's brow with iridescent wreath. Directly and indirectly, the sun is the light of the world. And I dare assert the same of Christianity and the intellectual world of our age. I have tested this in imagination by conceiving the annihilation of that Book, so indissolubly, so essentially associated with

Christianity. The Bible triumphs when and where Christianity triumphs. Let me be permitted to suppose somewhat, at least, of an approach towards the utter destruction of the Book. First, copies of the volume itself, in all shapes and sizes, in all tongues and versions, shall have been collected, heaped into pyramidal piles, and fired, until but dust and ashes remain. No Bible anywhere! This is but a very little thing, however, compared with that to be accomplished. Then all literature — prose, poetic, tome and folio, essay and sermon, drama and lyric, hymn and idyl — must be subjected to a process, either of utter destruction or of perfect, absolutely perfect, expurgation, so that no grace of style, nor elegance of allusion, nor aptness of quotation, nor felicity of metaphor, suggestive of or derived from the Book, shall remain in such volumes. Then visit the galleries, private and public, devoted to the exhibition of art. Here are walls frescoed with the products of old masters and new; here are pedestals and niches crowned and crowded with the triumphs of the chisel and the sculptor. Blot from that canvas the Last Supper, the Transfiguration, the Ascension, the Light of the World; pluck from that pedestal and from yonder niches the Moses and the David of Angelo, or such forms and expressions of majesty, tenderness, purity, and grace as their creators learned and caught from study of the teachings, or fellowship with the heroes of the Book. Then haste to the baptismal registries of the Church, and, instead of Mary, write Cleopatra; of Rachel, Messalina; of John, Nero; and of Peter,

Caligula. Erase whatever there reminds one of the Bible. Then on to the Libraries of law, and let all codes, statutes, enactments, constitutions, in which shall be found reverence for God, respect for liberty, protection for reputation, life, and person, defence of woman and of feebleness, and guarantee of equal and impartial justice for meanest plebeian, as for meanest plutocrat; — let all such as owe their humanity, their justice, their impartiality, to the genius and the teachings of the Book, vanish and be forgotten. Then, away to the *Cemeteries*, urban and suburban, civic and rustic; to the crypts and vaults; to the stately minster and to the humble chapel; — where sleep the dead, and on whose tombs Hope, Faith, and Love have carved the blessed texts in which the widow found a balm and the despairing, consolation. See, see! 'T is a November midnight. Nor star nor moon rides the cloud-draped heavens. No light, save the fitful flash from yonder moving form. *That* is one of the myriad conspirators against the human race, who, on this grim night simultaneously visit the graveyards of the Christian world, that from the slab and obelisk they may blot out the Bible. See! he bends, and with light of lantern reads: "I am the resurrection and the life;" "Blessed are the dead;" "In my Father's house are many mansions." Now he seizes chisel and mallet, and begins. Chip! chip! chip! The lone night-winds as they travel o'er the spot take up upon their dusky wings a burden sadder than they ever bore, — the sob, the sigh, the low-toned throb of heart-chords snapping;

for, henceforth, the chamber of the dying shall be one of horrors, death's rule a "reign of terror," and the graveyard "the abomination of desolation." I need not imagine more, though the half is not yet pictured; for the fruits of Christianity in manners, in civilization, in treatment of criminals and of the insane; in homes for age, for orphans, for widows, for idiots, for outcast women; in popular education, and in kindred generous and gracious institutions, — these all must also suffer destruction before we shall have by any means attained unto the extermination of either the Book or the Faith.

5. Is the mission of Christianity a superfluity by reason of the results of our intellectual age? Let human nature, let man, reply. Is there any change such as to render the further existence of our faith unnecessary? As generation after generation arises, see we not the past repeated? Hear we not the same queries voiced by human hearts, human memories, human consciences? Amidst vast changes, if we go deep enough, shall we not find *man* unchanged?

(1.) Listen to the old, old question, and know that it is prompted by something in man other than accidental, in condition or circumstances. It is the question of "a conscience of sins," a sense of wrongdoing, and of guilt arising thence. You cannot bid down, so as to keep down, that question: "*How can man be just with his Maker?*" A homely question, indeed; ay, but one that can with earthquake might thrill the whole inner man, and in answering which man has steeped the earth in blood, bleached it with bones of weary pilgrims, and wrapped it in smoke of countless sacrificial altars. It must be answered. What hath modern science to say in response? Nothing that commands for one moment the acceptance of intelligent conscience. What has matter, as it rolls through space; marbles, though veined with beauty; gems, though aglow with fiery splendor; corals, though fashioned after the similitude of a palace; life, death, force,—what have they to do with a query sighed forth by a self-conscious and self-convicted spirit? "It's not in us," the solemn heights reply. "It's not in us," the dark, unfathomed caves of earth respond. Christianity has proven her power to meet the need. She owns that power to-day.

(2.) And *there is the demand for inner rectification of nature.* There is a deep-seated sore within. The ideal of right is there. The endeavor to realize it is made, but the failure is total. And this involves conflict the most stern and anguish the most bitter. "When I would do good, evil is present with me; the evil I *would* not, that I do." I pay a visit to the sages of physical and of transcendental wisdom, and with impassioned earnestness ask of their chief,

> "Canst thou not minister to a *mind* diseased,
> Pluck from the memory a rooted sorrow,
> Raze out the written troubles of the brain,
> And by some sweet oblivious antidote
> Cleanse the stuffed bosom of the perilous stuff,
> Which weighs upon the heart?"

Perhaps he will tell me that sin is a necessary stage in my moral development; and that wherever man is, — in the brothel, in the gin-mill, on the gallows, — he is on the way to God; and that the only possible error that can arise, is this, — that by lack of effort the man remains a little longer than he might in either one of the above-named localities. From such my inner being turns, as it utters, "Miserable comforters are ye all!" Christianity meets the want. It offers, and it has, — yes, it has effected, thorough renewal of the "hidden man of the heart." It has brought a clean thing out of an unclean. It is doing so to-day: in some one spot of this old globe, day by day, it is transforming and emancipating and harmonizing the inner principles and powers of man; for it is the power of God unto salvation to every one that believeth.

(3.) And man asks, — as he looks up into the vastness of creation, and round upon the strangely checkered aspect of life, and on through the dim, trackless future; when woes fill his cup of life, and disaster crashes upon disaster, and helplessness is the o'ermastering feeling of his sinking heart, — Is there One above all others to whom I may carry my load, pour forth my tale of desolation? Or is it indeed true that he heeds not, neither can help, — as helpless as

> "The gods who haunt
> The lucid interspace of world and world,
> Where never creeps a cloud, or moves a wind,
> Nor ever falls the least white star of snow,
> Nor ever lowest roll of thunder moans,
> Nor *sound of human sorrow mounts to mar*
> Their sacred, everlasting calm!"

Vain to lead me to "an altar with this inscription, 'To an unknown God.'" Ay, and as vain to tell me of a "power that makes for righteousness." I want "the living God." I am a person, and my God must be a person. Out of the light, ye sages, Spencer, Arnold! Let me to His side in whom resides wisdom, at least, — at least as great as yours, that to my heart's longing cry, "Show me the Father!" I may from his own lips catch the words of strength and solace: "He that hath seen me hath seen the Father."

(4.) And, once again, man asks for light. It is as he sits yonder in darkened chamber beside his dead. To her in youth's jocund days his heart went out, and round hers twined its tendrils. They were lovely and beautiful as they grew in wisdom, confidence, and love. But the ruthless blast swept o'er her, and in the very pride of motherhood she gave up the ghost; her sun went down while it was yet noon. And soon he must "bury his dead out of his sight." What is thy mission and what thy meaning, O Death? Dost thou, indeed, end all? or through thee pass we back again, as raindrops, into the vast immensity of THE ALL, — individuality, personality, forever lost? or shall we live again? It is not sentimentalism that thus speaks. Strongest minds have heaved the lead in these mysterious depths. Mightiest hearts have quaked with strange terror in presence of these problems. He who *is* Christianity, Himself replies. In *word* he answered; better far, in *work* he responded; best of all, in his *own person* he grappled with, wrested the sceptre from, the king of terrors, and o'er his prostrate form marched forth from death's dominion with the note of triumph on his lip: "I am the resurrection and the life." "He brought back, not the shadow, but the substance of immortal man," as said R. Hall. "For now is Christ risen from the dead, and become the first fruits of them that sleep."

Friends, these are the truisms of our faith. Through these, attended by the grace of the Lord and Giver of life, Christianity hath won her way hitherto. Nor is there trace of feebleness or of age in her fair form to-day, nor hectic flush on her cheek, nor halt in her gait, nor haze in her eye. She is mighty as when she went forth to vanquish the Vandal, civilize the Celt, hallow the Hun, gather in the Goth,' and win the worshippers of Woden from the fierceness of their temple worship and their forest sports. She is entering new regions, and intends to conquer; and they feel this, and are troubled. Hoary creeds and gory superstitions tremble at her approach. She comes to make men *think*, and, thus, to overturn. Revolutionist, indeed, she is! Monopoly of power, of thought, of joy in life, she comes to overturn. Her mission is race wide and is full of mercy, without partiality and without hypocrisy; knowing no man after the flesh, nor giving flattering titles unto any; her smile is hope, her presence a benediction. Judging from former victories, and studying her in the light of prophecy, we look forward with assured confidence of ultimate, universal supremacy. Her Head "ascended that he might *fill all things.*" And he is achieving his intent. His ideas, principles, are silently but surely permeating society,—in commerce, honesty; in law, justice; in government, liberty; in art, purity; in society, gentleness, tenderness, mutual helpfulness, world-wide charity. As she advances in her career,

> "Flowers laugh before her on their beds,
> And fragrance in her footing treads;"

for
> "She doth wear
> The godhead's most benignant grace;
> Nor know we anything so fair
> As is the smile upon her face."

With full assurance of faith we anticipate the time when through her influences her Founder shall fulfil the glowing prophecy, "And on his head were many crowns." I see the grand procession gathering to the coronation. Yonder are Herschel and Kepler and Copernicus and Galileo, at the head of the astronomic sages. They draw nigh to crown him; and as he stoops to receive the gift, I hear them exclaim: "The heavens are the work of thy hands, the moon and the stars which thou hast ordained." And yonder I see the great chiefs of geologic science, and their sumless followers: there are Hugh Miller, and Buckland, and Dana; and as he stoops to receive their offering thus they declare: "Of old didst thou lay the foundations of the earth; the strength of the hills is thine also." And, see, yonder the great old masters lead up their ranks,—Angelico, Angelo, Da Vinci; and as they present their tribute, I hear them say: "Blessed are our eyes, for we have seen the King in his beauty."

And there is another surpassing far all these in power to touch his heart. It is woman,—"redeemed, regenerated, disenthralled" woman; and at the head of the illustrious throng there is the first mother of us all, and by her side *His own*. To them he stoops,—is there not haze in his eye?—and as their gentle hands place in his their choicest diadem, thus they exclaim: "When thou tookest upon thee to deliver man, thou didst not abhor the virgin's womb." It is enough. Let us conclude by chanting, in harmony with such a prospect,—

> "All hail the power of Jesus' name;
> Let angels prostrate fall;
> Bring forth the royal diadem,
> And crown him Lord of all."

IV.

THE PLACE OF CONSCIENCE.

By REV. MARK HOPKINS, D.D.

IV.

THE PLACE OF CONSCIENCE.

By REV. MARK HOPKINS, D.D.

THE PRELUDE.

IT is one thing to lecture to an audience, and another thing to lecture to the general public. It was my intention, when I agreed to speak here, to discuss the subject as I did when I spoke last before the Lowell Institute, — working directly upon the blackboard, and not reading at all; but when I noticed the reports of the lectures given, and understood the wishes of the committee, I saw that it would not be in the line of what had been presented on this platform, if I should deliver a lecture which could not be reported so far as the use of the blackboard was concerned.

It was the custom of the distinguished founder of this lectureship to begin with a prelude, and I follow the custom. As was fit, his preludes usually consisted of a discussion of some popular subject or topic of the day. The subject of "Man's Upbuilding *versus* Development" is hardly that, and yet I venture to adopt it as having been so much before the public, and also as somewhat connected with the lecture that is to follow.

We find ourselves in the midst of an orderly universe. Everywhere around us we find unity in the midst of variety, giving us at once the principle of order and of beauty. The perception of this unity, as now known, is due to modern science. It was so far removed from the primitive and unaided thought of man, that he supposed the heavens, the ocean, and the regions below to be subject to different gods, and to be ruled by different laws. It was a great step, and the cause of a high joy, when man was able to extend the laws which govern matter on the earth to the heavenly bodies; and, again, when he was able to find, by means of light, that the same substances which are found here on the earth are discovered in the sun and in the remotest star. And the unity and order thus found around us and throughout a measureless space are equally disclosed among the different species of organized beings that are shown by the microscope as peopling a drop of water.

But this was not always so. It is equally the doctrine of science and of revelation that there was a time when chaos reigned, and when this planet was devoid of order and of life. The accepted doctrine of science at present is, that the material of the whole system, celestial and terrestrial, was originally stardust diffused in space, that has at length, after untold ages, been condensed and brought to its present order. Allowing this, we naturally inquire by what causes and in what manner this result has been reached.

In doing this there are three words, development,— or, what is the same thing, evolution, — growth, and upbuilding, each indicating a different process, which I wish to consider.

Of these, the first is development. What, then, do we mean by that? In strictness, it presupposes a whole that is enveloped, and is then enlarged and unfolded by a process from within. Of this a rosebud is a good example. In that, all that is to be lies in miniature, enveloped in its covering, and, by a process from within, it is brought out, developed into largeness and beauty and fragrance. But in its use in common life the term is not confined in its meaning to a strict development and unfolding; it is applied in any case where a whole already existing is enlarged by a process from within. Thus we say of a muscle, that it becomes developed, and of the boy, that he may develop into a fine man. In every case, if the word be used according to the definition in any dictionary, or according to the usage of common speech and the conceptions of those who use that speech, there must be, either in idea or in reality, a previously existing whole.

Now, what I object to is, that this word, thus definite in its meaning and well understood, has been so used as to involve a practical fallacy. It has been so used as to imply that there was in the original stardust the whole of what we now see, and that the present order has come out of that, with no external agency, by the process known to the common mind as development. The whole subject is vast and obscure; in the minds of common men it lies in a misty way, and when by the use of a common term they hear the process of world-making identified by men of high scientific standing with one with which they are familiar, they readily accept what is said, and suppose they understand that process.

But while the development theory has had the advantage of this fallacy working insidiously and unconsciously, the ablest advocate of the theory, Mr. Herbert Spencer, has found it necessary to frame a definition of development, or evolution, which entirely excludes the idea of any whole, either ideal or physical, and which is, moreover, equally applicable to processes of the most diverse and even opposite kind. His definition of evolution is, that "it is a change from an indefinite, incoherent homogeneity to a definite, coherent heterogeneity, through continuous differentiations and integrations." There! Now you know what evolution or development is, and we will proceed to apply the definition to the process of making a world out of star-dust.

This star-dust was the indefinite, incoherent homogeneity. That it was indefinite and incoherent we know, but how he could know, or have a right to say, that that out of which was to come such a variety of substances and beings was homogeneous, I do not know. But, be that as it may, there began to be differentiations. One part of this indefinite, incoherent, homogeneous star-dust began to differ from another part, and these differentiations were continuous. A part, we may suppose, became oxygen, a part carbon, a part gold, and so on, of all the so-called simple substances of which this globe was originally composed. Previous to these differentiations, however, or in connection with them, there must have been one great integration without differentiation, by which the star-dust was brought into a mass. After that, different integrations might go on, forming water and granite and lime-rock and trees and men.

In all this it will be noticed that there were different processes, involving different forces. There was first the process of aggregation, by which the indefinite and incoherent particles were brought towards a centre and became condensed into a mass. This was effected by the force of gravitation. But these particles, atoms, molecules, whatever they were, being originally incoherent, needed to cohere, and so the force of cohesion came into play. Again, it was not sufficient that alien particles should cohere. What has happened since was foreshadowed at that early day. There were affinities, and immense excitement in consequence. The amorous oxygen rushed to its hydrogen, the acid to its alkali, and the two became one. No particle missed its true affinity, and hence marriages were formed that have known of no divorce for these thousands of years. The frequency of modern divorce finds no countenance in the doings of those ancient days. If, now, we bring these several affinities under the common name of chemical affinity, we have a new force by which, in connection with gravitation and cohesion, all the substances on the earth were formed up to the point of organization, all the different processes being covered by the one word, development; and, if we allow that the original substance was homogeneous, being really a change from an indefinite, incoherent homogeneity to a definite, coherent heterogeneity, through continuous differentiations and integrations.

Having now brought the earth up by the definition to the point where it has a sufficient basis for organization, let us try it upon that. And here we will take an egg, — the white of an egg, for it is from that that the chick is formed. This white of the egg is the indefinite, incoherent homogeneity. It seems at least to be homogeneous. But after the application of heat for a few days differentiations begin to show themselves, and these are continuous. The blood-vessels, the bones, the lungs, the eyes, the bill, the little feathers, begin to appear, and to form themselves into definite, coherent heterogeneities, till at length the perfect animal is formed. It then, by means of a little prominence that had been accidentally developed on the top of its bill, chips its shell and comes out, and, if it be a chicken, listens to the cluck of its mother, but if it be a duck, regardless of the cluck, makes for the nearest water by an instinct that was originally developed from the definite, coherent heterogeneities, and transmitted by heredity.

You see, then, that the definition applies equally to the formation of a world and the formation of a chicken, and I ask you of what value a formula of words can be that can cover such diverse and opposite processes? If I were to define a horse as a being, and a calf as a being, thus covering both by one definition, and should then infer that a horse is a calf, it would be but a trick of words; and this is the same.

But it is time to inquire whether the process just spoken of is one of development. It is not, unless we confound, as is wrongly coming to be done, development with growth. *Growth*, which is the next word and process of which I wish to speak, is a special process which starts from a cell or germ that is *alive*, and is carried on through the agency and superintendence of what we call life. It was said at one time that protoplasm was the condition of life. This may be true, but there is dead as well as living protoplasm, and no chemist can tell the difference, or find out what that subtile thing is without which, protoplasm or no protoplasm, there will be no growth. I would discourage no research; but it is my belief that my friend, Dr. Barker, who seemed, in his recent speech here in Boston, so confident that he and his coadjutors will soon capture life, will do that when the boy who chases the foot of the rainbow shall find the pot of money that is buried there. Not protoplasm, then, but living protoplasm, is the condition of growth; and this process, I insist, is to be distinguished from that of development. There is in growth no previous whole, no miniature parts, nothing in that from which the growth starts to indicate what the outcome is to be. Is it said that the chicken is in the egg potentially? Yes, but only as the ship is in the trees of the forest and in the iron unwrought. The material from which the chicken is to be formed is there, but the bones and the bill and the muscles and the tendons are not there. There is nothing there but the material out of which the animal is to be formed and an unknown something which we call life. Nor is there any one centre from which the growth of the animal starts in such a way as to indicate what may be called development from a centre. Each bone starts from a centre of its own and pushes out towards the other bones, and becomes joined to them, not organically but mechanically, by sutures and ligaments, so that the putting together of the skeleton is singularly like the putting together of any piece of machinery in a mechanical way. The process is totally unlike any other. Even in the egg, where the whole material for the formation of the animal is given, the only similarity between that and a proper development is, that the process is carried on by an agency that is not discerned as separate from the material. But how if we take a bunch of grapes? Here the whole process is carried on through a stem not the tenth of an inch in diameter; and by an agency and with a skill of which man knows nothing the minor stems are formed, and the delicate covering, and the pulp, and the seed for the growth of other grapes, while the material for the whole is gathered, not at all from the seed from which the vine sprang, nor from the vine itself except as an instrument, but from the earth and the air and the ocean. This being so, what significance is there to the word development, or evolution, when applied to such a *process? No, it is *growth*, by which word a process is indicated, the antecedents and conditions of which we know, but of the cause and method of which we know *nothing*, absolutely *nothing*, and we may as well say so.

That the process of growth, whether of the chicken or the grapes, is covered, equally with the condensation of star-dust and the formation of worlds, by the definition of Mr. Spencer, I agree; but how far does development, as thus defined, go to account for either? If not put forth to account for them, it is commonly supposed to be, and to do it. Does it do that? Let us see. "Evolution," it is said, "is a change from an indefinite, incoherent homogeneity to a definite, coherent heterogeneity." It is a *change*, and that change is a continuous one, leading to a result. That is all that the definition says; that is all that development, according to the definition, is or does. But does the statement of the fact of a change account for the change? or of the fact of a result account for a result? No. Taking this definition of evolution, and regarding it as an attempt to account for the present state of things, it would read thus: "A change from an indefinite, incoherent homogeneity to a definite, coherent heterogeneity, through continuous differentiations and integrations, is the cause of a change from an indefinite, incoherent homogeneity to a definite, coherent heterogeneity, through continuous differentiations and integrations."

It only remains in this connection to speak of *upbuilding*, as distinguished from both development and growth.

Why do we never speak of a house as developed? For two reasons. One is, that in the building of a house the agent is seen to be distinct from the material. It is seen that that which moves the material is outside of it, and cannot possibly be a property or tendency of the material to be thus moved. But the main reason is the want of continuity. There are such breaks between the foundation and the superstructure, and between the different stories, that what is above could not possibly have originated from what is below. This would necessitate for the building of the house an agent outside of the house. This is the turning-point, and is seen to be so by those who hold to development. Hence, mainly, the interest in the question of spontaneous generation. Hence the violent supposition by Professor Tyndall that there may have been sensation originally in the star-dust, and probably is now in the rocks. Hence his supposition — I think I may say the absurd supposition — that an eye might be formed by the action of light falling on an undifferentiated organism vaguely sensitive all over. Hence the anxiety to show that there is no essential difference between man and the brutes; and hence, as you have seen in the definition of Mr. Spencer, the word *continuous* as applied to differentiations. Now, what we affirm is, that there is no such continuity. We say that there are breaks in the upward progress of nature such that

THE PLACE OF CONSCIENCE.

there could be no power in the lower to pass over into and produce, or become, the higher.

These two modes of conceiving of the upward progress in nature and of the relation of its forces may be represented by two forms of a pyramid. On one the side will be an inclined plane with no break. On the other there will be breaks, and the pyramid will be composed of different platforms.

[The lecturer here illustrated upon the blackboard, by means of pyramidical designs, his statements.]

So I represented it some years since in lectures given before the Lowell Institute. In this pyramid each platform represents a new force, and one which, as I affirm, could not have been developed from the force or forces below. It is contrary to all our conceptions of causation, that a force which reveals itself only as it overcomes a lower force should be developed from that force. But that is the relation of the forces here. If cohesion were not a stronger force than gravitation, everything would be at a dead level. What prevents the wall above us from coming down? Nothing but cohesion as a stronger force than gravitation, which is constantly endeavoring to bring it down. Or, take the force connected with the growth of vegetables as it is related to the three lower forces on which it is conditioned, and how could the vegetable get its food as it lies combined in the earth and floats in the air, if it did not overcome cohesion and chemical affinity, or how could it lift its material one hundred and fifty feet into the air if it did not overcome gravitation? And shall we suppose that a force working not only in opposition to lower forces, but in absolute defiance of them, was developed from those forces? And as the three lower forces were an absolute condition for vegetation, so was vegetation an absolute condition for animal life, since it is the one great function of vegetables to mediate between inorganic matter and animals by furnishing them their whole food, which vegetables can, and animals cannot procure directly from that matter.

We have, then, inorganic matter with its three forces as a foundation for the building; we have vegetables as the first story, the lower animals as the second, and man as the third; and what we say is, that at every upward step there must have been a supervising agent to introduce the superior force, and to correlate it with the forces below.

But, as bearing on the upward continuity of movement, which is essential to the development system, there is one point which may not be omitted. I refer to the sexual relation as it exists both in vegetables and in animals, and which might almost seem a device for the very purpose of excluding the possibility of such an hypothesis. A single case might be explained away; but when we see this relation running through the whole animate creation, so that the continuance of its higher forms is dependent upon it, and reflect on the impossibility either that the sexes should have been developed *pari passu* through the untold ages required by the system to reach the needed point, or that the individuals should have been preserved in any other way, we must see how formidable the difficulty is, and how much more reasonable it is to suppose that in the beginning "God *created* them male and female."

The plausibility of development is derived in part from the fact that the force seems to reside in the material, but more from the way in which the different forms of vegetable and animal life seem to run into each other. But on the supposition of upbuilding by a wise Master Builder, this is accounted for by the need there is in the system of symmetry and of sympathy. If the points of transition in the upbuilding from one story to another were visible, the apparent symmetry and unity and beauty of the whole would be impaired. I remember to have seen an account of a piece of cabinet-work so deftly joined that the point of juncture could be found only by the preternatural power of touch possessed by a blind man. This perfect joining was required for unity and beauty, while the pieces were as really separate as if they had been divided by the wide Atlantic. And so symmetry requires that the points of juncture in nature should be invisible, while such points there must be. As between plants and animals, however the plant may simulate animal movements, there must *be* a line, on one side of which there is sensation and on the other not. We may be as unable to decide when or where it enters as we are to decide when or where the first ray of the morning enters the darkness, but a when and a where there must be.

And so of sympathy. I know of nothing more

wonderful than that close analogy between men and animals that comes from their sharing a common animal nature that so brings them into sympathy, while there is yet such a disparity that the animals are naturally subject to man.

Thus, from the need of symmetry and of sympathy, do we account for the apparent uniformity in the upward movement of the creation; while we find, too, those lines of separation between the different stories of this earthly building which renders it impossible that the higher should have been developed from the lower.

On the whole, then, I find myself agreeing with each of two propositions laid down by a man who lived nearly two thousand years ago. With the first of these I am sure you will agree, and with the second I hope you will agree also. These propositions are: 1st, That every house is builded by some man; and, 2d, That he that BUILT all things is God.

THE LECTURE.

In passing to the lecture, we do not leave upbuilding altogether. In the lectures already referred to, entitled "The Outline Study of Man," I attempted to show not only that there was an upbuilding from the lowest force in nature to man, but also in man himself, and that the principle on which the upbuilding was carried on was the same throughout. I attempted to show that in nature the principle was one of perfect subordination, as one force was a condition for another, and of limitation on the part of each lower force to such action as might best serve those above it. In the functions of the body, even, I attempted to show that there is a gradation as higher and lower according to the same law, and this, notwithstanding the circular and interdependent nature of all vital action. Then in the mind, taking its three great divisions, intellect, sensibility, and will, I sought to show that intellect was lowest, sensibility next, and then will: The faculties, or functions, of the intellect, as presentative, regulative, representative, and elaborative, I sought to arrange in the same way; and so of the sensibility and the will, till the whole man was constructed. That was the completion of one work. The man was constructed and put into possession of himself.

At this point the work of upbuilding on the part of God ceased, but only that it might be taken up by man on the model which God had set before him. Man, having faculties, and especially active principles, constructed in regular gradation as lower and higher, was to use them in accordance with the same gradation. The powers which were intended to rule he was to cause to rule, and those intended to serve he was to cause to serve, holding every lower principle of action in its place by the law of its limitation, and giving full scope to the highest as having nothing above to limit it. Thus doing, intelligently bringing each lower spontaneity and principle under its law, he was to build up his activities, and so his character, after the model set him by God in the upbuilding of his universe.

What we need to know, then, at this point is, what the active principles of our frame are, and how they are related to each other as higher or lower, as subordinate or supreme.

In regard to some of these there is a general agreement. The appetites, as a condition for the continuance of life, and so for all the others, are the lowest. These are good in themselves, and, held in their place, are only good. Then come the instincts, which seem, as sometimes impulsive, and sometimes regulative, to be, when acting on their own line and without being thwarted, a kind of divine reason, and when acting out of that line, a kind of idiocy. Next we have the desires, the cravings of the mind for those things needed for its own well-being, as the appetites are for things needed for the well-being of the body. The natural affections, as of parent and child, are next in order. These have in them an element of desire, but it is a desire for the good of others. They are strong and beautiful in the lower animals, but become doubly beautiful when comprehended and irradiated by a higher nature.

Up to this point our active principles are impulsive, as distinguished from rational. By this it is meant that each principle has, standing over against it, its own object from which it, or rather the being, is to derive gratification, and that it goes out towards its object as by an impulse from behind, and, without reflection or regard to consequences, rests in it till it is satiated, if that be possible; or if, as in the desires, that be not possible, till some one desire becomes the ruling passion, and so insatiate. If all our active powers were of this kind they would become a mob. We therefore plainly need rational or governing powers.

The rational principles of action, therefore, come next. They are called rational because they imply a comparison between different principles of action, authority over them, and a choice between them by a being who stands above and comprehends them. These principles are said by Bishop Butler, Dugald Stewart, Dr. Wayland, and writers on morals generally, to be self-love and conscience. This enumeration I think defective. I have never seen, for example, in any list of the active powers, *Rights* put down as among them. But I would inquire of this audience whether they do not think that rights are among the most underlying, general, and powerful of our principles of action? What will a man fight for sooner than his rights? What but his rights ought he to fight for? Our conception of these comes in connection with every active principle. Among the first, if not the very first, of our moral ideas, is that of a right to ourselves, — that is, of a right to use every power we have for its appropriate ends; and when that right is interfered with, our nature is stirred to its lowest depths. If the idea of a right, or of rights, be thus an active principle, it is of course rational, since no one except a rational being can have a conception of rights.

But a greater omission, in my view, is that of LOVE, — moral and rational love. We have the power of

disinterested action. We have the power of making
the good of others, without reference to complacency
in their character, the object of our choice and effort,
and that good may stand over against our power of
rational choice, as food stands over against appetite,
or as money stands over against the desire of the
miser. The good of others may be so apprehended
that the pursuit of it shall become an absorbing passion. This love is not a mere emotion. Its central
element is choice, rational choice, and no emotion
that is sacred can belong to a love that does not
follow this. This is the love required in the Bible
as the central spring of our actions; and it is remarkable that Christian moralists should have constructed their systems so as to exclude this, or, at least,
that in any enumeration of our active powers they
should not have given it the place where it is put
by the Bible, and where, by a fair analysis of our
powers, it belongs. Instead, therefore, of accepting
self-love and conscience as a complete enumeration
of our governing powers, I would make them to
be rights, self-love, rational and moral love, and
conscience.

But here comes the question about the place of
conscience. Almost universally it has been placed
at the head of the list, with its object over against it,
like the rest, and not differing from them except
as supreme. The question is, whether it ought to be
so placed. Let us see. We have at the bottom of
the list appetite, say hunger, and over against it food.
We have instinct, say the instinct of the migratory

bird, and over against it a warm climate. We have desire, say of power, and for its object power. We have natural affection, as of the parent, and for its object the child. We have rights, and for their object those things to which we have a right. We have self-love, and over against it our own good. We have moral love, and over against it the good of others. Now, shall conscience be placed next, and over against that, right, or the right? This is what has been done. It has been, and is, supposed that right, or the right in an action, is immediately and intuitively perceived by the conscience, and that the action is to be done solely for the sake of that, with no regard to consequences or the good of any one. Those who hold this view are generally careful to say that it is quite certain that an action thus done will result in good, but they affirm that it will lower its quality and tone if that fact be so known as to have any influence in determining the act. They seem to think that if the whole truth were clearly seen, the highest virtue would be impossible, thus making truth hostile to virtue. In fact, I once heard regret expressed that this regard to right could not be made to stand wholly alone.

But there is another view. It was said by Sir James Mackintosh, though it has been little noticed since, that the immediate object of conscience is the will itself. According to this the conscience will not, like the other active principles, have an object corresponding to it, and towards which it is to go out; but its office will be, when two objects of choice are presented, as there always must be when a choice is to be made, to prompt the will to choose the higher and the better. If this be so, it will at once change the place of conscience from the top of the list, and place it by itself behind the will, so that the man shall hear a voice behind him, saying, "This is the way, walk ye in it."

These different relations of conscience will be best expressed by their representations on the board. The first has been sufficiently explained. For the second, we need a line back of the list of active powers representing the man, the person who is really the governing power. We speak of governing powers, but we mean by it only the powers that ought to govern. In the last resort it is the man himself who decides and governs, and who is to be considered apart from all influences that can be brought to bear upon him. We may identify him with the will or the will with him, but it is not the will that decides, — it is the man who has the will; and we wish to know what the influences are that are brought to bear upon him when he acts morally in making a choice, since it is only in making a choice and carrying it out that he does act morally. In order to do this we will suppose a choice is to be made between the desire of power and moral love, and represent the influence of each by a line drawn from it to the man, one drawing him up and the other down. Then conscience, if it is to have, like the rest, its object before it, must be represented as behind the man, and its office will be to prompt him to choose to be influenced by moral love, and forbid him to be influenced by ambition.

If this view of the place of conscience be accepted, it will change the whole aspect of the moral problem. It being conceded that all moral action is in choice, and in carrying out choices, it will be seen that, according to this, the only object of choice there can be, must be from some one of the active principles represented as in front of the man, each of these presenting some form of *a* good either to himself or to others. It will follow from this that conscience never furnishes the primary motive for action, and never acts at all except for the enforcement of some motives not furnished by itself. If there were not a good beyond its own sphere furnishing the occasion for its action, it could never act. And not only must there be a ground for action aside from conscience, but it must be so far rational that it would suffice for itself, or conscience could have no basis for action. In other words, according to this view, conscience does not furnish the grounds of choice, but requires of us, in a peculiar manner, and with sanctions, the choice of ends and forms of good furnished by other principles of action. It supersedes no natural principle of action, and it restrains none, except it be by acting in conjunction with one that is higher than it. Thus doing, the conscience works in harmony with reason, which must always require the choice of the higher good, and also with each natural principle of action along the whole line, so far as it abides within its own bounds.

It will be perceived further, that, according to this view, the existence of moral ideas, and so of conscience itself, is conditioned on a sensibility, and on that product of a sensibility which we call *a* good. Each principle of action in the upward line can furnish a motive only as it is a form of the sensibility, and as there is, from its normal action, some form of *a* good in the sensibility. It is only as there is such a good from the action of these principles that the idea of rights or of obligation can arise, — of rights as belonging to ourselves, of obligations either as due from others to us, or from ourselves to others.

Certainly, if we had no conception of a good either for ourselves or others, we could have no conception of either rights or of obligation; but these are primitive ideas given by the moral nature, and without them the action of conscience would be impossible. And what has just been said of rights and of obligation in their relation to *a* good, will, of course, be true of benevolence and of justice. Without a sensibility through which there might be enjoyment and suffering, natural good and evil, there could plainly be no benevolence or malignity, no justice or injustice; and thus, without a sensibility and the idea of *a* good from that, as prior in the order of nature, there could be no moral ideas. We see, then, how impossible it is that any system of morals should be based on an intuition purely intellectual, unless we call that so which has for its underlying ground a good which is the product of a sensibility, and which is recognized through a sensibility as having value in itself. As I have said in "The Law of Love," "When it is said, as it has been, to be an *a priori* law that benevolence is right and malice is wrong, it cannot be so *a priori* and transcendental as to exist till there is a knowledge of what benevolence and malice are, and so of that good and evil [natural good and evil] without which neither of them could be."

But to this view there are objections. One is drawn from the consciousness we have of acting directly from a sense of duty, with no reference to anything else. That we have such consciousness I agree. The voice of conscience is imperative, and may occupy our whole thought. So may that part of a tree which is above the ground occupy our whole thought to the exclusion of the roots from which the tree grew, and whence its sap is derived. Certainly, among the motives which must be involved in an act of choice by a being so complex as man, a sense of duty may determine what the choice shall be, the mind may be fixed upon that alone, and man may feel a sense of dignity when that is so. There is a certain grandeur in quoting the passage, *Fiat justitia, ruat cœlum,* — "Let justice be done, though the heavens fall." That passage I would quote with as much emphasis as any one, but I would not have such a conception of justice as would make it of no consequence whether the heavens should fall or not. In the same way it is said that children have a sense of rights and of duties before they can estimate consequences. Yes, like other parts of our nature, the conscience acts spontaneously and impulsively. Before we are able to understand the reason of it, it impels us like an instinct; but when we come to understand it, we find it a part of a harmonious system, every part of which was intended to conspire for the good of the whole.

It is said, too, that this view does not comport well with what our Saviour said of self-denial, and suffering, and persecution, and losing our lives for his sake. It does comport with it perfectly, and is the only view that does. For what does he say? "Blessed are ye when men shall revile you, and shall say all manner of evil against you falsely for my sake, . . . for great is your reward in heaven." "Love ye your enemies, and do good, hoping for *nothing* again, and your reward shall be great." What a pity he said this last! Again, "He that loveth his life shall lose it, and he that hateth his life shall keep it — unto life everlasting." Even he himself, for the joy that was set before him, endured the cross. Can there really be anything wrong or in any way unworthy in a man's intelligently co-operating with God for his own best good? If there were time, I should like to speak at this point of the confusion by the positivists of a regard to self-interest with selfishness, and of the quixotism of their professed devotion to an abstraction, which they call humanity, by which they outquixote Don Quixote himself.

But would not this view lead to utilitarianism? Not as I understand the term. I recognize the distinction between a regard to duty and a regard to utility. I hold to obligation and its binding force as strongly as anybody. I hold to a moral nature, through which obligation is immediately and necessarily affirmed, but I hold that obligation is obligation to choose; and because I hold further that it is obligation to choose a good rather than an abstract quality of an action, I am regarded by some as a downright utilitarian. Utility is a good thing in its place, but that place is not at the basis of a moral system. I would choose a good, not for its utility, for it has none. It is the only thing I know of that neither has nor can have utility. I would choose it for its own sake, and also as under obligation to choose it; and this behest of moral law, uttered through the sense of obligation, may and should become a motive sufficient to lead me to choose that good under every extremity. Adopting here what I have said elsewhere, "It is one thing to say that the formation of moral ideas and the action of conscience at all — of the will even — are conditioned on a sensibility, and quite another to say that when these ideas are formed, and conscience utters its imperative as between a higher and a lower principle of action, conscience is not to be obeyed out of regard to any utility there may be supposed to be from the action of the lower. That conscience is to be obeyed implicitly I assert, and always have asserted, and the action is not made utilitarian because conscience sides with the principles that would give the higher good." It would be a disturbing element in the constitution, and an anomaly in the creation of God, if it did not.

But this subject I will not continue further. It requires a more thorough treatment than the time permits. It might, indeed, have been better if I had taken but one subject. I should at least have avoided the architectural blunder of making the porch larger than the house. If, however, I have succeeded in presenting to this audience clearly and fairly, so that its bearings are understood, the question of the place of conscience, it is all I could hope to do. The question I leave with you. How to reconcile the claims of the sensibility on the one hand, and the moral nature on the other, philosophers have not been agreed. They are not now. Some way of reconciliation there must be, and if what I have said has thrown but one gleam of light upon that way, I shall be satisfied.

V.

DEVELOPMENT: ITS NATURE; WHAT IT CAN DO AND WHAT IT CANNOT DO.

By REV. JAMES McCOSH, D.D., LL.D.

V.

DEVELOPMENT: ITS NATURE; WHAT IT CAN DO AND WHAT IT CANNOT DO.

BY REV. JAMES McCOSH, D.D., LL.D.

THE PRELUDE.

WHEN I was asked a few weeks ago to lecture in Boston, the question immediately started up in my mind: What can have induced anybody to invite me to speak in a city where, as I look upon it, every man is fitted by heredity, by birth and education, to be a lecturer? After puzzling my poor brain for a time, I gave up the question as unanswerable, resolving meanwhile to embrace the opportunity of meeting so enlightened a community. Being here, I feel that I should conform to the practice of the place and the hour; and so I begin with a prelude.

There are few people here who remember, or indeed ever heard, that some years ago I delivered in Boston a short course of lectures (afterwards published) on the topics which lie between philosophy and theology. Not claiming to be a prophet, I looked at the causes then in operation, and ventured to draw out a map of the road which a certain class of our young men were taking. I described Unitarianism, so full of life and hope an age ago, as dead and laid out for decent burial. Everybody saw, or was beginning to see, that the system defended by Channing, as founded on the Scriptures of the Old and New Testament, could not stand before an honest interpretation of these writings. Left without any divine authority to uphold it, the creed was like the icicles we see on the roofs of our houses at this season, clear but cold, not drawing our hearts towards it, and certain to melt away in the heat of a more fervent period. But I intimated my fear that those left without any revelation from Heaven to stay them might go down the sliding scale into a lower depth.

The causes operated, and the anticipations I sketched have so far been realized. Our youth have tried to live in a certainly wide enough region, supplied them by Herbert Spencer and his accomplished disciple and expounder in this country, Mr. Fiske, — the region of the unknowable to which they politely consign God and religion, where no one can see them, and where Professor Huxley has conveniently set up for them "worship chiefly of the silent sort," with no one to speak and no one to hear. But our active young men have felt a difficulty in living in a vacuum; and, seeking for something more substantial, they fondly expect to find air and food in materialism, which Professor Tyndall assures them has every sort of promise and potency.

Meanwhile, there have been protests against this

tendency, and persons have been eagerly clutching certain weak branches to stay their descent, but which, as they give way, will only, I fear, precipitate them the faster. Mankind have, after all, a deep underlying belief in something supernatural which seems to be pervading and surrounding the whole of natural operation. Some one said that when men cease to believe in God they begin to believe in ghosts; and there are numbers who, in the felt want of anything better, have lent a favorable ear to Spiritualists. Those who could not believe in Moses and the prophets, in Christ and his apostles, have listened eagerly to audible scribbling on concealed slates, which show, by their imbecility, that the spirits which return from the other world have lost there the high ability which some of them possessed in this world. Those who could not believe that God sent his Son into the world to solve the enigma of the universe, and to show how man, the sinner, is to be reconciled to God, the holy Governor, and how he is to be delivered from the bonds of iniquity, resolutely maintain that he sends spirits to untie the ropes which weak or cunning men and women have tied around themselves.

A much nobler outlet has been opened for this craving after the divine and the supernatural. The beautiful dreams of Emerson have been made to irradiate and gild a mysticism which has been brought from the East and supposed to be the Light of Asia, and an ideal philosophy which has come with other emigrants from Germany,—where I know it is in danger of being starved; and many have resorted to this castle in the air. The Concord School, which is an annex of literary Boston, has just been strengthened by the resort thither of an able and a most estimable man, who has taken up Hegelianism after it had run and ended its course in Germany. These philosophers open to us glorious views, if not into heaven, at least into the clouds, gilded by the shining sun. I do rejoice in all they say so eloquently of the infinities, the eternities, the moralities, and the idealities. There are not only beauty and elevation, there is also a truth in all these sentiments. But my rational nature requires me to know on what I am to ground my belief, and how I am to separate between the sober truth and the associated extravagances. This I can do only by carefully observing the laws of the mind, after the manner of the true American and Scottish philosophy, or by following the revelation of God in his Word.

Meanwhile, notwithstanding these side eddies, the deeper current is moving on. First, there is a doctrine of relativity, with which Mr. Herbert Spencer and Mr. Fiske start. According to this philosophy, we know nothing of things, which may or may not have a reality; all that we have are simply relations connecting unknown things,— a bridge with nothing to support it on either side. This has prepared the way for what we used to call Nescience and Nihilism, but which is now designated Agnosticism, which insists that nothing can be known. But it is proverbial that nature is stronger than speculative theories, and will return though repelled with a pitchfork. Its very advocates, though denying that there is such a thing as mind or matter, practically believe in such things as pleasures and pains, as money and position in society. What they regard as unknowable are simply God and good, immortality and a judgment day. As the issue of this discussion, there are numbers of our young men who are unable, or at least affect to be unable, to determine anything about divine or spiritual or even moral truths, and care about nothing more than catching the enjoyments of the hour. But meanwhile there is a higher nature within — a remnant and indication of their divine nature — which will not allow them to rest satisfied in their present creed. They are made to feel that they have stalks from which the fruit has been pulled. Craving for substantial food, they would find it in materialism, and would fain fill their belly with the husks which the swine do eat, only to find that they are " in want," with their hearts turning away from the repast with nausea and disgust. It is in this state of things that we find pessimism propagated, and accepted by some as their only refuge.

I am more hopeful of this hopeless state of things than of that self-satisfied, self-righteous one that went before. The ball has reached its lowest point and struck against impenetrable adamant; and it is ready for a rebound. The time for reaction has come. We are at the darkest hour; I am looking for the sun to rise. We may now sow as they did in ancient Egypt, for the waters are receding, leaving a soil ready to nourish what is cast into it. I am this day to endeavor to put out of the way an obstacle which is hindering many from accepting the truth. That obstacle is Development, which is cherished by some and repelled by others, as supposed to be capable of carrying on nature without the need of God.

THE LECTURE.

There is a perpetual reference in the present day to Evolution, or Development. There is an equally persistent avoidance of any explanation of its nature. Instances of it are given, and inferences, legitimate and illegitimate, are drawn; but there is scarcely an attempt made to specify what is involved in it.

The phrase is used to cover all sorts of things, clean and unclean. Scientific men discourse profoundly of the evolution of plants and animals, of individuals and of species, of genera and orders, from the monad up to man. But we hear also of the development of the resources of a country, of its wealth, its mines, its gold and silver; its crops and corn, its wheat and fruits; of its sheep and cattle and horses; of its industry, its trade and commerce; of its cities, their streets, houses, and harbors; of its education, its colleges and schools. They give you histories of the development of the sciences, of astronomy, chemistry, and geology; of the fine arts, as painting, sculpture, and architecture; and of the useful arts, as masonry, carpentry, and engine-making. They talk, too, of the evolution of things from a simpler to a more complete form, — of pottery, of wax-work, of metal-work, of vases, of dinner-sets and teacups. It must surely be a comprehensive phrase, or, quite as possibly, a loose and ambiguous one, which embraces all these things and a thousand more.

Just because of its capacity, it is apt to take up ✗ and carry with it all sorts of incongruous wares. In these circumstances, when any one is talking of development, for or against it, it is necessary to insist on his telling us precisely what he means by it. "I am sick," says the man of common sense, who is not to be taken in by high-sounding phrases, "of this pretentious development. I prefer the old way of speaking, when it was believed that all things came from God." But I ask this man of uncommon sense whether he is prepared to affirm that he was not developed from his good father and mother; whether he, the man of forty, has not grown out of that boy whom he remembers going to school at the age of six. "But I am a religious man," he tells us, "and believe that God and not development guides this universe." I ask him more pertinently whether God may not have made him grow by development, and whether this same God has not evolved the Christian from the Jewish faith, and the Jewish from the patriarchal. When we lay down for ourselves and abide by the principle that in the discussion we explain beforehand what we mean, we are in the better position to require the same on the part of our opponent, and to insist on knowing what he means by the evelution which he is defending: an evolution out of nothing; an evolution without a God to set it a going or to guide it, an evolution of life from the lifeless, of mind from the mindless, of man from the monkey, of the monkey from the mollusk, of the mollusk from the monad, and all from senseless molecules?

Development is evidently not a simple power in nature, like mechanical force or chemical affinity or gravitation. It is clear that there is a vast, an incalculable number and variety of agencies in the process, whether it be the development of the plant from its seed, of the bird from the egg, of the horse from its dam, of the threshing-machine from the flail, of the reaping-machine from the reaping-hook, of our present kitchen utensils from those used by our grandmother. The question presses: Is there any unity in the "thousand and one" things that form the process? I believe that there is. It is worth inquiring what it is, when it will be found to settle for us what truth there is, and what error there is, in the common expositions, that is, developments of development.

Development is essentially a combination of causes working towards a particular end. I call it an organized causation for ends, a corporation of causes for mutual action. At this point I am greatly tempted to enlarge and dwell on the subject of causation. I am not singular in holding that, after all these discussions about the conservation of energy, we scarcely know what causation is. Mr. Mill has shown successfully, as I think, that in all causes there are always two or more agents. "The statement of the cause," he says, "is incomplete unless in some shape or other we introduce all the conditions. A man takes mercury, goes out of doors and catches cold. We say, perhaps, that the cause of his taking cold was exposure to the air. It is clear, however, that his having taken mercury may have been a necessary condition of his catching cold; and though it might consist with usage to say that the cause of his attack was exposure to air, to be accurate we ought to say that the cause was exposure to air while under the effect of mercury. [Logic, III. 5.] The true cause comprises both the mercury and the state of the body. It is always dual or plural. I have shown that it is the same with the effect. [Divine Government, III.] The true effect consists in the mercury changed and in the body changed; the mercury is absorbed into the frame and the body dies. The true physical cause always consists of two or more bodies in a particular state, and the effect of the same body in a different state. A ball in motion strikes a ball at rest. It is not correct to say that the one ball is the cause of the other ball moving. The true cause is made up of both balls, the one in motion striking the ball at rest, and the effect on the one ball moved and the other stayed. A cold current blows on my body; this acts as a cause, and the effect, the air is slightly warmed and my body is made colder. So in every case of physical causation: the effect consists of the agents acting as the cause in a new state. According to the doctrine of the conservation of energy, the amount of energy, real and potential, in the causes and effects is always one and the same."

But I feel that I must restrain myself from wandering in a field where dykes and roads have not yet been made. I take up the subject only so far as it concerns my present purpose, that is, the relation of development to causation. Perhaps it might be said in a loose way that all causation is development. It consists in effects coming out of causes. All that I need to insist on is, that all development is a certain kind of causation.

Now, it has been admitted for ages that causation works through all nature; not only divine causation the source of the whole, but physical causation: that is, the ordinary occurrences of nature are all produced by agents working causally; in other words, fire burns, light shines, and the earth spins round its axis and rotates round the sun, and the consequence is that we have heat and light and the beneficent seasons. Men of enlarged minds do now see and acknowledge that in the doctrine of causation, in the doctrine of God acting everywhere through second causes, there is nothing irreligious. On the contrary, the circumstance that God proceeds according to laws is evidently for the benefit of man, who can thus from the past anticipate the future and prepare himself for it. On the same principle I hold that there is nothing irreligious in development, which is just a form of causation. It was my privilege in my earliest work to justify God's method of procedure by natural law. I reckon it a like privilege in my declining life to defend God's mode of action by development, by bringing the present out of the past. Only, it must be held resolutely, that as the forces of nature are exhibitions of the power of God, and as the laws of nature are the laws of his government, so development is one of the methods by which God unfolds his plans from age to age.

For my purpose it is not necessary that I should settle what are the original constituents of the universe. Some suppose these to be atoms, some prefer representing them as centres of force, some will only allow them to be centres of motion. I am inclined to regard them as atoms, with their forces or properties; perhaps we might expediently call them molecules, without defining what they are. Let us suppose that there are millions of millions of them working in the knowable world. As they operate they co-operate and combine. As they act they might, if left to themselves, work evil quite as easily and naturally as good, and the molecules might have been formed into destructive machines and pestiferous creatures: into flaming meteors with burning worlds; into mosquitoes, gnats, and serpents, devouring each other and arresting all forms of beauty and beneficence, and yet incapable of dying. But instead of this, these million agencies combine to accomplish good and benign ends, so as to show that there has been a mind disposing them and a power guiding them. Let us observe some of the beneficent issues, and we will soon come among these to development.

1. The combination of molecules acting as causes has produced general laws and beneficent order: in the seasons, in the growth of the plant, — first the blade, then the ear, then the full corn in the ear; in the animal, enjoying its season and handing down its life to a new generation. All this is not the action of simple properties of matter acting fortuitously or fatally; it is the result of the adjustment of numerous properties of matter, mechanical, gravitating, chemical, electric, all conspiring towards an end.

2. The combination produces special ends, such as those unfolded by Paley and other writers on natural theology. Take only two well-known examples. There is the eye. What a combination of independent agencies before we can see the smile on that friend's face! There are vibrations coming from the sun ninety million miles away; these have passed at various rates through an ether; they touch and are reflected from the countenance; some of them reach the cornea of an optical instrument called the eye; they go through an aqueous humor, thence through the gateway of the iris into the crystalline lens; they are there refracted and pass through the vitreous humor to the retina, where they impact on thousands of rods and cones and are sent on to the optic nerve and the brain; and we now see the smiles on our mother's face. Let any one of these be absent or fail, and nature would remain forever in darkness.

WHAT DEVELOPMENT CAN DO.

Take the ear. A sister utters a word, a vibration is started, it reaches our ear, is collected by the outer ear and knocks on the tympanum, is propagated into the middle ear, where it sets in motion the hammer and the anvil and the stirrup, thence into the inner ear, where it vibrates through a liquid, affects the thousand and more organs of Corti, is sent round the semicircular canals into the cochlea, and on through the auditory nerve into the brain; the silence is broken, and we are cheered by a voice of love.

But 3, and this more to my purpose, there is a combination, to produce evolution. The present is evolved out of the past and will develop into the future, all under a divine arrangement. The present is the fruit of the past, and contains the seed of the future. The configuration of the earth, its hills and dales, its rivers and seas, which determine the abodes and industries of men and the bounds of their habitation, have been produced by agencies which have been working for thousands or millions of years. The plants now on the earth are the descendants of those created by God, and the ancestors of those that are to appear in the coming ages. There is through all times, as in the year, a succession of seasons: sowing and reaping, sowing in order to reap, and reaping what has been sown, in order to its being sown again. This gives a continuousness, a consistency, to nature, amidst all the mutations of time. There is not only a contemporaneous order in nature, there is a successive order. The beginning leads to the end, and the end is the issue of the beginning.

This grass and grain and these forests that cover the ground have seed in them which will continue in undefined ages to adorn and enrich the ground. These birds that sing among the branches and these cattle upon a thousand hills will build nests and rear young to furnish nourishment and delight to our children's children in millennial ages. Every naturalist has seen a purpose gained by the nutriment laid up in the seed or pod to feed the young plant. I see a higher end accomplished by the mother provided for the young animal. That infant is not cast forth into the cold world unprotected, — it has a mother's arms to protect it and a mother's love to fondle it. Development is not an irreligious process; every one who has been reared under a father's care and a mother's love will bless God for it.

In this development there are usually *periodical* results in the epochs of geology and of history, and especially in the vegetable and animal kingdoms. This enables us so far to anticipate the future and to accommodate ourselves to it. The oak develops the acorn, and the acorn develops the oak. The bird produces the egg, and out of the egg comes the future bird, and the species is continued. A loving pair are joined in holy marriage union, and the offspring transmits the inheritance of both.

In development there is usually *progression.* At times there is degeneracy, chiefly the result of human sin, as we see in the degeneracy of the Indians. But as a whole there has been an advance in our earth from age to age. The tendency of animal life is

WHAT DEVELOPMENT CAN DO.

upon the whole, upward, — from all fours to the upright position, in which men can look up to heaven. Agencies have been set a going to produce these evidently intended ends. Causes that operated ages ago have called in other causes to co-operate with them, and have thereby added to the power and riches of the product. The geological changes have made our earth fit for the abode of man. Human beings have taken the places which in earlier ages were handed over to wild animals. There is a greater amount of food produced on our earth than at any earlier stage. There has been, as the ages rolled on, a greater fulness of sentient life and a larger capacity of happiness, The intellectual powers have been made stronger and firmer, like the trunk of the tree, and the feelings, like the flowers, have taken a larger expansion and a richer color by culture.

As we observe all this, there is one principle we are bound to carry with us; we are to see God in it throughout and from beginning to end. Because a rose, a dog, or a horse is gendered by natural causes, it is not less the work of God. Our finest roses are derived from the common dog-rose; that rose in its simple beauty by the roadside is the divine workmanship; but so is the richest rose, the fullest in form and the gayest in color in our gardens. God, who rewards us for opening our eyes upon his works, gives higher rewards to those who in love to them bestow labor and pains upon them. Dogs, it is said, have all descended from some kind of wolf. This does not make the shepherd's dog, or the St. Bernard dog, with their wondrous instincts, not to be the divine workmanship. Just as little does the hypothesis that our living horse is descended from the Pleiohippus, and this from the Miohippus, and this from the Eohippus, which used to tread with its five toes on marshy ground, prove that the animal we ride on, so useful and so graceful, so agile and so docile, is not the creature of the Creator who formed it, and gave to it its power of development.

Not only is development when properly understood not inconsistent with religion; it will be found that the combination and adaptation in it clearly argue design. Sooner or later there will be written a work on natural theology after the manner of Paley, showing that as there are plan and purpose in the well-fitted limbs and organs of the bodily frame of animals, so there is design quite as evident and as wonderful in the way in which by a process running through ages the bones and muscles have been adjusted to each other to produce the horse we drive or ride on. There is a manifest and a wise and beneficent end in the joints of our frame: in the joint backward and forward of the finger by which we grasp objects; in the ball and socket joint which turns all round at the shoulder; but there is quite as palpable a purpose in the way in which these joints have been moulded in the geological ages and handed down by heredity.

I therefore see design in development. There is an obvious end, and a means arranged to accomplish it. We see purpose evident in the development effected by man. The farmer uses a series of agencies to secure his end : he ploughs, he harrows, he sows seed, he weeds, and in the end he gathers in a crop. The teacher lays out a plan for developing the faculties of his pupils : he imparts knowledge, he corrects, he stimulates, and he reaches his aim, — the improvement of these faculties and a fitness for the duties of life. We see numerous cases in which there is need of co-operation in order to compass an end. A house is built and furnished because a number of people have done each his part : the mason, the carpenter, the plumber, the slater, the glazier, the upholsterer. A city becomes richer because the merchants have been far-sighted, and the manufacturers expert, and the tradesmen honest and industrious. The country prospers because the master and the servant, the schoolmaster and the minister of religion, are all and each doing their part. But there are still more wonderful evidences of a plan and a purpose in the succession of the seasons, and of the grass and grain and trees, and in the living creatures advancing in fulness and strength, in activity and beauty. It is not in the single object or operation that we discover such evidence of a purpose so much as in their organization, and orderly succession and development. Development is a sort of corporation in which each part, like the citizen, fulfils its office.

But while development can do much, it may not be able to do everything. There is a tendency among rash and rapid thinkers to push every new truth to an extreme. I am so old as to remember the feeling produced when Sir Humphry Davy made and published his brilliant discoveries. There were sciolists in our schools of popular science, among our newspaper editors and lecturers, who made electricity explain everything, even life and mind itself. This disposition, never encouraged by the great discoverer, soon ran its course, and died out in the struggle for existence as new discoveries were made. Development is at present running through a like crisis. The work of the past age has been to show what it can do; that of the coming age is to determine precisely what it cannot do. Like all creature action, it will be found to have very stringent limits. We may fix on some of these.

1. Development cannot explain the origin of things. This is implied in its nature and its very name. It is a procession out from something which has gone before. It implies a set of arranged substances which seems to imply a creator and organizer.

2. It cannot account for the collocations, as Dr. Chalmers, followed by Mr. Mill, calls them, or, as I designate them, adaptations necessary to carry on the operations of the world beneficently. A train without a hand to put it on the right track and to guide it might work only destructively.

3. It cannot account for the law, the order, the beneficence that pervade nature.

4. There are products which cannot be developed from the original elements of nature. I have declined to dogmatize as to what these are, atoms or centres of force or motion. I call them molecules. These atoms or centres cannot give what they have not got.

WHAT DEVELOPMENT CANNOT DO. 133

If heredity has a gift committed to it, it may transmit it from parent to offspring, and from one generation to another. I have shown at an earlier stage of my lecture that in physical causation the effect is merely a changed state of the agents acting as the causes. There is no power in the effects which was not in the causes. If a new power appears in the effects it must be from superadded causes. Let us look at the things that have been effected, and inquire whether they could all have been in the original molecules.

Was there life in the original molecule? If not, how did it come in when the first plant appeared? Was there sensation in the original molecule? If not, how did it come in when the first animal had a feeling of pleasure or of pain? Was there mind in the first molecule, say a power of perceiving an object out of itself? Was there consciousness in the first molecule or monad, a consciousness of self? Was there a power of comparing, of judging, of discerning between two things, of noting their agreements or differences? Was there a power of reasoning, of inferring the unseen from the seen, of the future from the past? Were there emotions in these first existences, say a hope of continued life or fear of approaching death? Perhaps they had some elements of morality or loving attachments to each other, or a sense of justice in keeping their own whirl and allowing to others their place and rights in the dance! Had they will at the beginning, and a power of choosing between pleasure and pain, between the evil and the good? Perhaps they had some piety and paid some worship to God!

It is needless to say that there is not even the shade of a proof of there being any such capacities in the original atom or force centre. If so, how did they come in? Take one human capacity,— how did consciousness come in? Herbert Spencer, the mightiest of them, would have us believe that he has answered this question, and yet he has simply avoided it. In his "Psychology" he is speaking of nerves for hundreds of pages; he shows how in their movements there is a succession of a certain kind, and adds simply that "there must arise a consciousness." This is all he says, bringing in no cause, or link, or connection (see Part IV. 1). Thus does he step over the gap,— a practice not uncommon with this giant, as he marches on with his seven-leagued boots.

How, then, did these things come in? How did things without sensation come to have sensation, things without instinct to have instinct, creatures without memory to have memory, beings without intelligence to have intelligence, and mere sentient existence to know the distinction between good and evil? I am sure that when these powers appear there is something not previously in the molecule. All sober thinkers of the present day have admitted that there is no evidence whatever in experience or in reason to show that matter can produce mind, that mechanical action can gender mental action, that chemical action can manufacture consciousness, that electric action can reason, or organic rise to the idea of the good and the holy. I argue that we must call in a power above the atoms to produce such phenomena. I may admit that a body may come out of other bodies by the operation of the powers with which they are endowed; but I deny that a sensible, intelligent, moral-discerning soul can proceed from the molecules of matter. New powers have undoubtedly come in when consciousness and feeling and understanding and will begin to act. They may come in according to laws not yet discovered, but they are the laws of the Supreme Lawgiver.

An attempt may be made to avoid the force of this by a far-fetched supposition. It may be urged that there has been a latent life in these molecules; a consciousness, an intelligence, a conscience, with benevolence and power of choice, which developed, some in thousands and some in millions of years or ages. It may be allowed that this is a thing imaginable, but there is not the slightest proof of it. Even if I discover proof of it, I would also find proof of design in the way in which these latent powers have come forth and acted from age to age in organized plants, in sentient animals, in organized man. Choose your horn. If all these endowments were in the primary molecules, it is clear that they must have been the creation of intelligence, and their appearance in their seasons the arrangement of intelligence. If they were not, there must have been a subsequent creation, or, if any dislike the phrase, a forthputting of divine power.

5. There is evidence that there has been from time to time a special action of God, at the first creation and at the subsequent appearance of new powers.

The account of the progressive work of creation in Genesis is in accordance with geology. This has been shown satisfactorily by the three men on this continent best entitled to speak on the scientific question,— Professor Dana, of Yale, Principal Dawson, of Montreal, and Professor Guyot, of Princeton. It can be shown that it is equally consistent with development as revealed by recent science. I believe that in the beginning, or origin, God created the heavens and gave the original constituents their potencies, which began to act by the command of God, and there was light. But neither religion nor reason requires me to believe that he gave to these life, or sensation, or reason, or love. I believe that when these were added, whether by law or without law, it was according to the will and by the power of God. There were days or epochs in the same procedure, and at the opening of each was a special act of God. The earth was without form and void. When the evolution began, there was first the development of light; then the elevation of the expanse of heaven; thirdly, there was the separation of land and water, and the earth was ready for plants. On the fourth day the sun and moon appeared as distinct bodies, all in accordance with the theory of Laplace. On the fifth day animals appeared, the lower creatures, *tannim* or swarmers, then fishes and fowls; on the sixth day the higher animals, and, as the crown of the whole, man. Man's creation must have been a special act, and is so represented in Scripture. When man appeared, there was something which was not there before, and this Godlike, after the image of God. In all this, Genesis and geology are in thorough accordance. There are two accounts of the creation of man. One is in Chap. i. There is council and decision. "Let us make man in our image." This applies to his soul or higher nature. The other account is in Chap. ii. 7: "And the Lord God formed man of the dust of the ground, and breathed into his nostrils the breath of life, and he became a living soul." This is man's organic body. We have a supplement to this in Ps. cxxxix. 15, 16: "My substance was not hid from thee when I was made in secret and curiously wrought in the lowest parts of the earth. Thine eyes did see my substance, being yet unperfect; and in thy book all my members were written, which in continuance were fashioned, when as yet there was none of them." This passage used to be quoted by Agassiz. This is my creed as to man's bodily organism. I so far understand what is said. Man is made of the earth. There is a curious preparatory process hinted at, a process and a progression going on I know not how long; and all is the work of God and written in God's Book. I understand this; and yet I do not understand it. Socrates said of the philosophy of Heraclitus that what he understood was so good that he was sure the rest would also be good if he understood it. So I say of this passage. I so far understand it, and get glorious glimpses of a divinely ordained process; and yet I do not understand it, for it carries me into the secret things which belong unto the Lord our God.

I affirm with confidence that there is not in the geological or biological science any truth even apparently inconsistent with this statement.

All my thoughts have been developed, some may think, without much purpose being seen in the development. As there are speculators in our day who are as infallible as the Pope, and *savans* who claim the Divine attribute of omniscience, and lecturers who know all the work which God does not do from the beginning unto the end, I must remind you, ere I close, that development has not yet given to men all knowledge. "We know in part." Yes, we know, but we know in part only. We who dwell in a world "where day and night alternate," we who go everywhere accompanied by our own shadow — a shadow produced by our dark body, but produced because there is light — cannot expect to be absolutely delivered from the darkness. Man's faculties, exquisitely adapted to the sphere in which he moves, were never intended to enable him to comprehend all truth. The mind is in this respect like the eye. The eye is so constituted as to perceive the things within a certain range; but as objects are removed farther and farther from us they become more indistinct, and at length are lost sight of altogether. It is the same with the human mind. It can understand certain subjects and to a certain distance; but as they reach away further they look more and more confused, and at length they disappear from the view. And if the human spirit attempts to mount higher

DEVELOPMENT: ITS NATURE. 139

than its proper elevation, it will find all its flight fruitless. The dove, to use an illustration of Kant's, may mount to a certain elevation in the heavens; but as she rises the air becomes lighter, and at length she finds that she can no longer float upon its bosom, and should she attempt to soar higher her pinions flutter in emptiness and she falters and falls. So it is with the spirit of man. It can wing its way to a certain distance into the expanse above it; but there is a limit which, if it endeavors to pass, it will find all its conceptions void and its ratiocinations unconnected.

Placed as we are in the centre of boundless space, and in the middle of eternal ages, we can see only a few objects immediately around us, and all others fade in outline as they are removed from us by distance, till at length they be altogether beyond our vision. And this remark holds true not only of the more ignorant, of those whose eye can penetrate the least distance; it is true also of the learned; it is, perhaps, true of all created beings, that there is a bounding sphere of darkness surrounding the space rendered clear by the torch of science. Nay, it almost looks as if the wider the boundaries of science are pushed and the greater the space illuminated by it, the greater in proportion the bounding sphere into which no rays penetrate, just as (to use a very old comparison), when we strike up a light in the midst of darkness, in proportion as the light becomes stronger so does also that surface become black and dark which is rendered visible.

VI.

A CALM VIEW OF THE TEMPERANCE QUESTION.

By CHANCELLOR HOWARD CROSBY, D.D., LL.D.

VI.

A CALM VIEW OF THE TEMPERANCE QUESTION.

By CHANCELLOR HOWARD CROSBY, D.D., LL.D.

THE object of temperance societies is to prevent drunkenness. The cardinal principle in these societies is total abstinence from all that can intoxicate. That total abstinence, if adopted by all, will prevent drunkenness, no one will dispute. The object of temperance societies would be gained.

But two questions arise, after contemplating these propositions: first, will this plan of total abstinence be adopted? and, secondly, ought it to be adopted? The first question is prudential; the second is moral.

1. *The Prudential Question.*—Will the plan of total abstinence from all that intoxicates be received by men in general? We desire to use in all measures of reform a plan that is practicable. We cannot be satisfied with mere testimony to a theory that will be unproductive of results. Herein reform differs from religion. Religion demands adhesion to a truth stamped by the conscience, even though that truth find no other adherent. But reform lies in the do-

main of the expedient. It seeks to make society better, and if it cannot raise society to the highest level, it will raise it as high as it can. It will not prefer to let society wallow, because it cannot place it in an ideal Utopia. The most religious and conscientious man will be glad to see men leave off strife and discord, even if they do not act from the highest motives, or attain to the heights of a genuine charity. His conscience will not be injured by their improved condition, however much he would like to see them still more enlightened. It is an important point to make clear to the mind this distinction between the conduct of reform and the movement of personal religion, for confusion here has led to much false action. A common argument of the radical agitator is, that his conscience cannot stop short of total abstinence in the temperance question, and on that ground he will not have any affiliation with one who seeks to subdue the intemperance of the land by any other method. But his argument is a complete *non sequitur*. His conscience concerns his own personal habits. In the matter of other people's habits he is simply to do the best the circumstances allow. The conscience that prescribes his personal habits may make him long to see others like him, and may make him work to that end, but it cannot rebuke him if that end is not attained, but only an approximation is gained; nay, it should make him work for the approximation with all zeal.

Too often that which is called conscience is mere obstinacy of opinion and personal pride. A large part of the fanaticism that history records has been made in this way. Men have gone to the stake as martyrs, or sufferers for conscience' sake, when the heresy they professed never went deeper than their sentiment, and might readily have been altered by a free judgment. While this fact does not justify their persecutors, or palliate their guilt, yet it certainly detracts from the merit of the martyrdom. In this matter of arresting the progress of drunkenness we may have very different views of the means to be used, and we may conscientiously adhere to our own plan of working toward the end, but we connot *conscientiously* object to the means employed by others unless they contain an immorality. Nay, more, we *must conscientiously* wish them success.

If this principle of sympathy and co-operation on the part of all who seek the abatement of intemperance were once established, we should see effects that are now thwarted by the divisions and mutual hostility of those who profess to have the same end in view. One of the reasons for this confirmed hostility of the total abstinence advocates against the reformers who do not adopt that principle is found in the power of a false usage. I refer to the word "temperance."

The word has been violently wrested from its legitimate meaning. By a persistent use of a moderate word for radical measures, the great unthinking public, so far as they are seekers for the common good, have been led to see in these radical measures the only path of duty. They have learned to con-

sider all that was opposed to the party called by the
name of Temperance as inimical to temperance, and
so have enormously swelled the radical ranks by
their unenlightened adhesion. The label has been
affixed to the wrong goods, and the unsuspecting
purchaser has not noticed the fact. So potent has
been this deception, that I undertake to say that
there are thousands of worthy citizens who have no
other idea of the word "temperance" than that
it means the total abstinence from all that can intoxicate. With such we have to begin with first
principles. We have to show them that the Latin
temperantia signifies the moral quality of moderation
or discreetness, and that the English word "temperance," as used in all good standard English works,
means precisely the same thing. We have to show
them that the temperate zone does not mean a zone
which totally abstains from cold or heat, but a
zone that is moderate in both; that a temperate
behavior is not a behavior that totally abstains from
severity, but one that is steady and reasonable in its
course, as Cicero says (Fam. 12. 27): "Est autem ita
temperatis moderatisque moribus ut summa severitas
summâ cum humanitate jungatur." And while quoting Cicero, I may quote his definitions of temperance
as given in his De Finibus, first, "Temperantia est
moderatio cupiditatum rationi obediens" (2. 19. 60);
and, secondly, "Temperantia est quæ, in rebus aut
expetendis aut fugiendis, rationem ut sequamur
monet" (1. 14. 47). Now, what a fearful prostitution
of a noble word is seen in the popular use of the

word "temperance" to-day! And this prostitution is a work wrought within the last fifty years. From its high position, as signifying a grand moral subjection of the whole man to the sway of reason, it is degraded to the maimed and mutilated function of representing a legalism that prohibits man from any drink that can intoxicate. To what base uses has it come at last! This false use of a word has had special influence upon that portion of the unthinking public who rightly reverence the Scriptures. They see that temperance is put in the list of Christian virtues, and as temperance now means total abstinence, what can they do, as loyal believers in the Scriptures, but sign the pledge; and, furthermore, count all who do not as aliens from God's truth? They are as honest and as enlightened as the good Presbyterian woman, who only needed to see the words "general assembly" in the Bible to know she was right and everybody else wrong.

Now the use of a false argument always reacts against the user, and, while the ignorant and semi-ignorant multitude will be deceived, the thinking classes of society will shun a cause that rests on misrepresentation. The word "temperance," as seized and appropriated by radical and intemperate souls, is a false flag, and, as a false flag, will disgust and alienate true and enlightened souls. Especially will this be the case when it is found to be only one of many false lights held out to attract the masses. Another of these deceptions (of course I do not say these are wilful deceptions by all that use them, I am only speaking of their absolute character), — another of these deceptions is the circulated theory of an unfermented, unintoxicating-wine. There is not a chemist nor a classical scholar in the world who would dare risk his reputation on the assertion that there was ever an unfermented wine in common use, knowing well that *must* preserved from fermentation is called wine only by a kind of courtesy (as the lump of unbaked dough might be called "bread"), and that this could in the nature of things never be a common drink. Cato (De Re Rusticâ, 120) shows how by a very careful method must could be kept for a whole year, and other Roman writers show the same; but who can pretend that these writers ever looked upon such preserved juice as wine, when their whole object is to show how it can be kept from becoming wine? Yet with no other foundation than this, the leaders of the total abstinence cause have published their bull, affirming that the good wines of antiquity were unfermented, in utter defiance of chemistry, history, and common sense. Because the grape juice could, by means of hermetically sealed vessels under water, be kept grape juice, therefore the common wines of antiquity, the wine of which writers speak when they use no qualifying phrase, must have been unfermented. This is the logic used by these infatuated defenders of the total abstinence principle.

A third deception in this cause is the twisting of Scripture to its advocacy. No unbiased reader can for a moment doubt that wine as referred to in the

Bible *passim* is an intoxicating drink, and that such wine was drunk by our Saviour and the early Christians. To meet this fatal blow to the total abstinence system in the minds of those who take the Bible as their guide, the advocates of the cause have invented a theory that is magnificent in its daring. It is no less than the division of the word "wine" by a Solomonian sword, so that the good and the bad shall each have a piece of it. Whenever wine is spoken of severely in Scripture, then it is fermented wine, and whenever it is spoken of in praise, or used by our Lord and his apostles, then it is unfermented wine. And, if you ask these sages why they so divide the wine, — on what grounds they base this theory, — they bravely answer that our Saviour could not have drunk intoxicating wine, and God's word never could have praised such, and, *therefore*, their theory. They start with the begging of the whole question, and then on this thin air they build their castle.

It is not now my purpose to argue with these strange logicians. I only wish to put this Scripture-twisting in the list of deceptive methods used by the representative total abstinence reformers to promote their cause. I could add in this item the false use of texts and the suppression of parts of texts, but I leave the matter here.

The three elements of deception entering into their cause is, as we have seen, the use of the word "temperance" for a totally different thing, the fable about unfermented wine, and the violent wresting of the

Scriptures. Now I unhesitatingly affirm that a cause having such falsehoods as its main supports can never be accepted by the public. Simple-minded people may be gained to it, but the thinking people will be repelled. It is true that some may adhere to it, in spite of its falsehood, for other reasons; but the three great untruths that are flaunted on its banners will disgust most men who have brains and use them.

A second reason why I believe the plan of total abstinence will not be adopted by the people is its *unmanliness*. To stop the use of anything because of its abuse is an expedient for the weak and diseased, an exceptional plan for exceptional cases; but to assert this principle among men in general would be to degrade the race and remove all the incentives and helps to moral growth. We know in the family how mistaken a method it is to remove everything the child should not play with out of its reach. The wise parent leaves the article in its accustomed place, and teaches the child its rightful use.

The other plan only makes the child more and more dependent on external checks, and prevents the growth of self-control. The same reasoning holds good in the human family at large. We are to develop self-control as much as possible. A true civilization always seeks to do this. A barbarous state of society requires man to hide everything valuable in places unknown to others, and to go personally armed to secure himself against attack. But a civilized condition reveals a very different state of things. Men live in houses full of valuables, and walk the streets unarmed and in security. Dependence is placed upon the common self-control, and it is acknowledged to be a far higher and more successful principle for the conduct of human life. Of course there is a limit to this practical trusting of mankind, and much wisdom is needed to mark this limit correctly in any given instance. But the general truth is evident, that true civilization is in the direction of personal self-control, and not in that of governmental prohibition. We expect law to *prohibit* crime; but we look to law only to *regulate* matters that do not involve crime, but contain risk under certain conditions. Now the selling or drinking of wine is certainly not a crime, and any legislation which prohibits it is open to the charge of putting it in a wrong category, and abusing the popular conscience. A prohibition for certain times or places may be defended without subjecting the act to this false imputation; but a total prohibition, the cardinal doctrine of the total abstinence people, at once brands wine-drinking with theft and violence. Things that are not vicious in themselves, but which may be readily abused to vicious ends, certainly need legislative regulation, and such regulation is a help to self-control, where prohibition would be a hindrance. Regulation is a hint to put the people on their guard, but prohibition is completely taking away the subject from the people's notice. Now the public mind revolts at being treated in this childlike way. It virtually says: "Give us certain wise rules about this thing, but for the sake of respectable and dignified humanity do not sweep it away from the earth." Remember that we are not arguing now on the merits of the total abstinence theory, but only on its feasibility. We do not say that it is a wrong principle. We only say that people will not adopt it, and we are showing the reasons why they will not. The community will not unreasonably (as they think) be put into leading-strings and kept in a permanent nursery, and that too by men who use manifest falsehoods as prominent arguments for their position. There is such a thing as the public conscience, and people will draw lines of distinction between things criminal and things indifferent. They will naturally, therefore, resist any movement that tends to obliterate these distinctions, and judge of it as the action of a tyrannic opinion and not of an ethical truth. They feel that their manhood is assailed, and if this assault is allowed in this form they may be exposed to other assaults in still more odious forms. Of course, it is easy for the radical reformers to say that this opposition is interested, and is only the struggle of evil against those that would fetter it; but there are too many good, conscientious, and thoughtful men who feel all this that I have said, for this allegation to be maintained. We cannot consent to go back to mediæval nonage, and have our day's allowance doled out to us by a few who arrogate to themselves the paternal management of the world. We cannot permit the system of sumptuary laws to take the place of an enlightened common sense. We cannot forego our reason on the plea that the world is in danger. Nay, we must all the more assert our reason against a false expediency that in curing, or attempting to cure, one evil, would create a hundred. The fact that there is a great danger is the very fact that should guard us from pursuing any false way. Great dangers must be met by great prudence, not by headlong impulse. It looks brave to shout and fall *pell mell* upon the enemy, but it is wiser to set our batteries in sure places, and to order line and reserves in the interests of a permanent victory. Too many of our reforms are pushed without regard to the character of the means, the end being insisted on as justifying all means. The temperance reform has been an eminent example of this heedlessness.

And here I put the third reason why I believe the plan of total abstinence will not be adopted by the people, — because of its spirit of *intimidation*. Of course, this is not inherent to the cause, but it has been the invariable accompaniment of it during its forty years' curriculum. And we now have to deal practically with historic facts, and not with mere abstract theories. Whatever may have been the cause, whether it be the weakness of the case or the unfortunate choice of leaders and defenders, the total abstinence propaganda has been an overbearing and tyrannical power. It has used a violence of language that can admit of no excuse. It has condemned every one, however faithful in all moral and religious duties, who has refused to enter its ranks. It has confounded all ideas of right and wrong, calumniously declaring the man who drinks wine moderately is as bad as, nay, worse than the drunkard; asserting that all drinks, whether vinous, malt, or distilled, are alike poisonous; vilifying those who teach any other doctrine by calling them traitors to the truth, — Judas Iscariots betraying the Master, — and exercising where it could a fearful proscription in driving good men from the pulpits of the land because they would not and could not conscientiously pronounce their Shibboleth. The principal printed organs of this propaganda have been full of these fierce onslaughts upon the character of respectable men, and the harsh and cruel judgments spoken of have been carried out with the spirit of the Inquisition. The political world has lately invented a word for this way of settling a disputed question. They have called it "bulldozing." It makes peace by creating a desert. It produces unanimity by shutting the mouths of the other side. The world is apt to think that such conduct indicates a cause that cannot be sustained by reason, and the reaction is likely to be excessive. It is exactly that reaction which is now making the cause of rum and ruin more successful than ever. Men in their revolt from tyranny rush into licentious extremes, and however honest the tyranny may have been or however true the cause it supported, it has only itself to blame for the harm it does. A man may put his hand on the safety-valve and exclaim, "See how I have stopped the noisy escape of the steam!" and certainly everything looks calm and peaceful; but a few minutes afterward, when the steam has had time to gather its strength, our hero will have a different cry. A little success here and there by the total abstinence crusade may impress many with the idea that this is the true way to make men temperate. A partial success in Maine has been proclaimed as proving the question against the painful failures everywhere else; but no careful observer will either approve the specimen or take it as a proof against our general position. Maine is but a small part of our country, and has no great seething population made up from every nation on earth. It has a highly educated people, who can bear an experiment in morals with something of a philosophic spirit. A few strong-minded and high-minded people can become ascetics, but the great world cannot, and we must legislate for the great world. Even Maine cannot permanently keep its Maine Law.

There is a general notion in the public mind that the present condition of Maine in regard to the liquor question is that of a temporary repression; and, whether that notion be right or wrong, it belongs to that public opinion which has to be regarded in all prudential planning. The general thought of the community concerning this repression is that it belongs to a system of intimidation, that can never be a permanent institution in this land.

I have thus far considered only the prudential question. The total abstinence scheme may be in strict accordance with theoretical virtue. It may be the grand end to which all reforming processes should tend. All that we have endeavored thus far to establish is, that it is a plan that cannot succeed, if we are to judge it by its past history and methods, as well as by its intrinsic principles, and that therefore to push the plan is to defeat the great end we should all have in view,—the cessation of drunkenness, with its fearful ruin to body, soul, and society. We have endeavored to show that the public mind will not receive a system whose principal agencies have been falsehoods and intimidation, and whose principles they consider to be at war with a proper manliness or self-respect. We repeat (that no one may mistake us) that these falsehoods and intimidations are not necessary parts of the system, but have been its constant adjuncts in point of fact, and we also repeat that our argument regarding manliness is not (so far as we have gone) so much a charge against the system, as a statement of what a very large portion of respectable and virtuous thinkers think of it. It is from such considerations, we hold, that the plan of total abstinence as a method of eradicating drunkenness and its attendant vices will never be adopted by the community. One other thing I desire to repeat before taking up the other branch of my subject; and that is, that I make no charge of purposed falsehood on any of the total abstinence leaders. Their main arguments *are* falsehoods as I have shown, but I am quite sure that the excellent men who are often found leading the crusade are honest in their use of these false statements. They take up these weapons without sufficiently examining them. They see that they can be made effective, but do not stop to inquire whether they are legitimate. Their praiseworthy zeal outstrips their judgment and prudence. I honor the heart and energy of very many of these men. They show a philanthropy and consecration, involving often self-denial and loss, which demand our admiration. They are indeed too often mixed up with low, hypocritical self-seekers, who make the temperance cause a mere lever to raise money, but that does not detract from the sterling devotion of these noble souls. And while I differ from them altogether in my views, and am thoroughly convinced they are doing unmeasured harm to the community by retarding practical reform and disseminating pernicious principles, at the same time I would not refrain from yielding this honest and hearty tribute to their intentions, and disclaim any personal reproach while criticising the system they advocate.

2. *The Moral Question.* — The prudential question being thus treated, I turn to the *moral* question before us. "Ought the plan of total abstinence to be adopted?" Is it a healthful and legitimate method of doing away with drunkenness? A man stands at a great disadvantage who argues in behalf of his belief that the total abstinence system is immoral, because he at once exposes himself to the assaults of slanderers who impugn his motives and deny his honesty. Radicalism has so ruthlessly mobbed down independent thought by its intimidating processes, that editors who have no faith in the total abstinence system still uphold it in their columns, and ministers deem it prudent to say nothing against a cause so popular in religious circles. Men are loth to come forward

and be bespattered with mud thrown in the name of truth and godliness. They are loth to lose the support and good-will of the many whose fanaticism despises argument and brooks no opposition. Hence, if any one is constrained to speak, he is tempted to come forward as a humble apologist and modestly plead his cause with many concessions and compromises. Surely this is not for the advantage of the truth.

In this address I take no apologetic position. I carry the war into Africa. I have no contest with men, but with false principles. I assert that the total abstinence system is false in its philosophy, contrary to revealed religion, and harmful to the interests of our country. I charge upon this system the growth of drunkenness in our land and a general demoralization among religious communities. And I call upon sound-minded, thinking men to stop the enormities of this false system by uniting in reasonable and wholesome measures for the suppression of drunkenness, for the lack of which this false system has all its present success. Between fanaticism on one hand and licentiousness on the other, there ought to be a large mass of solid folk, whose union and efficiency would moderate and reduce, if not destroy, both extremes.

1. The first moral error of the total abstinence system is in turning a medicinal prescription into a bill of fare for all mankind. That a drunkard should carefully avoid every form of alcoholic drink nobody can deny. He is a diseased man, and his restoration

depends on this restriction. Now by what logic does this man's duty become mine? Because I have admitted total abstinence as a correct principle in his case, am I bound to admit it as a correct principle for all? Are the sick to be the norm of the well? Is the matter of diet to be regulated by the needs of the drunkard? Why not, then, by the needs of the dyspeptic? Ah! but (say they) it is to save you from *becoming* a drunkard. Well, is the logic any way improved by this explanation? You would put me on a sick regimen to keep me from becoming sick! Because total abstinence is absolutely necessary to a drunkard's recovery, you would make it necessary to one who is not a drunkard. Do you not see that, if you are going to prove your latter proposition, you must have another premise than your former one? The two are wholly unconnected. It is an offence to the moral sense of the community to spread over it the restriction of the drunkard, as it would be to imprison all the community with the imprisonment of the thief, lest by liberty they should all fall to thieving.

2. A second moral error of the total abstinence theory is its assumption that moderate drinking leads to drunkenness. The millions upon millions of our race who have been accustomed to drink wine, and who never knew drunkenness, stand up against this atrocious dogma. And yet this dogma has actually become an *axiom* with the total abstinence reformers, and they would disdain to argue it. They are so determined to have it true that they have performed the

paradoxical operation of putting the moderate drinker in the place of the drunkard as the criminal to be punished with scorn and contumely. This strange *mixing* of things reminds me of the calling good evil and evil good, which a high authority makes a mark of very deep depravity. You will find that the principal shafts of the total abstinence literature are directed, not at the drunkard, but at the moderate drinker. The drunkard is pitied and coddled, while the moderate drinker is scourged. Now, this sort of moral jugglery is not beneficial to the community. It distorts and perverts judgment, and involves moral distinctions in chaotic confusion. It overthrows the ordinary reason that is so useful in all the relations of life, and leads men to clannish obedience to some ruling mind. It is the old trick of the Jesuits, to weary the mind in mazes, so that it may, in sheer fatigue, seek to be guided by them.

3. A third moral error of the total abstinence theory is its want of discrimination between things that differ. Everything that has alcohol in it must be tabooed. As if all the drinks that had alcohol in them were of the same effect when drunk. Brandy and hock wine and lager beer are all alike the devil's poison, and must be banished from the lips of all true men. This assault upon common knowledge is a blunder that has the proportions of a crime. To say that certain drinks that are wholesome and beneficial are the same as certain drinks that are pernicious and destructive, is a moral outrage which the whole community should indignantly repel. Beers and un-

brandied wines are promoters of health and strength when used judiciously, especially by those who have not robust health. They are tonic, anti-scorbutic, and gently stimulating to the digestion. As Dr. Parkes, who is a strong opposer of the use of distilled liquors, says: "For the large class of people who live on the confines of health, whose digestion is feeble, circulation languid, and nervous system too excitable," mild wines and malt liquors are beneficial. The fact is, that (as another writer well says) outside of the sick-room the distilled liquors are comparatively noxious, the fermented comparatively harmless. What we desire to emphasize is, that the two classes of drinks are altogether different in their character and effect, and that a theory which destroys that difference has therein a moral stain.

4. A fourth moral error of the total abstinence system is its assertion that all drinks that contain alcohol are poison; that the presence of alcohol thus justifies the confounding of different sorts of drink just referred to. Dr. Anstie has clearly shown that alcohol in small quantities is not a poison but a true food, and that it is a stimulant to the system in precisely the same sense as that in which food is a stimulant. He has shown that there is an essential difference between the effects of large and small quantities of alcohol, a diference of *kind* and not of degree. The effect of the small quantity, he says, is often beneficial; the effect of the large or narcotic quantity is injurious. Dr. Binz defines *food* as both building up the tissues and supplying the warmth and vital force necessary for the

body's functions; and he shows that, while small quantities of alcohol have not the former quality, they have the latter, and he further shows that alcohol in moderate quantities is entirely assimilated in the human system. In the light wines and beers, where alcohol forms only from three to ten per cent of its liquid, we have the alcohol in the form best adapted for this beneficial effect, while in brandies, rums, gins, whiskeys, and all distilled liquors the alcohol is in dangerous proportions for a beverage. To say that everything containing alcohol is a poison, is therefore a false assertion, as false as to say that fruit is poisonous because prussic acid, which is a deadly poison, is found in it. Nature has in her alembic turned a powerful and dangerous element into a beneficial minister to human wants, and all nations have recognized this vital difference between a moderate and an excessive use of stimulants, and have testified to the wisdom of using Nature's provision without abusing it.

5. A fifth moral error of the total abstinence system is its dependence upon a contract rather than on a moral sense. Instead of regulating a man from within, it would apply a strait-jacket. Instead of allowing a free play of the man's individuality, and then endeavoring to instruct and educate the man's reason, it would in a moment of the man's emergency tie up his conscience with a pledge, which, when the emergency is past, he will bear irksomely and endeavor to nullify or evade. This is a most pernicious instrument for debauching the conscience. In the

first place, it manufactures a new sin, always a dangerous experiment, bringing about a reaction which sweeps the soul into real sin from its experience in committing the constructed sin; and, secondly, it gives a ready excuse to the conscience against any moral argument for temperance by covering it with a suspicion of conventionality. The pledge is always an injury and never a help to a true morality. It is a substitute for principle. It is a sign, not of weakness (for we are all of us weak enough), but of readiness to reform. The true reform would demand a change of the underlying principles of life. *That* the pledge-taker refuses to make. Instead of that he reforms the surface. Instead of turning the stream into a new channel, he contents himself with throwing up earthen dykes to prevent an overflow. You can get thousands to sign the pledge where you can get one to reform. Of course the pledge is not kept, except in the cases where it was not needed, where the reform took the place of the pledge, where the man would have reformed without any pledge. Surely such a wholesale defiling of promises is a profane dealing with sacred things, and marks a very corrupt system. Man's moral nature is not to be curbed by pledges. His outward conduct may be restrained by imposed law, but so far forth as that conduct has a moral element in it, no action of the man himself can effect it except a moral reformation. Government, by its threatened punishment, may stop a man's drinking so long as he thinks himself in danger of punishment, but a pledge that has no punishment for its breaking will command no obedience, while the moral convictions remain unchanged. It is only an invitation to further sin.

6. The sixth and last moral error of the total abstinence system to which I shall refer is one which I bring forward not as a philosopher nor a moralist, but as a Christian who believes in the divine authority of the Holy Scriptures. This error I have already adverted to in my prudential argument, and therefore need not enlarge upon here. It is impossible to condemn all drinking of wine as either sinful or improper, without bringing reproach upon the Lord Jesus Christ and his apostles. There has been an immense amount of wriggling by Christian writers on this subject to get away from this alternative; but there it stands impregnable. *Jesus did use wine.* I will not waste my time in proving this proposition, and answering those wild *bashibazouks* of controversy, who assert with childlike confidence and simplicity that the Bible wines were unfermented grape-juice. Their learned ignorance is fairly splendid with boldness. They disarm criticism by their overwhelming dash. Such little questions as why the epithet *wine-bibber* should have been opprobrious, why deacons should not be given to *much* wine, why the Corinthian communicants should become *drunken,* why the Apostles at Pentecost should have been accused of wine-drinking as the cause of their strange utterances, — all such trifling questions they utterly disdain to notice in the magnificent sweep of their assertion. It is a small thing, too, with them, that the Apostles never hint at two kinds of wine, a good unfermented wine and a bad fermented one,

when it would have been so easy and natural for our Lord or for Paul to say, "Drink only the unfermented wine." Instead of that, they lead us into great danger by their unguarded remarks about wine as if there were but one sort; nay, worse than that, Paul even tells the deacons not to drink *too much wine*. Did Paul mean the fermented wine? Then he allowed the deacons to use it as a beverage. Did he mean unfermented wine? Then why did he limit the amount? This dilemma and all the other arguments from the Scripture are as mere cobwebs to the lances of these valiant knights, who are too free and fiery to be checked by reason or overcome by a syllogism. To a foot-pilgrim like myself, however, these Scriptures are convincing and end the controversy, and therefore I have to charge the total abstinence propaganda with wresting the Scriptures and despising their authority.

I know that there is a wing of their army which acknowledges all that I have said of Scripture record, and which holds that times are so changed that the Scripture examples and precepts are now obsolete, that they were made for an Oriental people eighteen centuries ago, and are wholly inapplicable in the great Occident in this nineteenth century. But this wing of the host is a very weak wing, and is often very thoroughly snubbed by the loud leaders who count their position a giving up of the contest, as indeed it is. For who will believe that Christ and his Apostles, on great moral questions and matters of moral conduct, gave example and precept that would not last? The argument runs this way: Christ and his Apostles said that we may drink wine, but that was a local and temporary matter. Now, under new circumstances, we must not. Christ and his Apostles said that Christians must not be mixed with the ungodly world, but that was local and temporary, when idolatry was rife. Now, under new circumstances, Christians and the ungodly world may so intermingle that you can't tell one from the other. The Apostle of Christ said that women must keep silence in the churches, but that was local and temporary, when women were not much more than slaves. Now, under new circumstances, women may mount platform and pulpit as exhorters and preachers, for, verily, under the gospel there is no difference between male and female! I said, Who will believe all this? Alas! there are many who do. And I charge them with undermining the authority of the Word of God. If moral questions that are not in the Scripture are to be thus treated, who is to draw the line where you are to stop? why may not the Christian merchant say of the New Testament command, "Lie not one to another," this is local and temporary, when trade was sluggish and men's minds were dull? Now, under new circumstances, when emulation needs every help and Wall Street sharpens men's wits, you *must* lie or go under. This departure from the Bible sentiment and example on moral conduct in us who believe in the Bible is a very dangerous thing. Of course, for the Buddhists, who have lately become fashionable in our country, it is of no consequence. And to them this division of my argument is not addressed.

I have now endeavored, in a very brief way, to point out the reasons why the total abstinence system as a cure for intemperance will not and ought not to be adopted. Of course, I am, therefore, bound to propose a system that *ought* to be adopted. I do not dodge the issue. No man is more keenly alive to the frightful ravages of drunkenness than I am, and it is because the prevailing system of a total abstinence crusade is hindering the cure of the evil by keeping just methods from the field and by disgusting men's minds with the very name of temperance, so cruelly bemired, that I denounce it, and ask good men to rally around a truer and purer standard.

The right system must be one that recognizes practically the difference between excess and moderation, and the difference between injurious and harmless drinks, and will thus appeal to the common sense of reasonable and thinking men. It must be a system that deals honestly with history, science, and Scripture, and does not invent theories and then support them by garbled quotations and imaginary facts. It must be a manly system, that has no cant or foolery of orders and ribbons, degrading a matter of high principle to the hocus pocus of a child's play. Such a system would be found in the exclusion of distilled liquor from common use as beverage both by public opinion and by law, and the wise regulation in society and in the State of the use of vinous and malt liquors. Society should put away all the drinking usages that lead to excess, such as furnishing many wines at an entertainment, or "treating" others, or putting brandied wines upon the table; and the State should limit the number of licensed sellers to at most the proportion of one to a thousand inhabitants of each town, and these sellers should be under heavy bonds not to sell to minors or drunkards, and not to allow disreputable characters to gather at their places. The law should likewise make the collection of evidence against a licensed seller easy, and the penalty of breaking the law should be imprisonment as well as fine. On a basis like this, that does not sweepingly condemn every drink that has alcohol in it, the great majority of the people could work accordantly, and therefore effectively. The wild radicalism of the teetotalers is just what the rum-sellers and their advocates enjoy. They know that this absurd extravagance disintegrates the army of order and renders it powerless; that so long as temperance is made to mean "total abstinence from everything that can intoxicate," the great multitude of order-loving men will shrink from joining any temperance movement, and hence these wholesale destroyers of the race can go on in their nefarious work with impunity. Now, what is needed is the union of all good men who desire to stop the fearful drunkenness of the land, with its attendant crimes and misery. That union never can be effected on the principles of the total abstinence propaganda. But it can be effected on the principles of truth and common sense, and they who prevent this union by their tenacious adherence to a false and fanatical system are responsible before God and man for the spreading curse.

There is no more important question before the American people to-day than this, "How shall we stay this surging tide of intemperance?" And it is to be answered on one side by the practical voice of society, and on the other by the edicts of our legislatures. We should act with an even mind on so grave a subject, and see to it that every step we take is solidly founded on right reason. We should urge before our legislatures plans that are free from the taint of crude prejudice and instinct with practical wisdom; and when we do this, we shall be surprised to see how many, whom we took to be enemies, there are who are ready to join us in the work and establish foundations of order and peace in the land, that shall save us from a moral slough.

Let me, in conclusion, distinctly say that I do not oppose the principle of total abstinence from all that intoxicates *for the individual*. Every man is at liberty to abstain, if he will, and it is his duty to abstain if his own conscience command it. That against which I contend, and which I hold up as the hindrance to true reform and the promoter of the drunkard's cause, is the total abstinence *crusade* or *propaganda*, the forcing total abstinence upon the community as the duty of all, the putting under the ban every one who does not follow that standard the insisting upon total abstinence as the only safety against drunkenness. It is this headlong movement which virtually cries, "The Koran or the sword!" and tramples alike on reason and Scripture in its blind rush, — it is this, and not private total abstinence, against which I inveigh. And let me also repeat that I am attacking a system, and not persons. I have no war with men, but with error. I can honor the men who uphold a pernicious system, for I can believe in their purity of motive and singleness of aim. And for this reason I the more earnestly and hopefully urge them to consider their ways, and abandon a course which is only confirming the dreadful curse we all abhor and desire to remove.

APPENDIX.

As some replies to the above lecture have been made by Mr. Wendell Phillips and others, whose rhetoric is superior to their logic, it may be well for me to add a few words to those who might mistake assertion for argument and epithet for proof.

1. That I am behind the age I freely confess, but I am more than the "fifty years behind" which these gentlemen affirm. I am eighteen hundred years behind. I am with Christ and his Apostles against an age that makes light of the inspired Word and prefers man's methods to God's.

2. All the eloquence expended on my opposition to total abstinence is *brutum fulmen*, as my whole argument was against the total abstinence *system*, and not against total abstinence. The system I defined at the beginning as demanding total abstinence from all liquors that may intoxicate, on the part of every-

body, as a moral duty. It is this *giving law to the world* on the subject that I denounce.

3. A picture of the terrible ravages of drunkenness is no answer to one who objects to a false mode of meeting the evil. The false mode will only make those ravages the greater. It is a favorite method with Mr. Phillips and the stereotyped "temperance lecturer," to attack the opponents of the total abstinence system with harrowing pictures of the distress and misery caused by drunkenness, thus *assuming* that their system is the right one. Suppose a fanatic tells me that Boston ought to be destroyed because of the abominable vice in it, and I should in reply suggest that there might be a better way of meeting the emergency, what would you think of his counter reply by exclaiming at the fearfulness of these sins committed in Boston? The teetotal fanatics coolly assume that we who oppose their wild theories are either unaware of the terrible evils of drunkenness or else wilful abettors of the depraved classes.

4. The two-wine theory regarding the Scriptures, silly as it is, cannot help the teetotalers, for the wine drunk at the Lord's Supper by the Corinthians intoxicated them, and yet the Apostle never thinks of telling them that they took the wrong kind of wine. So the command to the deacons and others not to be given to *much* wine shows that the Apostles had fermented wine in view.

5. The oft-quoted text, "If meat make my brother to offend, &c.," only shows that a man must *judge for himself* as to the use of his privileges. The Apostle

Paul, on this very matter of meat, told the Corinthians to eat what was set before them and ask no questions, but *if a special case occurred* to refuse to eat it. It was *on special occasions* they were to abstain, not perpetually; and, accordingly, who supposes that Paul gave up eating meat for the rest of his life? Now apply the Apostle's precept and example to the other matter of wine. On *special* occasions, of which each man is the *only judge*, we are to abstain. *That is the whole of this abused argument of expediency.* The teetotalers turn expediency into law.

· 6. The man who drinks brandy, and quotes another that drinks wine as his example, is as wilful a liar as the man who smokes opium, and quotes the man that smokes tobacco as his example. The drunkard who quotes a man that drinks wine in moderation as his example is as wilful a liar as the thief who steals a diamond pin to wear, and quotes Mr. Phillips wearing a diamond pin as his example. The "example" idea is a mere ruse that he holds up to deceive silly folk. He himself sees no example in it.

7. The comparison of moderate drinking with slavery as equally upheld by the New Testament, and yet now to be abolished, is altogether lame. Our Lord drank and made wine. Did he buy, sell, or own a slave?

8. So all classification of drinking wine with crimes, and therefore the demand of a like treatment for both (see Mr. Phillips's pretty passage on "gambling hells" and "flash literature"), are the errors of a juvenile reasoning.

9. The improvement in the social customs with regard to drinking, the result of prayer and labor on the part of all good men, is pleasantly appropriated by the teetotalers as *their* work. I like that. It is bold.

10. An honest, upright, manly course, in which we call things by their right names, and make no sweeping assertions that confound good and evil, is the course that effects most for the truth in life and conduct. Then the conscience and the regard of the men we desire to turn from immoral ways will be touched, for they immediately see that we act not from passion, but from reason. The fanatical system only antagonizes the class we wish to convert. I am sure Mr. Phillips will forgive me if I seek to restore the system of reason and common sense, which, under the progressive inventions of the teetotalers, is in danger of taking its place with "the Lost Arts."

VII.

OLD AND NEW THEOLOGIES.

By REV. GEORGE R. CROOKS, D.D., LL.D.

VII.

OLD AND NEW THEOLOGIES.

By REV. GEORGE R. CROOKS, D.D., LL.D.

THE signs of a demand for a new theology are so many, that he who runs may read them. As specimens, let us quote a few. A leading Baptist minister of this country says: "Doubtless there will be in the future a new theology, an outgrowth of the old, an expansion and deepening of sacred truth made precious to the church by many centuries of rich experience."

Dr. Crosby is quoted as saying that it "would be wise to broaden the terms of subscription necessary to church membership and church ministry"; this would be a letting go of some ideas once sacredly cherished. A leader of the English Congregationalists, J. Baldwin Brown, expresses a desire "to see a great dogmatist once more." In the spring of 1878 the United Presbyterians of Scotland added supplementary declarations to the Westminster Confession, which practically nullified some of its important statements. Dr. William M. Taylor, who has passed from Presbyterianism to Congregationalism, in commenting on this action, has expressed the hope for "a shorter, simpler, less metaphysical and more comprehensive creed." Principal Shairp, of St. Andrew's, Scotland, echoes the opinions of the Americans quoted. "It needs no divine," he writes, "to tell us that this century will not pass without a great breaking up of the great dogmatic structures that have held ever since the Reformation or the succeeding age. From many sides, at once a simplifying of the code, a revision of the standards, is being demanded." Dr. Philip Schaff, in the Presbyterian Alliance at Edinburgh, practically called for a recasting of the confessional statements of the Reformed churches, saying: "Every age must produce its own theology, adapted to its peculiar condition and wants. Thus we have a patristic theology, a scholastic theology, a Reformation theology, and a modern Evangelical theology, not to speak of the various shades of denominational theologies. Divine truth, as revealed in the Scriptures, is unchangeable, the same to-day, yesterday, and forever, but it must be ever reproduced, newly appropriated, and represented in all its phases. Every true progress in theology is conditioned by a deep study and understanding of the Word of God, that is ever new, and renewing the church, and will ever remain the infallible and inexhaustible fountain of revealed truth. The Scriptures may have been studied more intensely and devoutly in former ages, but they never were studied so extensively and with such an array of facilities and advantages as at the present age. Every progress in exegesis must have its effect upon systematic theology and the symbolic statement of trust." [Harmony of the Reformed Confessions, pp. 36, 37.]

What is the meaning of all this? Are the foundations of truth giving way? Is this reaching out after new formulas of faith a symptom of dissatisfaction with the verities of Scripture? Is it a sign of religious progress, or of religious decay? Were this call for re-statement of doctrine accompanied with a disposition to abandon Scripture, it might excite alarm; but they who utter the call profess, and we may believe possess, a deep reverence for the Word of God. Let us observe, however:—

All theology is progressive. It has advanced from delicate germs to its present stately growth. We can, as we go back along the line of the Christian ages, stop at the successive points of time when the present accepted doctrines of the church, one after the other, reached a definite form. In the history of our religion Scripture is original, systems of doctrine are derivative. Scripture is divine, theology is human. We all know that the doctrinal systems are the product of the action of the human reason upon the contents of the Word of God. Sometimes truths of the gospel have been obscured for ages and recovered again, as in the Protestant Reformation. That justification is by faith alone, and that Scripture is the sole standard of appeal in matters of faith, are the doctrinal positions for the reassertion of which we are indebted to the Fathers of the Reformation. Their present prominence is not much over three hundred years old; and yet they have been so powerfully operative that they have changed the character of modern civilization. On these two, as cornerstones, the fabric of Protestant theology has been built. We owe, therefore, whatever is distinctive of Protestant culture, society, politics, to doctrinal ideas, whose formulation, as we possess them in our creeds, is comparatively recent. The truths are old, as old as the gospel, but they have had a resurrection unto life.

It does not follow, because we admit that theology is progressive, that we are ready to forsake old faiths. It does not follow, because leaders such as we have quoted desire re-statements of points in their doctrinal confessions, that they are about to surrender the substance of Orthodox doctrine. It does not follow, because they desire to relegate some of the matters of belief to the category of matters of opinion, that they are about to surrender the essentials of Christianity. "Every man," says Neander, profoundly, "is in one sense an historical production; the ideas which form his life have come to him through the course of development in which he moves." And so we may claim that every theology is a historical production. Whether clearly Scriptural or divergent from Scripture, it represents some tendency rooted in human nature, and of which we can give an historical account. But of that body of doctrine in which the Protestant churches agree, we may say that it is hallowed to us by the prayers and labors of sainted men; the blood of martyrs has sealed it; the nations that have risen under its inspiration to high planes of civilization are witnesses of its power. How, then, are we to explain the present unrest?

It is not easy to give all the answers to this question; but a notice of some facts in the religious movement of the century may help us towards some answers. What is religion essentially? Is it right knowledge? If so, piety is the equivalent of Orthodoxy. Is it right external practice? If so, piety is the equivalent of morality. Or is it a right feeling toward God and man? If so, then piety is the equivalent of a certain inner life. In this sense piety is conditioned by knowledge, and works itself out in moral practice. The characteristic of the religious revival which we have inherited from the past century is, that it has drawn attention to the true centre of subjective religion. That centre it makes to be the sense of forgiveness, or, as it is sometimes expressed, the consciousness of redemption. Religion, under its teaching, appears less as a dogma to be received than as a life to be lived. Thus we have experimental Christianity, as distinguished from catechetical Christianity, or sacramental Christianity. But this change in the view of subjective Christianity has led on to a new view of objective Christianity. Those doctrines which minister to life — the atonement, its freeness and fulness, the immediacy of the Divine answer to faith, and the direct action of the spirit at the moment of regeneration — have come forward into prominence. Thus our later and living theology is a theology of the spirit. The growth of subjective religion in this form has not only projected into prominence corresponding doctrines of theology, but has tended to obscure others, which were once considered of paramount importance. This revival of subjective religion was, however, but a return to the first period of the Reformation, the period of its glow, its ardor, its early experience of redemption without the mediatory offices of the church. Luther had made the exegetical discovery that "the just shall live by faith" long before he had translated his exegesis into experience. During his long and memorable journey to Rome, and especially in his hours of weariness and sickness, the Pauline formula, "The just shall live by faith," was continually present to his mind. Not till he had personally appropriated Christ's merits by faith was the Reformation born in him; the discarding of the Latin Church doctrine of penance, and of the mediatorial character of the priesthood, following therefrom of necessity. The recovery of the idea of the priesthood of the people, to which he was led both by Scripture and his experience of redemption, delivered the church from the bondage of a thousand years. The Reformation, as it was born in Luther, was a heart-birth as well as a brain-birth; its material principle, justification by faith, pointed to a fact of the inner life; its formal principle, the supreme authority of Scripture, pointed to the light which guides us to that fact. But the scholastic habits in which the leaders of the Reformation were trained were too strong for them. There followed the period of glow and a new life, a period of cold confessionalism, of distrust and dissensions, of the strife of conservative and radical reform, — a period marked by a tendency to consolidate almost every theological opinion into an authoritative dogma. Each church was gathered as into a fortress, and the walls of the confessions were built up high, so that those who were within might not get out, and those who were without might not get in. In a word, it was a period in Protestantism of alienation and mutual repellency.

In the nature of the case such a condition of the churches could not last. A prophet might have predicted such a religious revival as would loosen the tightness of confessional bonds. In the middle of the last century there came such a renewal of the church's life. State-Churchman and Dissenter, Calvinist and Arminian, alike shared in its blessings. Though its results are gathered into organized form in one ecclesiastical communion, it was limited to no one. Its first effect was, through increase of Catholicity, to weaken the binding power of separative dogmas. I may be allowed, I trust, in this presence, to quote one of the leaders of the Evangelical movement, John Wesley. In a letter to a friend he writes: "You have admirably expressed what I mean by an opinion, as contradistinguished from an essential doctrine. Whatever is compatible with love to Christ and a work of grace is an opinion." [Journal, May 16, 1765.] And again: "I am sick of opinions. I am weary to bear them. My soul loathes this frothy food. Give me solid and substantial religion. Give me an humble, gentle lover of God and man, a man full of mercy and good fruits, without partiality and without hypocrisy; a man laying himself out in the work of faith, the patience of hope, and the labor of love. Let my soul be with these Christians, wheresoever they are, and whatsoever opinion they are of." [A Further Appeal to Men of Reason and Religion, sec. IV. par. 10.] Once more, for the words of this teacher, though spoken more than one hundred and thirty years ago, singularly coincide with the temper of our times. "It is a poor excuse to say, 'O, but the people are brought into several erroneous opinions.' It matters not a straw whether they are or not (I speak of such opinions as do not touch the foundations); it is scarcely worth while to spend ten words about it. Whether they embrace this religious opinion or that is no more concern to me than whether they embrace this or that system of astronomy. Are they brought to holy tempers and holy lives? This is mine, and should be your inquiry; since on this both social and personal happiness depend,—happiness, temporal and eternal." [A Further Appeal to Men of Reason and Religion, sec. IV. par. 14.] Thus we may say that one of the early fruits of the Evangelical revival was a discrimination between the essential and the unessential in dogma; between the credenda and the cogitanda between those facts of the creed which minister more directly to the life, and those which, whether determined in one way or another, leave the life untouched.

There has run parallel with this practical revival

a corresponding movement of religious philosophy. Schleiermacher, who drew his religious life from Moravianism, lays down the principle "that the essence of religion is not knowledge, but feeling. He defines religion to be rooted in the absolute feeling of dependence, and of a conscious relationship to God originating immediately from it." The Christian religion is that in which the sense of dependence is accompanied by the consciousness of redemption through the merits of Christ. The feeling of dependence becomes in the Christian religion a feeling of dependence on an infinite Saviour. Grant, if you please, that Schleiermacher fell into the error of making the Christian consciousness a primary source of doctrine. Grant, if you please, that this error, by setting aside the Divine Word, ends in the corruption of the Christian consciousness itself, yet the principle can be held with a full recognition of the supreme authority of the Scriptures in matters of belief. I for one can, therefore, fully agree with Van Oosterzee, when he says: "Only where objective truth finds a point of contact in the subjective consciousness does it become the spiritual property of mankind and can it thus be properly understood and valued. So far, and so far only, does the Christian consciousness deserve a place among the sources of dogmatics. But since the doctrine of salvation can be derived neither from reason nor from feeling nor from conscience, and the internal consciousness only attests and confirms the truth, after having learned it from Scripture, this last must always be valued as the principal source." [Christian Dogmatics, Vol. I. sec. 10.]

If there are Scripture truths capable of such subjective attestation, then they form an important part of the whole body of dogma; they furnish a common standing ground for Christians of diverse confessions; nay, more, their coming forward into prominence must loosen the hold of the differentiating dogmas of the churches upon the people. In order that this point of attestation may be made clear, let Van Oosterzee be quoted again: "So long as I do not consciously accept a truth for myself, it remains a truth, external to and above me, but is not a truth for me and in me. And, therefore, the gospel looks for a point of union in man, and finds in it the highest aspirations of his heart, intellect, and conscience. Where it is faithfully accepted, a spiritual agreement springs up, and consequently an inner consciousness of truth. This consciousness of experience not only may but must be reckoned among the sources of our knowledge. Where it is utterly wanting, there the most accurate knowledge deserves only the name of dead knowledge. A man's own experience leads to much deeper insight of things than the best attested testimony." [Christian Dogmatics, Vol. I. sec. 10, par. 3.] Morrell, the author of the "History of Philosophy in the Nineteenth Century," and of the "Philosophy of Religion," recognizes this attesting power of the Christian consciousness, and finds in the neglect of it the source of rationalism. As this is a point collateral to the subject of discussion, he may be cited here. "The only distinct idea," says

Morrell, "which I am able to attach to the term Rationalism, is the effort to reduce the whole essence of Christianity to a logical or scientific product, and the denial of there being anything contained in it, beyond the facts which actually are, or which can be contained in a connected series of propositions. The Rationalist begins by laying down his propositions in approved form; he goes on next to deduce certain conclusions from them; and then follows up his train of reasons, step by step, until he has brought his entire faith into a complete logical system. This system, according to his view, *is* Christianity; the profession of its truth is the profession of Christianity; and to believe the propositions in question is to be a Christian. To me Christianity in its essence appears a deep inward-life of the soul, — a life which cannot be accounted for by any scientific analysis, which cannot be expressed in any number of propositions, but which in its evidences, in its conceptions, in its holy impulses and anticipations, lies quite beyond the region of the logical understanding. If I possess the Christian life, I have the witness of the truth within me. If I possess it not, I may, it is true, possess a system of formal doctrine; but that system, as it appears to the logical faculty, has much the same resemblance to Christianity itself as a skeleton has to a living man." [Philosophy of Religion, Preface, pp. 16, 17.] If this be true, Rationalism is the divorce of the heart from the head in theology.

One of the great teachers of our age, Neander, has applied this living principle to the interpretation of church history, and thereby has reorganized that department of theology. To his mind the history of the church is before all else the exhibition of Divine power, in the unfolding of the work of redemption, and thus becomes "a school of Christian experience, a voice sounding through the ages, of instruction, of doctrine and reproof, for all who are disposed to listen." "The theology of the heart" is that to which alone he looks for the pacification of the clashing confessions of the fatherland, and the victory of Christian truth over rationalistic unbelief. I beg attention to his weighty testimony: "When, at the commencement of my labors," he writes, "I dedicated my work to the friend who was about to leave me, I affixed to it the motto of our common theology and of this exhibition of history: 'Pectus est, quod theologum facit.' We need not be ashamed of this maxim; shame rather to those who were bold enough to ridicule it. It was the watchword of these men who called forth theology from the dead forms of scholasticism to the living spirit of God's Word." [Preface to General Church History; second edition.] And again he writes: "As for my relation to all who hold the conviction that faith in Jesus, the Saviour of sinful humanity, as it has shown itself since the first founding of the Christian Church to be the fountain of Divine life, will prove itself the same to the end of time, and that from this faith a new creation will arise in the Christian Church, and in this part of the world, which has been preparing amidst the storms of spring, — to all such persons I hope to be bound by the bond of Christian fellowship. But I cannot agree with the conviction of those among them who think that this new creation will only be a repetition of what took place in the sixteenth or seventeenth century, and that the whole dogmatic system, and the entire mode of contemplating human and divine things, must return as it then existed." [Preface to History of Training and Planting the Christian Church.]

What dogmatic changes Neander anticipated, he has nowhere placed on record; but he doubtless foresaw that the "theology of the heart" would lift into greater importance certain vital doctrines of theology, and reduce the importance of others which have thus far stood in the foreground of the confessions. Dr. Philip Schaff, a pupil of Neander, who worthily illustrates the catholic spirit of his teacher, discussed in 1877, before the Presbyterian Alliance, the desirableness of a new confession of faith for the great body of Reformed churches. Let me quote his words: "The preparation of such a confession would afford an excellent opportunity to simplify and popularize the Reformed system of doctrine, to utter a protest against the peculiar dangers and errors of our age, and to exhibit the fraternal attitude of this Alliance to the Evangelical churches, which have sprung up since the Reformation, and have been blessed of God. It ought to be truly evangelical,— evangelical-catholic in spirit. A confession which would intensify Presbyterianism and loosen the ties which unite us to other branches of Christ's church, I would regard as a calamity. We want a wall to keep off the wolves, and not a fence to divide the sheep ; we want a declaration of union, not a platform of disunion." [The Harmony of the Reformed Confession, pp. 60, 61.] The following passage is entirely in the line of the argument of this lecture : "No Reformed Synod (at least on the Continent) could now pass the rigorous canons of Dort against Arminianism, which, after a temporary defeat, has silently leavened the national church of Holland, and which, through the great Methodist revival, has become one of the most powerful converting agencies in England and America. The five knotty points of Calvinism have lost their point, and have been smoothed off by God's own working in the history of the church." [Harmony of Reformed Confessions, pp. 49, 50.]

Thus we have shown that the Evangelical revival has changed the relative importance of dogmas, that it has found a secondary basis in a philosophy of religion, that it has led to the desire for a closer doctrinal consensus among all the churches that hold to the consciousness of redemption through faith in Christ as the vital fact of Christianity. The time when such a desire is likely to be realized is no doubt far off; but its expression is not a sign of the decadence of the churches, it is a symptom of growth. As for these uneasy, unstable, unsettled teachers, who are blown about by every theological wind, who cannot be found to-day where they were yesterday, and who will not be found to-morrow where they are to-day, and that other class, who court popularity by surrendering what they ought to defend, who are all things to all men in a sense of which Paul never dreamt, — the less said about them the better.

It remains to notice the reactions against the Evangelical movement, that has now maintained itself for nearly one hundred and fifty years.

1. The Anglo-Catholic revival. This originated in the perception that the Evangelical movement necessarily meant the downfall of sacramental Christianity, and the relaxation of what are known as strict church principles. The universal priesthood of the people, which is an outcome of the pure Evangelical faith, implies the extinction of the priestly conception of the ministry. John Henry Newman, the leader of the Anglo-Catholics, has stated very candidly the purpose cherished by himself and his associates. "My battle," he says, "was with liberalism; by liberalism I mean the anti-dogmatic principle and its developments. From the age of fifteen, dogma has been the fundamental principle of my religion; I cannot enter into the idea of any other religion; religion as a mere sentiment is to me a dream and a mockery." [Apologia pro Vita Sua, pp. 95, 96.] "As to the high church and the low church, I thought that one had not much more of a logical basis than the other; while I had a thorough contempt for the Evangelical." [Apologia, p. 91.] And again: "The vital question was, How were we to keep the church from being liberalized? There was such apathy on the subject in some quarters and such imbecile alarm in others. . . . The Bishop of London of the day, an active and open-hearted man, had for years been en-

gaged in diluting the high orthodoxy of the church, by the introduction of the Evangelical body into places of influence and trust." [Apologia, p. 79.] Newman had the penetration to perceive that Evangelical principles, when carried into civil life, created political liberalism, and this aroused in his mind a strong repugnance to the Evangelical faith. Speaking of his life in 1832, he writes: "Shortly before there had been a revolution in France: the Bourbons had been dismissed; and I believed that it was unchristian for nations to cast off their governors." [Apologia, p. 79.] So intense was his dislike of the progress of civil liberty on the Continent of Europe, that he says of himself in this year: "It was the success of the liberal cause that fretted me inwardly. I became fierce against its instruments and its manifestations. A French vessel was at Algiers; I would not even look at the tricolor. On my return, though forced to stop a day at Paris, I kept indoors the whole time, and all I saw of the beautiful city was what I saw from the diligence." [p. 82.]

This is the explanation of the motive of the Anglo-Catholic revival by one of its leaders. To set up a barrier against the Evangelical movement was a brave undertaking; and the undertaking could not have fallen into more capable hands. Ardent, richly cultivated in classical lore if not in theology, clear-sighted enough to perceive the nature of the battle they fought, honest to the core, they did all that intellectual energy, combined with the pleading of the authority of patristic antiquity, could do. They have appeared, and from Protestantism at least some of them have disappeared, and the Evangelical movement still moves on.

2. The Agnostic reaction, which limits the knowledge to the realm of sensible experience, and denies the possibility of knowing the supernatural. It substitutes the knowledge of law for the consciousness of redemption. This system carries us to the polar zone of thought, and leaves us there

"To starve in ice,
Immovable, infixed, and frozen round."

To others belongs the task of dealing metaphysically with the Agnostic system; it is only in place here to notice it as one of the reactions of the age, in which the possibility of religion is denied. But if I am to do no more than learn the laws of the universe, there is a mistake in the make-up of my constitution. I ought to have been all brain. The study of these generalizations of sensible experience which we call laws can never dry a tear, never heal a heartache, never ease the consciousness of sin which we carry with us, never relieve the sense of guilt. My heart and my flesh cry out for the living God, and I am told to rest in abstract law; that is to give me a stone when I ask for bread. They who speak to me thus tell me only half the truth. I would rise above law to One who is heart to my heart, love to my love; who has in him an infinite pity and readiness to help. The Agnostic reaction denies the best part of my nature all its rights. It cannot last long, for the imperishable wants of man demand a positive faith.

3. The last reaction against the religious life of the age is the Gospel of Culture, so eloquently proclaimed by Matthew Arnold. But this gospel is, in its last analysis, a Gospel of Selfishness. Here the law is self-activity; in the Christian religion the primary law is recipiency. Here man's centre is in himself; in religion, he is taken away from himself, and his centre is Jesus Christ. The goal of culture is self-developed perfection; the goal of religion is the outgrowing of our imperfection through the vigor of One greater than we are imparted to us. The spirit of culture is independence; the spirit of religion is dependence. The tendency of the Gospel of Culture to an absorbing self-consciousness has been clearly pointed out by Principal Shairp. "Its starting-point," to cite his statement, "is the idea of perfecting self, and though, as it gradually evolves, it tries to forget self and to include quite other elements, yet it never succeeds in getting clear of the taint of self-reference, with which it set out. While making this objection, I do not forget that Mr. Arnold, in drawing out his views, proposes as the end of culture to make reason and the kingdom of God prevail; that he sees clearly and insists strongly that an isolated self-culture is impossible, that we cannot make progress towards perfection ourselves unless we strive earnestly to carry our fellow-men along with us. Still, may it not be said that these unselfish elements — the desire for others' good, the desire to advance God's kingdom on earth — are in this theory awakened, not simply for their own sakes, not chiefly because they

are good in themselves, but because they are clearly discerned to be necessary to our self-perfection, elements apart from which this cannot exist? And so it comes that culture, though made our end never so earnestly, cannot shelter a man from thoughts about himself; cannot free him from that which all must feel to be fatal to high character,— continual self-consciousness." [Culture and Religion, pp. 92–93.] But all the reactions of the age, the Agnostic, the Sacramentarian, the Rationalist, only serve as a background to show more clearly the bright light of the Evangelical movement. Out of it what is most characteristic of the religion of our time has grown. It waits for a historian, but can wait till its work is completed in the renovation of theology itself. That theology will be pervaded throughout by the consciousness of redemption. When the song of the freed slave, "I'm redeemed, I'm redeemed," floating over the land, attests the power of the gospel, surely we in the centres of culture need not be ashamed to declare that we are determined to know nothing among men "save Jesus Christ and him crucified."

VIII.

FACTS AS TO DIVORCE IN NEW ENGLAND.

By REV. SAMUEL W. DIKE.

VIII.
FACTS AS TO DIVORCE IN NEW ENGLAND.

By REV. SAMUEL W. DIKE.

THE two words most significant of our American life are probably *business* and *home*. Business rests directly upon the institution of property, and the home upon that of marriage. Sir James Mackintosh said: " Almost all the relative duties of human life will be found, more immediately or more remotely, to arise out of the two great institutions of *property* and *marriage;* they constitute, preserve, and improve society; upon their gradual improvement depends the progressive civilization of mankind; on them rests the whole order of civil life." [Law of Nature and Nations, p. 76.] It may be said further, that since, with most people, the home is the great incentive to labor, and to the accumulation of its fruits in capital; so in the last analysis *marriage* is the fundamental institution of modern society. "The contract of marriage," wrote the learned Story, " is the most important of all human transactions. It is the very basis of civilized society."

The President takes the same ground in his last annual message, when he says, "The sanctity of marriage and the family relation are the corner-stone of our American society and civilization." "The stability of the family," writes an historian, "is the surest criterion of the moral character of an age." Whether, then, you come as men of business, as citizens or as the friends of good morals, as well as Christians, to listen to the facts as to divorce in New England, you are occupied with a topic second in importance — let me say — to no other moral question discussed on this platform.

I am to give the facts for New England only. This is not a serious limitation. For the New England idea, whether we find it East or West, is the most representative idea of our country, and any study of it is practically a study of American principles. It conquered at Appomattox. It is, and will be, at least for four years longer, represented in the chief executive office of the nation. But it has more work to do, East and West, North and South. For this work it needs to be watched, and to receive from time to time fresh power from its original sources.

Now, divorce is a New England idea, — not *the* New England idea, but rather a Yankee notion, apparently indigenous to the soil of Connecticut, — from which it has spread, with other and better notions, over large sections of the United States. Let us look at it with neither pessimistic nor yet with optimistic eyes, but with that manly New England courage that is ready to see its worst self to-day that it may be better to-morrow. The merest outline only can be given in an hour, and I try to seize on such points as, it seems to me, will best give you an idea of the facts and the field they cover, leaving out a hundred things that ought to be said. Unrighteous divorce, in its destruction of the marriage bond, destroys the family and necessarily affects the three great ends of marriage and the family; namely, the preservation of chastity, the giving of pure life to the world, and the help of the individual to the highest perfection and to the greatest social power, as a preparation for and foretaste of the life to come. What, then, are the facts?

First, as to divorces. Beginning with Connecticut, we find that Benjamin Trumbull, in 1785, mourned that 439 divorces had taken place in Connecticut within a century, and that all but 50 had occurred in the last fifty years. About twenty years later, when the corrupt influence of French infidelity had reached its height, President Dwight was alarmed that there was one divorce to every hundred marriages. The increase of the evil, however, seems nearly checked until 1843, when "habitual intemperance" and "intolerable cruelty" were added to the two existing causes for divorce. Even then the increase was small. But in 1849 several causes, including the notorious "omnibus clause," were added, making *nine* in all, and jurisdiction was taken from the legislature and given wholly to the courts. That year divorces numbered 94; the next year, 129; and in 1864, 426. Then for fifteen years they averaged

446 annually, varying less from year to year than the reported births or marriages or deaths. During this period the ratio of divorces to marriages was 1 to 10.4. The repeal of the "omnibus clause" in 1878 reduced the divorces of the next year to 316. Another slight change in the law for the better was secured a year ago.

Vermont grants divorces for six causes. There were 94 divorces granted in 1860, and from the close of the war they increased to 197 in 1878, with the ratio to marriages of 1 to 14. That year an amendment to the laws resulted in a reduction of divorces in the year following to 126.

Rhode Island grants about 180 annually, and her ratio is 1 to 13.

New Hampshire prints no statistics either of divorce or marriage, but it has been found that there were 159 divorces in the entire State in 1870, 240 in 1875, and 241 in 1878. Three counties, that had only 18 in 1840 and 21 in 1850, granted 40 in 1860 and 96 in 1878. There are fourteen causes for divorce, but no more inclusive, probably, than those of most other States.[1]

I do not know that the divorces of Maine have ever been reported. I have secured an examination

---

[1] The number of causes for divorce is a very uncertain guide to the facilities afforded by the laws of a State. Massachusetts has more causes than Maine, and yet parties go from the former to the latter State for divorce. Much depends upon the phraseology of the law. Of course some of those causes, like nullity and bigamy, are not, strictly speaking, causes for divorce at all. Though classified as such, they are really reasons for annulling the marriage.

of the county records in that State giving the divorces of the sixteen counties of the State for the year 1878. In these sixteen counties there were 478 divorces in that year. It is also found that in the five counties giving the number for 1880 there was an increase of more than one third in the latter year,— from 166 to 223.[1] Penobscot County granted 84 divorces last year.

And now take Massachusetts, which I have reserved to the last, because she is the heart of New England, and for the facilities she affords for studying this whole problem. This State, following closely English law, granted divorce for only two causes until 1860. That year there were 243 divorces, or 1 to 51 marriages. Then, by a series of acts passed, chiefly in 1860, '67, '73, and '77, the causes for absolute divorce became *nine*, Massachusetts copying a Connecticut vice just as Connecticut began to forsake it. In 1866 there were 392 divorces; in 1870, 449; and in 1878, 600. The ratio to marriages, 1 to 51 in 1860, became 1 to 21.4 in 1878. It is probable that in Massachusetts the increase still goes on.

If, now, we sum up for New England, there were in the year of grace 1878 in Maine, 478 divorces; in New Hampshire, 241; in Vermont, 197; in Massachusetts, 600; in Connecticut, 401; and in Rhode Island, 196; making a total of 2,113, and a larger ratio in proportion to the population than in France in the days of the revolution, though far less than

[1] Complete returns for 1880 show that there were 510 divorces granted in the entire State that year.

in the city of Paris. In France, the ratio of *separations* to marriages latterly is about 1 to 150; in Belgium, of *divorces* to marriages, 1 to 270, with a few separations; and in England, of *petitions* for both divorce and separation, 1 to 300. On the basis of population by the present census there was one divorce to every 1,357 inhabitants in Maine; one to 819 in Penobscot County, the seat of a theological seminary; one to every 1,439 in New Hampshire; one to every 1,687 in Vermont; one to every 2,971 in Massachusetts; one to every 1,553 in Connecticut; and one to every 1,411 in Rhode Island. But no State except Maine is likely to have a larger divorce rate than Massachusetts, unless the laws and discussion speedily check the evil, for the reason that the changes in the law have not had time to produce their full effects.

But the Catholic marriages are, in four States, twenty-seven per cent of the whole.[1] Assuming, what is very nearly true, that there are no divorces among these, the ratio of divorces to marriages among Protestants is 1 to 11.7 for the four States together; it being 1 to 15 in Massachusetts, 1 to 13 in Vermont, 1 to 9 in Rhode Island, and 1 in less than 8 in Connecticut.

But what of divorce in the West? Has not this practice, in going West with the New-Englander, run into greater extremes? Few States, if any, west of

[1] In 1878 the Catholic marriages were 31 per cent of the whole number of marriages in Massachusetts, 24 per cent in Connecticut, 28 per cent in Rhode Island, and 12 per cent in Vermont.

Ohio, collect statistics of divorce. In Ohio, the ratio for many years averaged 1 to 25, and now it is about 1 to 18. Indiana has changed her laws for the better, while Illinois has, it is said, adopted better forms of procedure. No city has had a worse reputation in divorce than Chicago. Yet the records of Cook County, with a population of about 600,000, for the five years 1875–79, show a ratio of divorce suits *begun* to marriages licenses *taken out* of 1 to 9.4. But for the year 1875 it was found that one fifth of the petitions heard were denied. Making this allowance, — and the more strict practice of latter years fully justifies it, — the ratio becomes 1 to 12. Chicago is not as bad as Hartford or New Haven.[1]

So this wretched business goes on, apparently wherever New England people are found, and it seems to spread elsewhere in some measure. Yet it exists only where laws render it possible. But loose laws and loose court practice, of which there is too much in certain courts, — chiefly perhaps in Maine and Connecticut, — cannot account for all of this increase. New Hampshire is in point. There has been no change in the law there, of any account, since 1854, and, I am told, very little for nearly a century. Yet the increase is as marked as in other States. Even in St. Louis, where there were few divorced until 1876, there were, it is estimated, 430 cases tried in 1879, and 205 divorces were granted last year. "I have as

---

[1] The Rev. Charles Caverno, of Lombard, Ill., has found that there were 6,603 marriage licenses taken out in Cook County, Ill., in 1880, and 830 divorce suits begun. The ratio is 1 to 8.

yet," writes a correspondent in St. Louis, "found no one who is able to give an explanation of the increase, beyond the fact that like a deadly epidemic it began to rage with greater violence about that time, because all the previous conditions of our social life had been favorable to such an outbreak." He adds: "You will also discover, from the names, that most of the parties are of foreign birth." Yet in Boston I find very few unmistakably foreign names on the divorce docket. There are 333 divorces reported for the city of San Francisco in 1880.

Not one fourth of these divorce cases are for adultery. Desertion and severity are the chief causes. The courts are crowded with unhappy couples, and often the cases are despatched with unseemly haste. A pastor once spoke to the judge in the lull of business one day,— a member, I think, of his church, and chief justice of the State. Another man approached. "Excuse me a moment," said the judge. In less than three minutes the judge turned to the minister and said, "Do you know what I have done? I have divorced a couple quicker than you ever married one!" There is a daughter of a prosperous farmer, still a young woman, who has been divorced from three husbands, each of whom is living and married to another wife, while she has lately been married to a fourth husband. Nor is this the only or the worst case of the kind reported in the State of Connecticut. Two Vermonters deliberately swapped wives by aid of the courts. Young people coolly reckon on divorce in contracting marriage. A Vermont couple married "on trial for six months," agreeing to get a divorce "if either party did not like." An advertisement appeared in a Boston newspaper for some time: "Divorces legally and quietly obtained. Can pay by instalments." Out of seventeen cases tried at one term of court in Vermont, in the opinion of members of the bar, all but one were collusive.

It is said that this is not wholly an evil. Said a minority report to the Massachusetts Legislature, many years ago, it is true, " The consequences of this course of legislation, so far as the undersigned can judge of them, have been to increase the happiness of married life, to promote lawful marriages, and to prevent licentiousness." And this opinion is frequently expressed in newspapers, and held by many very intelligent citizens to-day. It has had much weight with legislators.

This leads me to present a second class of facts, not so much, however, to refute this opinion as to throw light upon the whole discussion. I take Massachusetts, because her admirable Bureau of Statistics gives facts not accessible in other States. I find in the report of that Bureau for 1880, that for the twenty years ending 1879 the population of the State increased 50 per cent. In 1860, there were 12,404 marriages, — the largest number ever reported up to that date, save once. The highest number since is 16,437, — a gain of 32 per cent only, while in 1879 they were only 11 per cent more than in 1860.

Take crime. The report shows that, leaving out of account the liquor cases, fluctuating for obvious reasons, all crime in the State for twenty years increased 20.4 per cent, or two fifths as fast as the population. But how is it with the licentious crimes? I can learn of no essential change in the laws or in their enforcement, except that in Suffolk County the convictions for keeping houses of ill-fame for the last five years are only two fifths the number in the preceding five (206 to 523), and that the convictions for the kindred offence of night-walking have scarcely increased. Leaving out these two offences for Suffolk County only, — as a concession, if you wish, to increasing virtue in Boston, — and combining two that belong together, — fornication and lewdness, — we have these results for the entire State. Each of these ten offences of a licentious nature has steadily increased in each quinquennial period since 1860, until convictions for every one of them, with a solitary exception, have more than doubled in the twenty years, while convictions for that one have risen from 16 to 28. The totals are, for each five years: 1860–64, 719; 1865–69, 851; 1870–74, 1,164; 1875–79, 1,972. Note the per cent of increase over the preceding five years in each period, — $18\frac{1}{2}$, 37, 70. While, then, crime generally has increased 20.4 per cent, the population 50 per cent, this class of crimes has increased 174 per cent, or eight times as fast as crime in general, and more than three times faster than the population, and with accelerating rate.

I add that the exceedingly cautious report of the specialist employed will make Boston appear in the census as having 1,770 professional prostitutes, notwithstanding the reported decrease in convictions of the classes already named! Put these facts alongside the divorce statistics, and keep it in mind that this increase of licentious offences is found over nearly the entire State, with little variation. It is as noticeable in Berkshire, Franklin, and Plymouth counties as it is in Suffolk and Middlesex.[1]

Add to this the fact that the number of children born out of wedlock in the State has risen in the same period from 8 in 1,000 to 17, and the most rapid increase has been in the last six years, while in just those years England has as rapidly improved. And so far as I have examined the few registration reports of the other States, I find similar facts, whose force, however, is modified somewhat by the fact that greater care in securing returns tends to increase the number reported in later years.

You now ask, as I did, do these statistics fairly, or in any good degree even, represent the condition of things here and all over New England? Are the statistics given even half true? Is there not a better public conscience, a stricter enforcement of the laws? That I might do a little to meet this inquiry, and throw more light if possible on the general subject, I

[1] The value of statistics of crime and divorce would be greatly enhanced if the States should require the courts to make record in all cases of convictions for crime, and divorces granted, of the nationality, residence by town or city, age, number of the marriage severed by divorce, and length of time married, with all other social facts that in any way will exhibit the origin and causes of crime and divorces.

sent a list of questions to a hundred or more gentlemen in nearly all parts of New England, mostly judges, state-attorneys, lawyers, police officers, large numbers of physicians and specialists, with a few clergymen. Nearly all responded. About seventy letters are of value for the purpose of classification. These cover probably one hundred towns and cities, giving the opinions of nearly two hundred persons who were consulted in their preparation. I form, so far as these letters go, the opinion that there is probably less of open and coarse vice of certain kinds in many respectable country towns than there was seventy or eighty years ago, — very likely less than fifty years ago. But, with this exception, which covers a few only of our country towns, and occasionally a city, as correct a summary of opinion as I could give would be like this : In three fourths of the localities reporting on this point licentiousness is said to be increasing. In nearly as many the destruction of unborn life goes on as fast, or faster, than ever. Physicians are very emphatic on this point, and many speak with great indignation of the wicked practices of some church-members. In one half the places licentiousness and drinking are found together, while one quarter report more licentious than intemperate persons in their communities. Nearly all find the increase among the native population, while several call attention to the recent increase among persons of foreign birth, and especially their descendants in the second generation. Several speak in emphatic condemnation of the mischief done by commercial travellers, and others complain of vice in shops. Very few report an improved public conscience, or stricter punishment of vice and its crimes; while on no point do I find so near an approach to unanimity as in the opinion that the public conscience is dormant, and that these offences are punished less frequently than formerly. And all the while there is, if we may depend on the statements of one who ought to know, a vast amount of obscene literature poured over the country.

This is not an agreeable report. I know it is largely mere opinion, to be taken with allowance. But I submit that it is worthy of careful consideration, and should stimulate the most diligent private and official investigation. We are better, probably, in respect to religion, in education, and in some phases of morals, than we were; but in chastity I fear we are not.

See how this question of morals among us is regarded. The French Commission to the International Exhibition of 1876 reported, concerning us, "the need of a complete organization of regular moral instructions," and called attention to the fact "that the family and church have little power over the young, and that the increased contagion of vice has a bad influence on public morality." It is said that Dr. Legge, after showing some members of the Chinese legation from London over the University of Oxford, asked one of them — a young man quite in sympathy with Christianity — his opinion as to the merits of the Chinese and English systems of education. "I think," said the young man, "that for the purposes of science and general information the schools in England are infinitely better than any teaching we have in China. But then, for *moral* purposes, making men good citizens and moral ones, discharging all the duties of humanity, my impression is that our schools in China are better than those in England!" And yet the French commission thought us especially lacking in this very matter. Does any one point, for answer, to the immorality of China? I reply, Let him wait until our institutions are a quarter as old as those of China, and our population half as great. "America," to quote Mr. Cook, "is in the gristle yet."

Here let me take the testimony of two American witnesses as to the effect of the evils of divorce and the related vices. The first shall be in regard to the peril to our institutions. The venerable ex-president of Yale College, who has given us our best American works on political science and divorce, wrote at the close of the War of the Rebellion these words, — and there is no man more careful in his statements than Dr. Woolsey, — "Rome is a most interesting study for us Americans, because her vices, greed for gold, prodigality, a coarse material civilization, corruption in the family, as manifested by connubial unfaithfulness and by divorce, are increasing among us. We have got rid of one of her vices, slavery, and that is a great ground of hope for the future. But whether we are to decay and lose our present political power depends upon our ability to keep family life pure and simple." [Divorce, p. 49.] These are the words of a profound student of our political institutions, written fifteen years ago.

The other witness is a student of business and its laws, as well qualified, perhaps, as any man in New England to speak of the things that affect capital and labor. The State of Massachusetts puts Carroll D. Wright at the head of the Bureau of Statistics of Labor. She asks his opinion upon certain points. He gives it in his official report for 1880, as follows : " The study of the questions belonging to us to consider, extending over a half-dozen years, has taught us that the industrial and social condition of the laboring classes, as related to the permanent prosperity of the productive industry of the Commonwealth, is more affected by the presence of crime, poverty, and the disorganizing influences resulting from the decrease of marriages, increase of divorces, and kindred matters, than from many if not all the bad economical conditions resulting from want of comprehension of the true relations of labor and capital." [Report of Massachusetts Bureau of Statistics of Labor for 1880, p. 125.]

I have not said, you will observe, that divorce and licentiousness are as cause and effect to each other, though this is partly true. But I think that I have shown that the two evils are increasing together, and often you will find the increase in close relations. Let me call attention, for a moment, to certain facts as to the second object of marriage, — the giving of offspring to the world. I cite the well-known fact of the decrease in size of the New England family. The family of Massachusetts — including both native and foreign — fell from an average of 4.69 in 1865, to 4.60 in 1875. The marriage rate — that is, ratio of persons married annually to the population — has fallen in twenty years from a higher figure than reported in any European country to the level of Austria, and lower than in any country except Sweden. The number of children under five years of age in Vermont was 154 in every 1,000 inhabitants in 1830, and 113 in 1870, having fallen to 100 in 1860, and rising chiefly because of the foreign element. The birth-rate in New England is probably as low as in any European country; among the native stock, far lower. And there are certain losses of the maternal functions, well known to physicians, which are considered by them as exceedingly significant. It is not beyond the probabilities to say that if these things go on even at less than their present rate, the native New-Englander will practically disappear in less time than has elapsed since the landing at Plymouth. I am told the state of things is not much better among those who have settled in the West. Here is one of the stubborn facts of the times. Henceforth if the student of American institutions continues to visit Plymouth Rock, he must also take a good look at Castle Garden, and study the black population of the South.

Look at one more class of facts. In the Western Reserve — comprising the twelve northeastern counties of Ohio, settled mainly by emigrants who went from Connecticut long before that State made its new departure in divorce, and containing, it is said, a purer New England stock than can be found in the entire country, unless it be in parts of Maine — the ratio of divorces to marriages was 1 to 11.8 for the two years 1878 and 1879, while in the rest of the State it is 1 to 19.9. Nor is the worst of the Reserve in the cities. The ratio in Ashtabula County, among a farming people originally from New England, is 1 to 8.5. And in Lake County the proportion of divorce suits begun to marriages is 1 to 6.2, and of divorces granted, 1 to 7.4. Unless there be like counties in Maine, this is the worst county for divorces in the United States, except, for a few years, Tolland County, Conn. But if you go down to Gallia County, peopled with Welshmen and Southerners, the ratio is 1 to 50, and in Coshocton 1 to 47.2. The divorce rate in those counties of the Reserve is several times what it is in these and other counties. I am told, too, that the birth rate in Ohio is lowest where the divorce rate is highest. It is said that the people of these counties are the most intelligent and virtuous of any in the country, and that the law-abiding citizens of the Reserve go to the courts for divorce, while those in other counties do not. This latter may be partly true of people reared in the South; but I suspect not of the Welsh, nor of others, to anything like the extent necessary to account for the excess in divorces.

Is divorce, then, a virtue, in spite of the New Testament? An answer to this question is, that nearly all divorces occur among those outside our Christian congregations, and generally among people noted neither for intelligence nor virtue. It is neither a virtue, nor yet the proper safety-valve of our social life; for the evils it ought, in the opinion of many, to check are increasing. I suggest rather that divorce is one form of social disease appearing in a highly bred people like those of the New England type, just as other forms of life, when carried to a high degree of perfection, become liable to their own peculiar and insidious tendencies, which, unless carefully watched and checked, are constantly working to throw down the results of high culture to the lowest forms of degradation. It is generally true, I think, that divorce and kindred vices mostly appear among those who, while reared under the principles of our best New England life, fail to accept all those principles in their integrity, and are thus thrown by the influence of those they do accept into base perversions of the true New England ideas. It is not unlikely that Spiritualism, Free-love, Divorce, and the sheer materialism of large numbers all have some such origin. Mormonism and the late Oneida system of social life are in no small degree other forms of the evils under consideration. They are both largely Yankee notions in their origin and leaders. Joseph Smith, Brigham Young, and J. R. Noyes were all from Vermont.

It is significant that within the last twenty years it is approximately true that divorces and separations have doubled in New England, in England and Wales, in France, and in Belgium. Switzerland is said to have enacted a new divorce law in 1874, by which divorces are greatly facilitated. The ratio to marriages in some cantons is as high as 1 to 14; and the bill of M. Naquet, in France, was rejected in the Assembly only by a vote of 247 to 216.

This leads to the notice of some facts and opinions of still wider significance. For a long time society in Christian countries has been making more of the individual, and less of the family, as its organic unit. Sir Henry Sumner Maine sums up the conclusions of an exceedingly interesting part of his "Ancient Law" by saying, "The movement of the progressive societies . . . has been distinguished by the gradual dissolution of family dependency, and the growth of individual obligation in its place. The individual is steadily substituted for the family, as the unit of which civil laws take account." [Ancient Law, p. 163.] Though he uses the term "family" in a wide sense, it is inclusive of the stricter use of the term. "Contract," he says, " is the tie between man and man which replaces those forms of reciprocity and rights which have their origin in the family." And he concludes the chapter by saying that "the movement of the progressive societies hitherto has been a movement from *status to contract*." Nothing, it seems to me, could be truer of our American practice in marriage than its tendency to reverse the true order, and sink the *status*, to which the contract of marriage leads, in the contract itself. And the tendency reaches far beyond the marriage bond.

That remark, too, of Herbert Spencer has signifi-

cause, which declares that Individuation and Genesis are antagonistic to each other. Carpenter, I think, and others note the same law in physiology. Mr. Spencer says: "The development of society, as well as the development of man and the development of life generally, may be described as a tendency to individuate, — to become a *thing*." This is illustrated in a remarkable degree in the drift of New England social life. The decrease of marriages and births, the changes in the physical constitution of women, the disposition to seek not only the support of life, but its pleasures and great ends, outside the family relation, are patent facts. And when we think of the effects of that fundamental principle of Protestantism, — the right of the individual conscience — and of its formative power over our religious and political institutions; when we recall the influence of Rousseau and his social contract upon the minds of some of the political leaders of our country; when we consider the emphasis we have naturally given to the rights of the individual in the achievement of national independence, in giving freedom to the slave, and in doing a greatly needed work — in many respects at least — for the emancipation of woman, it need not surprise us to find the idea of the family, as the fundamental unit and great organizing element of society, somewhat obscured. This has been wellnigh inevitable while we were busy in behalf of human rights, and it has been greatly aided by the drift of nearly all civilized society. And to these forces must be added the effect of modern wealth, especially as developed under the influence of machinery and the laws of trade. There is an effect of these laws, which, if not the dominant one, is at least very powerful, and which is disintegrating to the family. Commerce is chiefly concerned with the mass and the individual. A tendency exists here to treat human life as increasingly individual, — each man struggling for himself, each woman for herself, against the mass, often with neglect or downright murder for the poor innocents. The modern factory and salesroom are in some considerable degree a grave peril to the marriage relation and the family.

It does not wholly surprise me to hear thoughtful and patriotic Catholics say, "Your whole theory of society is wrong. It is based on individualism. Your doctrine of human equality is the outcome of that false Protestant notion which asserts the right of the individual conscience to interpret the Bible for itself. Not only the old French Republic was utterly wrong, but the new is equally so. Even the American Republic is radically wrong. The logic and practice of Protestantism end religiously in atheism and socially in communism. See its inevitable fruits in your divorces, your lack of reverence for parents and civil authority, and in your godless Protestants, who care nothing for the church, God, or even morals." Here that church joins issue with us, and indeed with all modern society. Is the point well taken? and must the alternative become Rome or Rousseau? A large number of our people say yes, and eagerly accept individualism in nearly all its destructive forms; and this generally unchurched, often atheistic, and frequently grossly immoral class constitutes one of the most dangerous perils to our institutions.

If I have made myself understood, you learn from this rough outline that the family is suffering in four ways in New England. More than two thousand divorces annually, reaching twice that number of persons directly, and indirectly many times more, are destroying its vital bond with, as yet, but the beginning of an earnest attempt at reform. That is the blow aimed at the life itself. Secondly, licentiousness, as shown by the best accessible statistics of crime, is in most localities increasing, and rarely has been grappled with at all as earnest men and women are taking hold of intemperance. As divorce destroys the moral bond, so licentiousness corrupts the physical basis of the family, while it poisons its moral life. The physical basis of marriage is sex, which next to life is the profoundest fact in nature and society. Thirdly, marriage is giving fewer children to the world; and, fourthly, the growth of individualism, under the influence of civil and economical laws and social and religious forces, tends to lessen the influence of marriage, the family, and the home over the individual, and especially in society. Thus the bond and the threefold end of marriage suffer together, though, it may be, in varying degree.

A part of this evil is due to temporary causes,—slightly to the war, but more, I must think, to financial influences,— and greatly encouraged, in the case of divorce, by most careless and reprehensible legislation and court practice. Climate, food, and kindred influences are at work also. But to me the prime causes lie deeper, and run back into the most serious problems of modern society. For this reason I have preferred to outline the subject in its broader relations rather than go into the details of mere divorce. I do not think the facts as to divorce can be properly seen without much study in all these directions.

Now comes the question, What are we doing to meet this evil and its related vices? The Christian public is beginning to move in earnest for reform in divorce legislation, and ought to succeed. But there is other work to be done. Law is the expression of public opinion. That needs vigorous cultivation. When a religious newspaper devotes two solid columns — as one in this city did week before last — to the teaching of the simplest elements concerning marriage and divorce to an intelligent man, who, to all appearance, holds the notions of a heathen of the days of the effete Roman Empire, with the feeling that it has enough readers of that class to justify this use of its crowded columns, it is time the schoolmaster and tract-distributer were abroad.

But where shall we get the tracts? The obscene press is busy. What is the Christian press doing? Diligent inquiry of leading Protestant publication and tract societies having offices in this city discover two tracts on divorce, and less than a dozen — mostly cheap apologies for what we ought to have — on one to two only of the licentious vices and crimes. More than one or two societies tell me, "We have nothing of the kind." But a single temperance society has over seven hundred publications! Here is one way in which the Catholics take a wise care of their people that we do not of ours. You find no lack of good instruction in their publications on these subjects. It is also noteworthy that Massachusetts, in a term of years, changed her divorce system and was far down towards the level of Connecticut in actual practice, without — so far as I can learn — a single persistent protest from her Christian press or from the platform, and with probably only now and then a cry of alarm from the pulpit. And we have been holding up our hands in horror at Connecticut and Indiana, while Maine has gone beyond Connecticut in the business of settling family quarrels in her courts.

I know all that some will say about the difficulty of treating delicate subjects. President Dwight complained in his times that "the general prejudice against any public exposure of the evils attendant upon the violation of the seventh commandment has been carried to a length unwarranted either by the Scriptures or common sense." He refused to be bound by the false standard of the times, and a moral revolution was wrought in New Haven. Jonathan Edwards was thrust out of his pulpit, it is said, more for his plain dealing with the vices of the young than for any other reason; but the cause of religion and morality gained by his fidelity. If these things are as some allege, we had better expunge the seventh commandment, prepare an expurgated edition of the Sermon on the Mount, and cut out whole chapters of the Epistles to the Corinthians; in fact, revise the Bible and the Prayer-Book in the interests of prudery. But most of you will agree that no truth in religion or morals will have very much influence over private life long after it has ceased to be a frequent theme of the pulpit. There must be some way, therefore, in which vice can be wisely denounced, and chastity properly taught and encouraged, by public and private instruction. Intemperance and lust are the twin vices of society, together begetting most of its crime and misery. No attack upon the one is well made unless it is supported in some way by an assault upon the other.

We need a literature on this subject, scientifically sound and scripturally authoritative. *A thorough examination of the nature, the rights, and the place of the family in civil society is the duty of the hour.* In this work will be found the key to the whole problem. The study of the institutions of society, the teachings of biology, especially of human physiology, will show that our Lord did not lay more sure the foundations of personal liberty and individual perfection of character than he did the foundations of a stable human society in his doctrine of marriage and divorce; and we shall see that the safety of American society especially lies in our ability to use this organic unit of the family in all its completeness, and charged with all its created force.

And now we may reply to the criticism of Catholics. We do not see the use of fleeing to Rome to escape the evils of America. Italy and the Catholic countries of Europe are too full of illegitimate children for that; and we hesitate still more when we learn that Catholic Belgium has doubled her separations and quadrupled her divorces in the last forty years. All honor to the noble stand the Catholics of America have taken in the defence of marriage and for the protection of unborn life! But our hope, and their hope too, is in that grand old Protestant way of digging deeper into the Scriptures, especially those words of our Lord ending with that warning, "What, therefore, God hath joined together, let not man put asunder." Here Catholics and Protestants may join hands. When the family is recognized in its nature, as having both a moral and physical constitution, as possessing, next to individual existence, a life and unity of greater strength and importance than any other natural organism in the world, and is so respected and used, we shall not only find safety, but give new life and promise to American institutions. American institutions and Protestantism are no failure. There is more light in the Word of God for society.

We need to do vigorous work now because of the timeliness of this agitation. Growing Mormonism, for one thing, challenges modern civilization and is preparing to stand battle. We cannot evade the conflict. Especially that great antislavery sentiment of the North, which indicted slavery and polygamy as "the twin relics of barbarism," must stand firm here. "By giving up slavery," wrote F. D. Maurice of us, "by overthrowing the horrors which it introduced into the marriage relation, — horrors with which nothing in the worst records of polygamy can be compared, —

they have borne the true witness against Mormonism." [Social Morality, p. 63.] The President has put the issue on the right ground. As Dr. Wharton says, "Marriage is not merely a contract, but an international institution of Christendom. . . . Nor do the features of marriage derive their force from the legislation of any particular State. They existed prior to any territorial legislation." [Conflict of Laws, p. 122.]

But the Mormons will turn upon us when pushed with this doctrine. Already they declare that their peculiar institution checks vice, and they are not slow in making comparisons with us. We feel some of these things. Professor Phelps wrote, a year ago (I quote by permission): "We are not half awake to the fact that by our laws of divorce and our toleration of the 'social evil,' we are doing more to corrupt the nation's heart than Mormonism, tenfold. Vice, avowed and blatant and organized, to a large extent nullifies itself, so far as self-diffusion is concerned. But vice, lurking and still, trickles into all the crevices of society. A nation of Mormons is impossible, — not so a nation of libertines." That is the voice of Andover.

Look to the South. To one race of five millions the home has been but a chance, and marriage a mockery; while the other has been corrupted with the licentiousness of the two races. The tissue ballot is an evanescent evil; the fast multiplying black voter, a growing peril of vast proportions. Much as the South needs education, she needs the home more. The education that gives her the schoolhouse, or some other, must transform the negro hovel into a home. The philanthropy of the North will not complete its work until it has united, if possible, with the justice of the South in giving the negro a Christian home. The two great institutions of property and marriage have risen together, and exist in mutual dependence. Therefore the business interests of the South, as well as its social regeneration and political welfare, call for the soundest theory and the most correct practice of the family. The defence of Indian rights, too, has at last been made to turn on individual property in a home, thus melting away the ice of barbarism in the rights of Christian civilization.

Or, finally, if we regard our future as a whole, and think of hundreds instead of tens of millions of people, with wealth and resources beyond the dream of the wildest fancy of the Old World organized into gigantic corporations, and all these interests intrusted to universal suffrage, making wealth in some form the great coming question, or if we think of earlier perils when, at the next commercial crisis, European communist and native demagogue join hands, we need be sure that the bulwark of the family be set firm as the mountains to meet the shock, and that we may not, like the England of to-day, be toiling in the seas because her system of tenure of property in land forbids a true home to the masses.

The line of an old Roman poet runs like this: "He taught them divine laws, instituted marriages, and built spacious cities." "Nothing," said the writer quoted in opening, "can be more philosophical than the succession of ideas here presented by Calvus." America is fast building cities. Let her not forget the divine laws and the institution of marriage. For, by as much as she is to be more than the older nations, by so much must her corner-stone of the family be broader and more enduring than that of other countries.

Nothing, if I may say it, leads so surely into the heart of these living issues as does this question of Divorce. It is our opportunity, that we cannot fairly grapple with it without being compelled to bring the whole subject of the Family to the front. This extremity of the nation is the opportunity of the Christian Church. Let the Church so proclaim the doctrine of the Family that all the people shall take up the words of the President: "The sanctity of marriage and the family relation are the corner-stone of our American society and civilization," and make them known to every man, to every woman, and to every child in the land. They deserve to be cut into the rock of the mountain passes of Utah. Let California, if she must have something to calm her fears, write these words in Chinese characters at her Golden Gate. But let us continue to proclaim them as the right of the Indian and the best hope of the South; let us so set them that commerce shall read them and the unlettered immigrant inquire their meaning as he enters the harbor of New York; while we do not fail to cut them into the granite canopy over Plymouth Rock.

It will be time enough for Utah and the South to sneer at divorce and vice in New England when they shall have begun reform within their own borders. Massachusetts or New England will utter no word of censure for Utah or South Carolina which she does not intend shall be heard at home.

IX.

SIGNIFICANCE OF THE HISTORIC ELEMENT IN SCRIPTURE.

By REV. J. B. THOMAS, D.D.

IX.

SIGNIFICANCE OF THE HISTORIC ELEMENT IN SCRIPTURE.

By REV. J. B. THOMAS, D.D.

MY theme is "The Significance of the Historic Element in Scripture." I propose to follow in its discussion that inductive method which is usually characterized as "the scientific," but which may with equal propriety be termed the *natural* method. For every child is an inductive reasoner, when from two facts observed, namely, fire seen and pain felt in contact, he constructs the theory that fire burns; a hypothesis with which he is usually content without taking the further step necessary to satisfy the rigidly scientific mind, of repeated verification. It is certainly one of the illustrations of that "total depravity" of the human intellect, which the men of intellect are so apt to deride, that it should have persisted so obstinately in tracing its pyramids downwards, hanging them from an aerial apex; that it should canonize the man who insisted on taking the earth as a foundation. Perhaps nobody has of late years better illustrated the proverbial virility and clearness of the New England mind than Theodore Parker. He was wont to quote with gusto the satirical *mot* upon the Hegelians,—that "part of them were still milking the barren heifer, and the rest were holding the sieve." While at the same time Boston Brahminism was holding up its fine woven sieve to catch the ethereal drops wrung by him with rationalistic fingers from the udder of Transcendentalism.

The present time is more prosaic and more wise. It demands, first of all, a fact; then for comparison and inference other facts; then for verification again facts. Here seems safe journeying; for although our intermediate theory be but a tremulous wire bridge, it stretches from rock to rock.

I. PRELIMINARY SUGGESTIONS.

Still, however, precaution is needful, for our wire-spinners are capricious, and even the rocks, under the gaze of our atomic philosophers, have become clouds of vapor dancing in the sunbeam.

1. *Fact.* — Since we must begin with a fact, it is appropriate to inquire, "What is a fact?" And here, as we are more in danger of being cheated by sophistry than imposed upon by common sense, it is better to point out two or three misleading distinctions. The first I mention is the laying a heavy strain on the *antithesis between a fact and a phenomenon*, and insisting that the latter cannot be the basis of a logical induction. "First catch your hare," tauntingly says my scientific friend. But my hare when caught

is only a phenomenon. I seek the ultimate fact beneath; I flay him; I dissect him; I cinder him; I resolve him into his chemical constituents. The elements reached are not yet ultimate, although beyond microscopic reach; and I am told that when found each of this countless group of atoms will be a complex sphere whose movements are as immeasurable as those of the solar system, and involve a problem which no mathematician even knows how to attack. I think you will agree that the search is hopeless. Is it not better to accept the phenomenal hare as a sufficient basis, either of soup or logic, than to destroy it in quest of the reality, which is phenomenal after all? "Life" may be only a phenomenon, but it is quite as real a fact as "protoplasm," and is not explained by being ignored in behalf of "carbonic acid and water."

Again, confusion is introduced by *limiting the term to the phenomena of sense alone*, thus excluding all testimony from other sources. The eye is a fact, and so the image upon the retina and the tremulous movement of the optic nerve; and these being verifiable by sense are fit bases for induction. But not so the visual impression, the memory, the thought of that which was seen. The event seen is a fact, but the same event recounted has ceased to be a fact, having gone beyond the range of external perception. If this be so, the bulk of scientific induction and the whole of historic reasoning are baseless. The facts of consciousness and of belief on testimony may be less available for logical purposes, but they are not less real, because belonging to a different sphere. It is further *alleged, that nothing is to be accepted as fact that is beyond experience,* that is, that has not been proven. But this is to confound facts with theories. Facts are observed; theories are proved. Pregnant terms are sometimes used, which increase the confusion; as when it is said that no man ever saw a miracle, — for the term "miracle" involves not only a fact, to which the senses may testify, but the hypothesis of its supernatural origin. The fact may be accepted on the testimony of the plainest man; its occult cause may bewilder the philosopher. Moreover, it is worth observing that the sceptical attitude involved in this definition paralyzes inquiry with the first step; for our first fact must be verified by comparison with other facts, and by the trustworthiness of our own experience, while as yet we have no experience. It assumes, against all observation, that we are born Pyrrhonists. On the contrary, life itself is possible only upon faith in the fidelity of instinct and the observing faculties, and in the predominant truthfulness of men. It will be sufficient, then, to recognize as *prima facie* fit basis of reasoning whatever is given on the testimony of consciousness, of sense, or of unimpeached witnesses.

2. *Theory.* — A preliminary word is also needful as to the meaning and function of theory. And first, it is well to remember that *theory must rest on observation, and cannot, therefore, lawfully precede it.* To proceed to the study of the Bible on the assumption of its certain inspiration, or under a protest against its possible inspiration, is in either case to renounce

the inductive method and return to the "high *a priori* road." For inspiration is a question not of fact, but of theory. It cannot be observed, but must be inferred. There is this special danger also in the preliminary application of a theoretic term: that, while it is in fact to the last degree nebulous and plastic, the inquirer, starting out with a straight-edged conception of its meaning, is tempted either to blink incongruous facts, or to torture them into conformity to his straight line; or, failing this, to renounce the term altogether. To one man inspiration may mean faultless precision of syllable and date; to another, direct and oracular dictation of historic as well as didactic truth; to another, supervisory restraint against harmful error in doctrine; to another, only spiritual exaltation and suggestion, without release from human infirmity; and so on through all the hypothetic spectrum. False theories and imperfect theories there are certain to be, even upon the facts; but vain theories, scornfully ignoring the existence or repudiating the need of facts, there do not need to be.

Again, *erroneous impressions* are apt to arise, as to the nature and value of inductive theory, *from the use of sweeping phrases;* such as that which Mr. Herbert Spencer uses, when he proposes to establish his theory upon an "exhaustive induction" from all the facts of nature and humanity.

This would, indeed, be a task for Omniscience, and the residual conclusion very nearly a mathematical certainty. A similar implication is involved in the alleged methods of the positive philosophy. The original theoretic horizon, it is said, was the theological,—boundless, but, on exploration, empty; the lines were set closer in the metaphysical, but this proved also on trial a fruitless realm; and we are accordingly reduced within the tight rim of the positive, by the rigid and conclusive processes of experimental elimination. Let us seek an analogy in cosmology. Once this earth was man's universe; its measure boundless, the low-bending heavens ministering to it with torch-lights, that men called stars. We have reduced the illimitable boundaries of the earth, for we have gone round it. We have exploded the ancient superstitions as to the Hyperboreans, for we have visited them. We have weighed our earth and proved it, and found it solid, and our knowledge concerning it seems nearly as positive and spherically complete as the earth itself. But have we got the universe into our crucible and reached an ultimate analysis of it? Unfortunately for that hypothesis, Copernicus has meantime found his Archimedean fulcrum, and tilted our earth and our spherical philosophy with it into the illimitable. "The heavens have gone off," since our childhood, "and become astronomical."

And the continents of the skies have not ceased to be, or to challenge the reverent or unsatisfied soul, though islanded for a time in this corner of space, to a broader vision and a nobler hope.

The theoretic process is positive, not negative. Its results are obtained by collating our knowledge, not by sifting our ignorance; we proceed from the centre toward the circumference; and our results, so far as the universe is concerned, can be probable only, and not certain, as they might be if we proceeded from an explored circumference, with convergent lines, to a single centre.

It is manifest, therefore, that without omniscience and eternity we can never logically exclude the supernatural. The well of causes is too deep for our plumb, the rim of space too distant for our lines. The electric message seems supernatural to the savage, and a crimson star would have startled the ancient astronomers.

Again, an inductive theory, being *only a suggested explanation of the coincidence of certain facts, is not necessarily overthrown by casual contradictions;* at least in the absence of another theory more exact. The business of the theorist is not primarily to explain exceptions, but to discover a law. And this suggestion is important; since the critical instinct seems to find so much ranker growth in the mire of intellectual self-conceit than the love of affirmative truth. Too many men postpone the study of Scripture as a whole, until their sagaciously apprehensive nerves are quieted by being told "where Cain got his wife." Criticism has its place, to be sure; but it should be a finger-post at the crossing, not a toll-bar at the entrance of the road,—a pruning-knife, not an axe at the root of the tree. Phlebotomy has its uses in the hands of a skilful practitioner; but in the hands of an undeveloped and headlong critic, it resembles rather the singing of the mosquito, whose sting irritates without profit, and who becomes conspicuous only by the blood he borrows from creatures nobler than himself. Criticism, therefore, may not profitably supersede or antecede theorizing. Let the critic first tell me *his* theory, then we can match swords.

3. *Verification.* — Faith in miracles and prayer is challenged in our day to *accredit itself by experimental test*, or be relegated to that limbo of superstition which has been escaped by "all sensible men." Professor Huxley makes the test of reality to consist of a capacity of "being verified by experiment any time we like to try." Mr. Darwin thinks it worth stating, as an argument, that "no man ever *saw* a special creation." And Mr. Spencer gives the *coup de grâce* to the idea of creation itself by suggesting that it is "inconceivable." Now, in connection with all this, it is well to remember that we are reduced by physical philosophers to the necessity of faith in two fundamental theories; neither of which is verifiable by experiment, and each of which rests on an idea which is inconceivable. For the Newtonian theory of gravitation demands the action of a body where it is not, through a non-existent medium; and the commonly accepted theory of light rests on the assumption of a "luminiferous ether," which, according to the description of Dr. Young himself, while permitting us to live in and move through it without appreciable resistance, is yet "absolutely solid." Professor Jevons, in characterizing it, seems unconsciously to resort to a much-ridiculed phrase in our English

Bible, describing the space above us as "an adamantine firmament." It is clear, then, that hypotheses may still be admissible, which are directly verifiable neither by experiment, by reason, nor by testimony; if, taken as data, they give coherence and consistency to other hypotheses, which *are* so verifiable. If the assumption of a cause beyond the range of demonstration be a lawful resort as an explanation of facts otherwise inexplicable, why may not the assumption of a cause outside of nature be equally admissible as explaining facts for which nature cannot furnish an explanation? When cool-brained physics is driven to transcendentalism, it ought not to chide more docile faith for following. To those who have no scruple in believing that they themselves can bring back to life the shrivelled mummy of a boiled animalcule, we may well retort with Paul, "Why should it be thought a thing incredible *with you* that *God* should raise the dead?"

But even within the range of the verifiable, it is to be remembered that there are *planes of research that do not coincide*, and that a conclusion satisfactory in one may not be verifiable in another. The law of crystalline forms is geometric. There is strong temptation to prophesy that such symmetry will be still more marked as we ascend into the realm of biologic forms; but instead, the chief distinguishing mark of beginning life is the *breaking up* of symmetry. There is no lack of harmony, in the two lines of phenomena, but only of analogy. In like manner, the evolution of living forms by no means necessarily implies the evolution of the religious faculty. The history of human progress can no more safely be determined by the study of contemporaneous grades of society alone than geology can be concluded by the study of superficial geography. Our best effort in either case will be but a muddy guess. If there be a spiritual realm, therefore, it may safely be inferred that the certainty of its phenomena cannot be guaranteed, nor their nature perfectly interpreted, by processes purely physical or intellectual. These may create presumptions, or suggest partial analogies, but they cannot bring finality; for nothing in this lower realm is final. It is doubtless true that miracles are possible only to the believing. Faith, certainly, is a Scriptural condition. And the reason is obvious. No scientific study of external conditions, no practised keenness of scrutiny, can baffle the incredulity which, after it has exhausted the possibilities of ocular delusion, has still the inexhaustible realm of occult natural forces without, and of mental hallucination within, into which to retreat. The Dialectical Society tried spiritualistic phenomena, under precautions satisfactory to men so acute as Mr. Crookes and Mr. A. R. Wallace, and they were content. But of the remaining scientific world, "some mocked, and others said, We will hear thee again of this matter."

To sum up these preliminary observations: it will be my purpose to group together such pertinent facts as I may be able to gather from current observation, from monumental records, and from the testimony of men, living or dead, in Scripture or elsewhere, as to the "things which they have seen and heard," and also such as they have felt, and such as "have been most surely believed among" them; and upon such collection of facts to make such inferences as may seem reasonable in themselves, and not discordant with growing history.

II. THE BIBLE A FACT AMONG FACTS.

1. *The Bible and Christendom.* — The Bible is itself a fact as well as a record of facts. It does not melt before the gaze, nor crumble in the hand. It is overhung by an immense cloud of subjective personal experience, more or less indefinable and incommensurable; it is wrought into the foundations of various ecclesiastical organizations; its words are recast into divers symbols of faith and systems of doctrine; it is closely encompassed by a heavy growth of gloss and comment; it is the nucleus of an immense body of devotional literature; it is continually taking new phases in strange languages and in new translations in our own; and yet it is no more in danger of losing its identity and concreteness of outline by reason of these concomitants, than the light-house by reason of the floods of light it sheds, or the tree by reason of the fruit it bears. Unlike the Hindoo sacred books, — of which the original outline is gone, the substance being transmuted indistinguishably into the parasitic growth of comment that has infested and consumed them, — it bears but is not overborne. Like flower and bee, sealed up for future generations in the

amber of geology, the Old Testament was deposited in the Hebrew, which forthwith congealed, escaping henceforth the mutations of a living tongue; and the New Testament in the more fluent Greek (copied by many independent writers, whose very errors were to become in time, by interlacing testimony, reaffirmatory of the true text) was unwittingly hidden from the tampering or curious hand in dismembered sheets, under prosaic monkish essays, until the Greek language was also dead, and movable type ready to hide it from mutilation by stereotyped publicity. Then came forth the New and the Old Testament, linked henceforth in double and abiding testimony, — one book, the Book, to work its marvellous ministry in the earth.

If its errors be fatal, they cannot be remedied, for they are adamantine. No "ingenuity of exegesis" can avert the peril, for the original is in no cabalistic tongue, but is open to all scholarship. It seems, moreover, by the very sobriety and concreteness of its statements, to thrust itself purposely, as it has done actually, as a "stumbling-block" in the way of all travellers on the road to truth, which they may build upon or fall upon, but cannot miss.

Coextensive with the book is the realm which is characteristically known as Christendom. It has a distinct geographical area (the boundaries at least as clearly traceable as the kingdoms of physical science), a distinct literature, and civilization dominated by distinct ideas. I do not at this point assume that the Bible is the root of these; but only mark the exact coincidence of their range and the intimacy of their relation.

2. *The Old Testament and the Jews.* — If Christendom be an anomaly in the world, the Jews in Christendom and the world are no less anomalous, — a people without a country, without a civil nucleus, without a temple; a race poured out like a river into the salter sea, yet preserving its outline and its freshness to the farthest shore; malleable everywhere in the furnace and beneath the hammer of civil, social, and commercial custom, yet with domestic fibre utterly unbroken. So conspicuously do the old traits reappear, producing historic verisimilitude, that the mythic philosopher of the future can choose no fairer field than the essays of Macaulay, or the recent appeal to the Prussian king, placed beside the Scripture, to persuade the reader that the Scripture record was later than the nineteenth century, or that the record of our current history was mythical. For in Macaulay's time we find Mordecai still "sitting at the king's gate," and the essayist answering Haman's appeal against this alien people, "whose laws are diverse from all people; neither keep they the king's laws." And in the appeal of the German people we find the old Egyptian terror, because "the children ot Israel were fruitful and increased abundantly, and multiplied and waxed exceeding mighty, and the land was filled with them." Still, as of old, they seem to "dwell in tents," or rather, as when prepared for flight from Egypt, with "loins girded, shoes on feet, and staff in hand," as those who are "in haste." For, as

Professor Freeman explains, their persecutions have always arisen from their being *aliens*, and as aliens having no power to hold realty, but compelled to hoard their possessions in gold. Being thus by compulsion sojourners and capitalists, their presence has always inspired hate. Yet again, as in Egypt, "the more they afflicted them the more they multiplied and grew." Trodden under foot, ground to powder, scattered as chaff by the wind, their toughness has been the wonder of historians and the problem of ethnologists. "The Jew almost alone," says Professor Freeman again, "is sure of his pure blood" among all the nations.

And now, again, precisely coincident with Judaism is the Old Testament, treasured and read, not in modern vernacular, nor in the Septuagint Greek, although that is the work of their own scholars, but in the ancient and, as they insist, the original Hebrew. The splendor of their ancient ritual is gone; they speak many new languages, and wander amid strange peoples, surrendering much to courtesy or to rapacity; but their ancient Scripture they will not surrender. They find in it the core of genealogical pride, patriotism, political aspiration, and religion.

3. *The Bible in Relation to Current Facts.* — That there must be something more than a mere casual relation between the Bible and Christendom on the one hand, and the Old Testament and Judaism on the other, will, I think, be a natural suggestion to any candid mind. That the jagged edges of two sheets match here and there may be meaningless; but that

the irregular outline matches at every point, satisfies
the legal mind that they are counterparts, and that
their common indenture was designed.

Now, not only has the trend of progress been uniformly westward, outlining by its course the controlling influence of the Bible, as lines of verdure down the mountain's side in hot countries reveal the course of the running stream; not only does the world's history break asunder, as the Bible does, the one parting between the old Asiatic and the new European *régime*, as the other does between the Old Testament and the New, and at the very same era,—an era thenceforth stamped indelibly on all our coin and in all our literature, as though in perpetual reminder that the Lord and not Cæsar, by his stamp and superscription, claims these ages as his own. All this might possibly be attributed to a concurrence of natural causes,—the steady westward course to the uniform tidal drift of all terrestrial things following the sun (although the earlier migrations were clearly in diverse directions); and the change of civilization to a change of landscape, soil, and climate, although a like migration into the tempting Indian peninsula had ended only in a curdling lethargy.

But other circumstances to which I have alluded cannot be so explained. In the midst of this heaving flood, in which the ancient and petrified distinctions of language, race, custom, and traditions are lifted on the tumultuous wave, dashed against each other, and disappear, the mysterious Jew, tossed with the rest, and often submerged, alone, of all peoples, drifts on unbroken and unchanged. His phlegmatic conservatism is not due to his Semitic blood; for no nation of antiquity was more daring or progressive than the Phœnician, and none in modern times more aggressive than the Arabian. It is not due to isolation in business or life. He mixes in, and is pressed upon, by our civilization as by an atmosphere. Yet, while all other sects mingle, he resists intermarriage; European or American in sojourn, he remains an Asiatic in temper; transplanted out of the congenial past, he grows as an exotic in the unfriendly present, living a kind of posthumous life, a bush consuming yet forever unconsumed, like that which Moses saw. As the explanation of this anomaly, — this strange figure, looming against the horizon, among the whirling winds, spectral as a cloud, yet adamantine in outline, — I behold, clutched tightly in his hand, the ancient book which he himself accounts at once the record of his past, and the key to his present, existence.

4. *Origin of the Bible.* — That it is not the normal product of his national genius, no one will need to be assured who familiarizes himself with the Talmudic literature. The hand that in maturity produced such tawdry colors and incoherent forms, could never have created with unguided pencil the tranquil landscape of the twenty-third Psalm, or the Titanic splendors of Habakkuk's vision. That the Jew did not even comprehend the inner meaning of the priceless "oracles" committed to him, is confirmed by his rejection of the plainly prophesied Messiah. His

arrested development at that point, and the simultaneous outburst of new life in the believing Gentile world, clearly reveal the terribleness of his mistake. The book of which he, as the original custodian, thenceforth survives to be the appropriate witness, itself describes in prophecy his blind refusal and its consequence, — the forfeiture of his inheritance and the transfer of his destiny. Wearing the *tallith* in the synagogue to-day, he unwittingly republishes to every looker-on the Apostle's sad words, "the veil is upon their heart."

That their unique persistence against the tooth of time is due solely to their Messianic hope, seems so indisputable to Dr. Draper that in his book on the "Development of Civil Policy in America" he instances them, at the expense of his whole argument, as illustrating the power of an idea to master and reverse the otherwise overwhelming sway of Buckle's law. But the Messianic prophecy lies among the very germs of their history, and is interwoven with and moulds their whole record. It was not the fruit, but the root, of their development.

Professor Freeman also is so struck with the fact that their history is phenomenal — not having been shaped from without by natural force, but nucleated and vitalized from within by this extraordinary book — that he declares theirs "the strongest case in all history of a nation preserved in its purity by a marked and special religion." The case seems clear, then, that the destiny of this "peculiar people," lying outside the range of philosophic canons, has been developed in immediate connection with the book which was so long its special care, and which, though now a Gentile legacy, it still lingers to watch and confirm.

5. *The Bible and Modern History.*— To treat adequately upon the multiform relations of the Bible to modern history would be to honeycomb the whole realm of literature, science, art, politics, and domestic life. It is, as Professor Tyndall says, the "unquestionable antecedent" of our whole civilization. As flint in the soil at the root hides itself in the texture of wheat stem and oak, so the Bibles of Luther and Wickliff and their compeers, planted at the bottom of our printed literature, put fibre into and determined the very forms of speech through which State, school, and individual have poured their thoughts. The documents of diplomacy, judicial formulas, parliamentary routine, bear direct traces of Bible origin. It would be interesting to mark out, as time will not allow, the trend of the great courses of achievement in modern times; to observe how closely, as to period, they have coincided with eras of increased religious activity, and how far, as to great names, they have taken in believers and students of the Scripture. The men who have seen deepest into the mystery of things, and caught most of the prophetic breath of the coming morning,— such as Bacon, Kepler, Newton, Faraday, and others,— were earnest students of the Book in which they devoutly believed the heavens were truly reflected, and the earth's mysteries an "open secret." I trust a further study of the contents of the Bible

THE HISTORIC ELEMENT IN SCRIPTURE. 249

itself may vindicate the suggestion, that there is more than a casual coincidence in this fact.

It is interesting to observe how inevitably candid inquiry brings men back, by however circuitous a road, to the cardinal doctrines of the New Testament as the true goal of human perfectness. Mr. Herbert Spencer, building his colossal system of synthetic philosophy, after so wide and careful exploration, finds the tremendous pyramid converging at its topmost point to the truth which a "little child" might at the beginning get from Scripture. For in his "Data of Ethics" he sums up all in the humble hope and faith that "some reasoned form of the ethics of the New Testament" may yet become the life-core of society. He thus declares that this wonderful book, which has preceded the modern era, is still in advance of it, and its sublime ideal as yet unreached. Considering how slowly moral ideas are evolved, and the specially depressed condition of human society when the New Testament was written, the problem still remains unsolved, how, out of the least cultivated nation of that inferior age, there issued an ideal to which the nineteenth century looks up as still transcending its best attainments.

The conclusion seems fair, that some element unexplained and as yet inexplicable enters into the origin of these phenomena. The book did not "fall down from Jupiter" like the Ephesian image, it grew on earth; it was not written upon the sky in fire, but in human language in the earthly page; but though written by "hand of man," it seems to have been "under the wing of the cherubim;" its fruits and its unaccountable origin place it beyond the range of mere human phenomena.

III. HISTORIC INSIGHT.

From the relations of the Bible let us turn to its contents, seeking to learn thereby the secret of such power.

1. *The historic* element is unmistakable and conspicuous; it may even be said to be the controlling feature. For where, as in the Psalms or the Epistles, it does not take an avowed historic form, still it is instinct with the inner life of historic characters, and so a record of current facts, not the idle play of fancy. Indeed, in these features it supplies just those elements essential to the true picture of the passing time; elements once neglected, but, since Macaulay's day, recognized as essential to the very nature of true history. How diversified in authorship, in era, in locality, and in form: compendious statements of scientific truth; genealogies; state documents, like the Chronicles; idyls, like Ruth; statutes, like Leviticus; epics, like Job; lyric and didactic verse in Psalms; concrete earthly wisdom in Proverbs; pessimistic sighs in Ecclesiastes; commingled history, poetry, and oratory, as in the Prophets; unstudied memoirs in the Gospels; equally artless records of travel and experience in the Acts; Epistles which uncover the social and individual heart-history of the time; and the gorgeous vision of the evening, passing through night to morning, at the end!

But the record is as *comprehensive* as it is diverse, and being so comprehensive, how compact and clear in outline! Remember the grim criticism of Carlyle upon the disproportionate verbiage of our time compared with the severe sententiousness of the Pentateuch. In the hands of our modern chroniclers, he says, "the account of the burning of a Brunswick theatre takes more space than the creation of a world." As the quick sweep of Giotto's circle enclosed the rich revelations of his genius, as the oak lies in the acorn, so the whole Bible lies folded in the germinal sentence with which it begins. Mark the order of the unfolding universe: the spirit *moves*, the word is *spoken*, the firmament is *made*. We indeed approach these facts in an inverse order, "first natural, then spiritual;" but every new age makes clearer the truth that the coarser elements are the vehicles of the more subtile, — the spiritual was before, and is beneath, the material. In the light of the nineteenth century, when matter dissolved reveals light, heat, and electricity, and these again unwoven blend into the latest and central word of science, "motion," as the primal font of things, how strange to find this *last* word of science the *first* of Scripture! Again, in this time, when a *word* changes the boundaries and destinies of empires, holds the ponderous enginery in check or dashes it through the land, sends lightnings that they may go and say, "Here we are;" when brute force has receded and mind is supreme, — how noticeable that so long ago, in the very shadow of the massive pyramids, and of the Titanic despotism lying, like them, heavy on heart and hope, there came a vision so clear of a fact so deeply hidden, that mightier than the *hand*, the body's vehicle of power, is the *word*, the utterance of the soul.

The record thus beginning at the centre sweeps the whole circumference of history. It takes in the world, the race, the outer and the inner life. It accounts nothing insignificant or foreign that reveals a significant phase of human experience.

Yet, again, though so all-embracing, how symmetrically complete. It does not, like the childish Herodotus, pour an unassorted flood of gossip through its pages. It finds all history vertebrate, and along that vertebral line it moves, revealing the whole structure of the typical past. The Cainite races, the massive Egyptian, Chaldean, and Ninevite civilizations, the various changing fortunes of the world at large, are not overlooked, but put in their incidental and subordinate place; and so the perspective of history, unknown to the classic writers of a far later day, is recognized and preserved.

2. *Four underlying ideas* reveal themselves, namely:

a. The idea of structural unity. The universe is one; the groups in creation are single, yet make a complex unity; the human race is one; language is one; the Old Testament is one, sharply outlined, in its dominant conception of the *corporate and external*, from the New Testament, which is equally nucleated round the *individual and internal* life.

This sense of a pervading mental order is revealed also in the use of the type as representing the whole.

THE HISTORIC ELEMENT IN SCRIPTURE.   253

Israel is equally the man and the nation, and the nation reveals mankind. All history, thus having a symmetrical order, becomes, as Paul describes it in the case of Hagar, an "allegory." All nature becomes, as in the teaching of Jesus, a "parable." "How, then," said he, "will ye understand all parables?" The whole universe becomes a cryptogram, a "seven-sealed roll," which no man by earthly wisdom alone shall "prevail to open," but which may be unfolded, as in Patmos, to the devoutly open soul.

b. Historic continuity. The horizontal section of the plant gives a glimpse of its structural secret in ringed bark and curiously forming core; but the revelation is incomplete without the vertical section also from root to fruit, containing "seed after its kind." The one gives the mental, the other the natural order. The study of isolated facts is incomplete and misleading; and it can be remedied only when, having studied upwards and downwards, as well as right and left, our knowledge, like the perfect city, "lieth four square, its length and breadth and depth and height" being "equal." Geology must supplement geography.

In the history of man the study of contemporaneous social phenomena, ignoring the growing past, is in the literal sense of the word superficial. For it is man's special prerogative, as "a creature of large discourse," to look "before and after."

Now, the sense of the importance of historic order and continuity is specially prominent in Scripture. From Genesis to Revelation there is a steady flow, broken only at points such as the flood, and the gap between Old and New, where the breach is itself significant. The minuteness and emphasis of the genealogical record is conspicuous. Indeed, it seems sometimes, as in the broad wastes before the flood, to have scarcely any other purpose than by its scantiness of detail — as that "A begat B" and died — to remind us how vacuous the period was, but by the fidelity of the record to suggest the significance of unbroken continuity. The recapitulation of the register at the beginning of Chronicles and the Evangelists impresses us in like manner. We cannot fail, either, to notice the precisely logical order in which the necessarily antecedent forms take their place in the creative growth, — the simpler preceding the more complex, — and how in the unfolding of institutions there is an adapted progress, as they "are able to bear it." The line of progress is a growth, and not a mere superposition; hence every stage and item is significant.

c. Material and intellectual progress by empirical processes. The first man was houseless, and even tentless, garmentless, toolless, without writing or intelligent speech. He named the animals experimentally; he learned the awful secret of evil by the shock that threw his faculties off their spiritual centre, and his whole being out of gear with the universe, thenceforth "dim sounding on its perilous way." Outside Eden, tools, tents, and music were invented. The nomadic emerged into a more settled life; the tabernacle took root and solidified into a temple; tribes became a nation, and rural life and patriarchal simplicity gave place to the city, the tribunal, and the king. The "one lip and one stock of words" of the early world grew into dialectic divergence, not by the abrogation of the "stock of words," but by "confusion of lip;" so that phonetic reconstruction should show (as historically it does) the traces of a common primeval capital of speech, wrought into new languages, as the mutilated arches and columns of ancient temples have been wrought into the structures of later times. The accumulating knowledge of the fathers transferred to the children, as is often reiterated, is by them passed on, with elements added out of new experience, to their posterity, and so the "education of the race" (which is the idea not of Lessing, in its inception, but of Paul) went on.

d. Religious retrogression from ethical monotheism by intellectual apostasy, and moral suffocation under the weight of the physical. Paul, in the first chapter of Romans, makes a most logical inductive argument to show that heathenism bears the marks and shows the fruits of apostasy. He points to the indisputable moral degradation and the mental bewilderment of the time, and traces it back to the repudiation of an original knowledge which they "did not like to retain." This is an inverse statement of the facts as given in the historic record. The new-born man, uncultured and unripe, knew God by a direct intuition which is not further explained. Issuing from the fatal gate of departed "purity of heart," he no longer "sees God," but "gropes after him." Forthwith appear chaotic violence, animalism, — for they are "*flesh*," — and the cleansing flood.

Out of pervading idolatry Abraham is lifted. Israel perpetually topples into it as into an ever-surrounding gulf of corruption, until after long vicissitudes they are carried away into Babylon. There is here a marked antithesis between the successive stages of the intellectual and material on the one hand, and the religious on the other, — advance on the whole in the one, but equally definite decay in the other.

3. *Verification by Modern Research.* — Now, set this early conception of the inward anatomy and physiology of history beside the ultimate conclusions of the centuries accumulating testimony to this day.

a. Nothing is more conspicuous in modern methods than the introduction of the *comparative element* as enlarging and correcting the judgment upon single facts. Chemistry does not ignore the help of physiology, nor philology that of ethnology. The valley dweller cannot hope to judge the world without climbing the mountain-top for a wider horizon. Under that broader gaze the broken threads unite into a continuous design, — the mob of eccentric forms and forces fall into companies, regiments, divisions, and all wheel into line. The tangled meshes of the heavens are threaded out, the harp restrung, and under Kepler's touch the morning stars again break into song. It is upon the recognition of an underlying mental order, so rigorous that a single understood type becomes the key, — as when the bleaching skull took Oken into its confidence, whispering its secret to him, and the leaf grew transparent to the inseeing Goethe, — that science itself becomes possible. The more widely the sciences combine, the more manifest the convergence toward a *scientia scientiarum*, around whose single centre these disjointed arcs of knowledge may connect in an unbroken circle.

b. But *science has found its need as much of history as of comparison.* Its results in morphologic study are incomplete. It must know genetic relation also; its classification is not simply *artificial*, disclosing an ideal order, but natural, because there is a *real* order. Hence the emphasis upon all problems of origin, heredity, and growth. All studies tend to become historic. Humboldt and Ritter cannot understand the superficial *cosmos*, without lifting the crust of the earth, to study the underworking forces in their stratified historic chronicle. They see that the gaze must be deeper as well as wider, if they want the absolute truth of things. They find that knowledge must be also vertical. The scientific New Jerusalem, too, "lieth four square."

c. I need scarcely here dwell for a moment upon the further thought so well emphasized in our time, — the corner-stone of the system which Mr. Buckle, Sir John Lubbock, and others have wrought to such top-heavy proportions, — that *our civilization is normally the product of antecedent material and intellectual conditions.* It is plain that without telescope and microscope, opening our vision into the two worlds, hidden, one by its greatness and the other by its smallness, from our natural vision, the sweepingly inductive conviction of the all-pervading unity would not have naturally arisen. While the boundaries of the earth were unknown, its symmetrical structure could not be learned. Until, by long preparation, the social soil was fit for the seed, it could not grow. Imperfect statutes alone could befit imperfect Israel. They were not the best, but the best possible, considering "the hardness of their hearts."

I think it not inapt, therefore, to conclude that the marvellous insight which penetrated the fluent secret of this mysterious complex of nature and humanity, long before such vision could come in the order of natural development, — which saw the whole plant, leaf, flower, and fruit in the seed "before it grew," — was, somehow, touched with an element incommensurate with known and explored causes.

Is it rash to suggest that the eye, which gets to-day telescopic help beyond itself to range among the stars, may then have been enlarged by him who "*made* the stars also," and who "*formed the eye*"?

d. From every side direct testimony gathers, to the fact of a *Primitive Monotheism afterwards corrupted.* The monuments of Egypt, the ancient literature of India and Persia, the persistence of the original name of the "Heaven Father" from before the Aryan dispersion to our day (Dyaus piter, Zeus Pater, Jupiter, Unser Vater, Our Father), all combine to confirm the accuracy of the Scriptural statement. And this is the more noticeable because the exigency of modern theories had demanded, and their defenders had even passionately asserted, a contrary view. But that the believing in one God will not alone purify or perfect men, all history likewise assures us. The stagnancy of Hinduism, the barrenness of Mohammedanism, the decay of Persian civilization, are sufficient witnesses.

Not only is ethnic monotheism unfruitful in national life, it is not even self-preservative. Human nature seeks after a "sign," — a visible fragment of the Divine, — and slowly gravitates to the substitution of that for God. Thus in Athens, at its intellectual highest, religion is at its lowest. It was "easier" there "to find a god than a man," yet there was the altar "to the Unknown God."

IV. HISTORIC FORESIGHT.

1. *Facts.* — *a. Concreteness.* Christianity, says Dean Stanley, "alone, of all religions, claims to be *founded, not on fancy or feeling, but on fact and truth.*" The sobriety of tone, the circumstantiality, the precise, identification of locality and person by name, are specially remarkable in the Scripture record; because it is in these respects in contrast with the Oriental temper, and specially with the other sacred books of the East. The earlier part of Genesis is sometimes, indeed, called poetic, and this term is thought to carry with it a vague impeachment of its historic character. But to suppose that prose and poetry are synonymous relatively with truth and fiction, so that the poetic form makes false a statement which in prosaic form would be true, is like insisting that no portrait is trustworthy

which has not been laid out with rule and calipers. Poetry, it is true, deals largely in the symbolic; but it sometimes happens that the symbolic is the most direct, if not the only possible form by which the truth can be conveyed. "God said, Let there be light." How can the truth be more wisely shaped in words? Creation is beyond our analysis; but the energy which through imparted force produces light has its analogue in the human will, and the nakedest forthgoing of a will is in a word. "In the *word* of a king there is power." No physical formula, no philosophic circumlocution, can rival the accuracy of the world-old record, in whose sublimely simple utterance God's personality bursts into recognition, as light into the world.

The tendency to hero-worship and myth-making seems to be recognized and protested against in the case of Moses and Elijah, the two most likely candidates for apotheosis, by the unflinching disclosure of their frailties, — the emphatic after-reference to Moses as only a "servant," and Elijah as a "man of like passions" with us, — and by the clear statement how they were taken out of the reach of adoration while still men. Not only does the later Scripture recognize the literalness of the earlier, it insists upon and emphasizes it. The Sermon on the Mount assumes the reality of a former law-giving; the doom of Sodom is made the basis of present warning. Paul's argument in the Roman Epistle loses its leverage if there were no actual Adam, and he unhesitatingly rests the whole trustworthiness of the gospel on the literal resurrection of Christ from the dead. Mark the emphasis which Peter and John lay, in their Epistles, on the fact that theirs is original testimony, verified by eye and ear and hand, to the "flesh and blood" reality of the incarnation and resurrection, and not the outgrowth of "cunningly devised *myths*." So inextricably are the doctrines, the promises, and the claims of the Bible intertwined into its record of fact, that the effort to disentangle is sure to destroy them. To surrender the fidelity of the history in the Bible is to surrender the Bible itself; the Bible being witness.

b. Separate ages. Not less emphasized than the concrete verity of the events themselves is the *division of the history into distinct periods*, each usually parted from others by a conspicuous epoch, and having a certain unity and significance of its own. Many minor divisions of this character are traceable, as in the book of Genesis, where the recurrence of the formula, "These are the generations," etc., seems to indicate the beginning of a new era. But it will be sufficient for our purpose to distinguish a few more prominent ones after the apostasy. These are: the *Antediluvian* period; the *National* period of Israel, from Abraham to the Kings; the *Royal* period, thence to the Captivity; the *Teaching* period, thence to the Crucifixion; and the *Pentecostal* period, after the Resurrection. In the first of these nature reigned; the nations were all "suffered to walk in their own ways." Whereupon, overmastered by their conditions, they returned to the brutality of the primal "dragons in their slime," filling the earth with sanguinary "violence," until, like a dismasted and scuttled ship, the whole race settled out of sight in the seething waters. Thence began a new age, in which a "chosen people" were drawn out of the undistinguished multitude and "tried" under carefully devised conditions. The experiment was a protracted and painstaking one, but resulted at last in national decay and disheartenment. Anarchy reigned; for "every man did that which was right in his own eyes," and the "highways were deserted" because of freebooters. They lost even the tool-making art, sinking back into barbarian helplessness, in which, without "sword or spear among forty thousand," they were the easy prey of neighboring tribes.

Thereupon they were at their request remitted to their own wisdom, which they exercised in the substitution of a new *régime* for the Mosaic, making themselves "a king, like all the nations." Under this self-appointed experiment they grew rapidly to splendor under David and Solomon; but it was the splendor of the setting, not of the rising sun; whose light is crimson, too, with the vapors of decay. The "little finger" of oppression in the father grew to be "thicker" than his "father's loins" in the son; the leather thong became a scourge "of scorpions;" and the bruised and despairing remnants of the nation were dragged away into Babylon.

So ends the triple experiment which makes up the old *régime* and fills the outline of the Old Testament. Under the untrammelled tutelage of nature, under the sagaciously prescribed regulations of the Mosaic code, under the experimentally reached resort to regal rule, the problem has been fairly exhausted, as to whether a race or nation can be crowded to its true goal by the pressure of environment. It ends in heartbreak, exile, and the wail of the last prophet; which, turning toward the future, becomes a foreboding lest God "come and smite the earth with a curse." But through this foreboding sounds the tone of promise also; for Elijah the prophet shall return to prepare the way for the new kingdom of the heart. Not the old giants from before the flood, to hammer out massive weapons on cyclopean forges, nor Samson nor Shamgar to swing them in grotesque slaughter; not Moses, although, standing on majestic Sinai, bearing the adamantine tablets whose graven statutes can never be effaced, he be massive in character as the one and enduring in history as the other, — he shall indeed return at the Transfiguration, not to revive the old, but to bear witness that its hour is past, and to invoke acceptance of the new, for "the law made nothing perfect;" not Solomon, although "he made silver and gold at Jerusalem as plenteous as stones," and Jerusalem herself the crown jewel of the earth, — he "slept with his fathers" and does not awaken again, — not these, but Elijah the prophet, will link the Old time to the New. In this transfer of ascendency from the warrior, the lawgiver, and the king, to the prophet, and the predicted survival of the prophetic element alone from among the formative forces of that early time, we find clear testimony to the failure of the experiment of human perfecting by external means. The sword, the stone tablet, and the sceptre give place to the *word*. The true ruler is henceforth the "seer;" he only can foretell the future who can inwardly read the present and the past. Malachi, accordingly, turning the exploring lens backward along the path, sends its gleam also forward across the gulf, and beholds the coming enthronement of the WORD.

We pass on, then, to the new centuries. The intervening space is filled with turbulence and transition. The massive despotisms of Asia have been wrecked and ground up as in a flood, and the disintegrated elements of the ancient civilizations have been drifting westward to nucleate in a new continent in new forms. Among the Jews the teaching synagogue has been growing beside and threatening the supremacy of the temple formalism; the Jewish rabbi has breathed the effervescent atmosphere of Greek speculation, and is full of casuistry and debate; the rigid Hebrew language itself is giving way to the more fluent Greek, only tingeing it with the Hebraistic temper here and there; and the Sacred Oracles themselves have in the Septuagint version been boldly recast in forms of speech hitherto accounted profane. Meantime there is much questioning, but little satisfactory answering. The divers philosophic schools are in vain probing the muddy depths for a foundation stone. The Roman, weary of sophistry, but unable to return to animalism, asks restlessly, "What is truth?" Judaism likewise is broken into sects, alike dogmatic, alike dissatisfied.

Into such a receptive and expectant world the Messianic Teacher comes. Under so favorable conditions he proposes to try the new experiment of human renovation: no longer now by physical agencies reaching the corporate race or nation, but by intellectual forces remoulding the individual man. Forthwith we pass from history to biography, from the palace to the cottage, from questions of social and civil organization to those of personal experience. We are not busy with power, which cramps and mars, but with truth, which sets free. With the Great Teacher we return to the past and to nature, walking as in an Interpreter's House. He finds a fountain of love in the desert rock of the Law; he disenchants the dumb lily that it may utter its secret, of outward beauty through inward purity; he opens long vistas, through parable and miracle and well-matched incident, through which the open-eyed may look into the core of things. Cautiously, patiently, lovingly he leads on those who consent to be learners, telling them many things as they are "able to bear."

But with what avail? A few are led by curiosity, a few by love of "loaves and fishes," a few by gratitude, to follow him intermittently. Those whom by special appeal he attaches to himself are unsympathetic, dull, and untrustworthy to the last. "It is needful for you," he said, "that I go away,"— even "for *you.*"

So fails the last experiment of the four. It is noticeable how clearly the failure has been anticipated and announced. Not by ethical precept, by parable or miracle, had he, from the beginning, hoped to master and change the world, but by being "lifted up."

He saw but one cure for the heart of mankind,—
"Ye must be *born again*."

c. Genetic progress. And this suggests to us the third predominant idea of the Scripture record, namely, *the genetic relation of the successive periods.*

They have not followed each other at hap-hazard, but in regular gradation. The line of continuity, though often attenuated, has never been broken; and no epoch has been fruitless or void; for each has transmitted the unresolved problem to the next with some new elements toward its solution. As the earth born out of the waters, and life born out of the earth, brought forward each some elements of that realm from which it sprung, so Noah brought through the flood the arts and language of the perished world. Moses took through the Red Sea the training of Egypt. And the prophetic torch was passed on from the seers of the old covenant to those of the new. But as earth is more than water, and life than earth, so every new-born age has its elements of difference as well as those of identity. The risen body will by some unbroken thread prolong the identity of the present, for it is like the sheaf from the planted grain; but "the glory of the celestial is one, and the glory of the terrestrial is another." There is enough of identity to enable us to prophesy, enough of diversity to confound us, if we try to do more than "prophesy *in part.*"

The natural counterpart of this historic unfolding is the conception of a preordained plan, the outline of which becomes distinct through the events that fulfil it,—a "mystery" before, but in the growing years made plain.

2. *Theory.*—As to the meaning of all this we are not left in doubt. The Scripture itself plainly discloses a theory the truth of which we may readily test. It assumes—

a. *That precision of detail, including names and dates, will some day furnish clews for comparison with independent testimony, and so for verification of the date and genuineness of Scripture itself.*

b. *That the reasoned experience of mankind will some day disclose the deep anticipatory significance of the early experiences of the race, which were "written aforetime for our learning."*

c. *That history itself is germinant of prophecy, being the unfolding of an orderly series of events after a complete and unchanging plan, ordained "before the foundation of the world."*

3. *Verification.*—Let us consider these suggestions in their order.

a. Historic vindication. Near the beginning of the eighteenth century, the reaction from the mystic and scholastic methods of interpretation concentrated study more exclusively upon the text and narrative of Scripture. Beside this tendency in the theological, grew up in the region of classical study the school of destructive criticism, which sought to cut away the earlier portions of Roman and Greek history as mythical. The brilliancy of the method as proposed by Pouilly, the scope it afforded for the display of critical ingenuity, and the striking results it achieved in the hands of Niebuhr, could not but commend it to the adventurous and aspiring historical interpreter. Nor was so formidable a weapon likely to be overlooked in that arena where, as Farrar phrases it, the "human intellect" was making its "long struggle against the authority of the Scriptures." Accordingly, a phalanx of writers began along these lines, more or less directly, an increasing assault upon the genuineness, the integrity, and the veracity of the Bible history. Of the details of this warfare there is neither leisure nor necessity here to speak. Its results could in no case have been other than meagre, precarious, and unsatisfying; for they are almost wholly negative. "Niebuhr opened more questions," says Sir G. C. Lewis, "than he closed; and the critics have been at war ever since, because all alike are, in judging by internal evidence only, trusting to an *occult faculty of divination* rather than ordinary tests applied to modern history." So that each new history written from such a standpoint becomes "one guess among many." The great stress of adverse criticism on the Pentateuch is to show, for instance, that it is not the single work of Moses; but how much of it he wrote, and who wrote or compiled the rest, whether Samuel, Hilkiah, Jeremiah, Ezra, or some other, and when and where, and from what data, — to these questions the answers are almost as numerous and whimsical as the writers.

So far as reconstruction is attempted, it is on a purely theoretic basis. It is a rewriting of history (to accept the statement of Beaufort, who, although later than Pouilly, is commonly regarded as the founder of the method) "according to what it *ought to have been*, in order that things should have become what they afterwards were." That is to say, the testimony is to be weighed by the theory, after the scholastic method.

According to this canon, — requiring that whatever reveals insight or foresight extraordinary at a particular date, must, regardless of testimony, be assumed to have been written at a later date, when it would, in the progress of things, have become ordinary, — it is hard to see how the Scriptures can have been written earlier than the present century; and, in fact, as they keep steadily in advance of us, the next generation will probably be able to show that in our time they had not been written at all. Certainly the matchless architecture of the Great Pyramid as described by Ferguson "ought not to have been" in the age and land of protoplasmic mud; and by the same rule Professor Norton is abundantly justified in concluding that "it would be idle to argue against the supposition that alphabetical writing was known in the time of Abraham." Under its sanction Volney felt secure in ridiculing the faith of those who thought Babel and Nimrod and Abraham to have been realities rather than astrologic myths; and Kuenen still insists that nations must, from the beginning, have grown "by subjugation and assimilation," and not from a "genealogic root," as stated in the Pentateuch. The Dutch admiral refused to believe his sailors' testimony that the sun was literally above the horizon, because he had mathematically put it below. But the sun remained; and so do the pyramids, and the writings of the Abrahamic era, and the historic Abraham himself, and Nimrod, and Babel, and the concurrent proofs of patriarchy as the germ of political organization, to be "verified any time you like to try."

It surely must seem a striking coincidence to any fair-minded man, that just when this tide of adverse criticism had "come in like a flood," so loosening the foundations of historic faith that, as Keil complains, it had left "no objective ground or standpoint free from uncertainty," there has come a responsive outburst of direct testimony, such as has never, in so short a space of time, been given to the world before.

When the hypothetic reconstruction of the sacred narrative began, it had a free field; for all early history then hung loose and nebulous against the sky. Cloudland is facile to fancy, but troublesome to slow-footed faith. There were, indeed, strange written characters on Egyptian obelisks and in tombs; there were writings disclosed in the grasp of unearthed mummies, but the "book" was "sealed," we could not read it; there was a tangle of vision in the field of language, mythology, political and social growth, etc., but it had not been focused through comparative study, so as to reveal its secret; there were rich monuments lying beside the Tigris and Euphrates, but these were buried, not only under unattractive earth-mounds, but under two thousand years of human forgetfulness. For Xenophon, camping with his ten

THE HISTORIC ELEMENT IN SCRIPTURE. 271

thousand Greeks beside the ancient site, had forgotten the very name of Nineveh.

But now we are reminded how the Bible speaks of stone tablets "laid up for a testimony;" of a "book sealed up unto the time of the end;" of "risen witnesses," forthcoming in time of need. The century of literary scepticism has come almost to its close, its cautious insinuations have grown to a triumphant taunt, and there is no direct answer. In 1798 Napoleon is in Egypt on far other than theological business; his French soldiers (who are so benighted, religiously, that on the Mediterranean they have asked each other, wonderingly, why Palestine is called the "Holy Land") are at work in their military excavations; they turn up a dull basaltic stone, with a curious triple inscription; they do not know it, but in that Rosetta stone they have found the key by which the riddle of the Egyptian Sphinx shall be unlocked, and the statements of Scripture be confirmed. That pick-axe blow has broken open the sealed chambers of testimony, and we may read inscribed in the lasting rock, unobliterated and unmarred, the very words of contemporaneous witnesses concerning the times of Joseph and of Moses. The very dead seem to awake, under this talismanic touch, to unclasp the long meaningless papyrus rolls from their wasted hands, released from the custody of their long-guarded secret. So convergent and conclusive are these direct testimonies in answer to the theoretic cavils of the time, that Mr. Stuart Poole is able to cite the disinterested authority of the great Egyptologists, Lepsius, Brugsch, and Chabas, to the effect that the Pentateuch and the monuments are mutually confirmatory; and to affirm that the theory of a later date than the time of Moses, or of another locality than the banks of the Nile, for the production of the Pentateuch, is no longer tenable.

After the Rosetta stone and its revelations came the Behistun inscription, protected hitherto from careful notice and from defacement, not by burial but by its being lifted four hundred feet up the face of the rock. Almost simultaneously with its recovery, came the disentombment of the Ninevite and Babylonian world, to which it was to be the interpreter. In Genesis we read that the builders of Babel " had brick for stone, and slime had they for mortar." This statement, most natural if written in the midst of the massive stone-work beside the rainless Nile, reminds us at once, by contrast, of the perishableness of the ambitious tower, built of clay in a land of moist climate and water flood. Singularly, the very frailty of these structures has been the shield of their contents. The soft walls, melting inward, have formed a crust over the treasures within; beneath which, secure from sun and rain, the records written in crumbling clay have come down unharmed to us. By the light of these long-extinguished earthen lamps, rekindled from the flash of the Behistun inscription, we wander, as if by enchantment, in the corridors, and look along the vistas of an antiquity reaching nearly to the flood. For, not only do we here find the unquestionably synchronous record of the daily life of more than 2,500 years ago, but also in the royal libraries the memorials of a still more distant civilization, — so distant that already they had become fossilized in an extinct language. Babel and Erech and Accad and Calneh are no longer mythical cities, for their remains are visible; and scholars find no fitter name than that of "Accad" for the primeval language just mentioned. Nimrod is no astronomic demigod, but a historic mortal whose exploits are matter of record. In the very land where Genesis locates the Babel Tower and the "confusion of tongues," we find, in the library of Assurbanipal, a corresponding account, and the remnant of a tower which carries in its self-recorded name, Borsippa, a reminiscence of such an event. Moreover, we are compelled, in the language of Sir Henry Rawlinson, "by the mere intersection of linguistic paths, and independently of all reference to the Scripture record . . . to fix on the plains of Shinar as the focus from which the various lines had radiated."

It is needless to refer in detail to the daily increasing mass of translated Assyrian and Chaldean documents, in which the long list of names, once peculiar to the Scripture, recur as familiarly as household words; or to the Moabite stone, recovered in so romantic a way, which tells so freely the story of "Mesha, king of Moab," and interprets together the Hebrew and Phœnician, as the Rosetta stone had done the Greek and the Egyptian, and the Behistun inscription the Persian, Assyrian, and Babylonian; or to the testimony from the comparative study of language, ethnology, ethnography, etc., rapidly grouping in confirmation of the Scriptural account of the origin and growth of early civilization.

The stress of my argument is not upon the variety or completeness of the testimony as to matters of fact, but upon (1) the preservation of these unique and perishable memorials from so great antiquity and in so improbable ways, while the nearer, more abundant, and multiplied copies of the Greek and Latin classics have almost wholly perished; (2) their hiding through so many centuries, entombed in rubbish, or sealed up in occult languages, making their authority, when revealed, indisputable; (3) their almost simultaneous issuance, and the strangely coincident appearance of the several undreamed-of keys for their interpretation; (4) the exact response of the testimony so evoked to the very question in hand, namely, the antiquity and genuineness of the Scripture documents; (5) the abundance of points of contact, and consequently of test, between the new data and the Scripture, because of the circumstantiality of each; (6) the prescient minuteness of the Scripture in name, date, and circumstance avowedly for this very end. Surely "this also cometh forth from the Lord of hosts, which is wonderful in counsel and excellent in working."

b. Anticipated knowledge. We are assured in the Scripture that the things therein "written aforetime were written for our learning;" and especially as to the experiences of the people of Israel, that "these happened unto them for ensamples, and they are written for our admonition, upon whom the ends of the world are come." Rousseau and his comrades advocated a return to the *abandon* of "nature." Had they heeded the warning lesson of the early world, France need not have "become flesh," and sunk in a bloody deluge. Hero-worshippers ever and anon exalt the virtues of a "strong government," but the lessons of Cæsarism had been freely taught before Cæsar; and in the advent of Saul in Israel, we see the history of Napoleon written before the time; for he, too, solved by despotism the problem of anarchy arising out of the ill adjustment of highly developed institutions to an unfit people. Equally has the modern proposition of salvation by "culture" been anticipated, as we-have seen, in the matchless work of the Great Teacher in the propitious Greek era. But then, as always, the school, like "the law," "made nothing perfect."

It is especially noticeable, in the light of theories widely prevalent in our day, how precisely the emphasis is laid, in the typical history of the "chosen people," on those very formative conditions which, as we are now assured, have in them the "promise and potency" of a perfect humanity. The *first* of these conditions is *fitness of race.* The progenitor must be well selected and the stock kept pure. That is to say, we must begin, in science and in Scripture alike, with *Genesis.* Does it not meet the requirement, if a conspicuously worthy Abram be chosen, signalized henceforth as "the father," who will at the beginning protest against mongrel blood in Isaac's betrothal; who will so instil that sentiment into his progeny that it will henceforth reveal itself in scrupulous exactness of genealogic record, in the surrender of the fondest relations when in conflict with it, as in Ezra's reformation, and will survive as a passion in his posterity 4,000 years after him?

A *second* element is *fitness of environment*. The nation born into an unpropitious region fights an unequal battle. It cannot reach its destiny, except by the help of landscape, soil, and climate. Hence the prominence of *migration* among the agencies in human progress, — that is, of *Exodus*. Israel, wallowing in the luxuriance of the Nile valley, enervated by the caressing climate, dwarfed under the shadow of a landscape whose very mountains are tombs, can never become great. The decaying nation must first be got out of Egypt " by a strong hand;" then Egypt must be got out of them, by the sharp regimen of diet, exercise, and chastisement in the " desert of wandering;" then strong-tempered Canaan must stimulate, enlarge, and develop them into national manhood. Even to this day that insignificant strip of land between the river and the sea, — in the very centre of the triple continent, yet thoroughly secluded, — small in extent, but a very microcosm in diversity of landscape and product (having to-day, though itself not larger than the six northern counties of England, a flora twice as extensive as all Great Britain), — that land, I say, remains unique in the world as an ideal training-field of men.

A *third* prerequisite to national development is *fitness of institutions*. These, if they are to minister to growth, must recognize an unreached and inflexible ideal; but if they are not to dishearten, and so become fruitless, they must also recognize the " hardness " of men's " hearts," and so take on a temporary and practicable form. Precisely these "rudiments" of national legislative training are embodied in the next book of the Pentateuch, *Leviticus*, — the " primer " of Israel, — local and ephemeral in form, yet in spirit so perennially suggestive that it attracts and instructs alike the Puritan pioneer, the sanitary legislator, and the social reformer.

A *fourth* essential idea is *fitness of political organization*. This changes a nation into a people, fuses the elements into a corporate unity, and makes an organic life possible. How deftly this problem is wrought out in the book of *Numbers*, I need scarcely say. Military enthusiasm, family pride, religious devotion, all are there wrought in as buttresses of a structure which is itself single and complete.

Fifth and last in order is the element of *progressive adaptation of institutions*. *Fifth*, also, in order, closing the " five fifths " of the Pentateuch, is *Deuteronomy*, — the " second law." It is not a new statute, but a new phase of the old, — a revision adjusting it to a new life in a new land. It suggests by its very method and tone the subordination and plastic function of all forms, and recognizes some advance on the part of the people toward that conception. It hints of Christ's " new bottles " for " new wine," and Paul's " newness of the spirit " mastering the " oldness of the letter."

But enough : the Pentateuch was clearly written before our new day, in which world-wide research and wiser methods of study have made luminous the pathways of the race; before the human mind had aroused even to curiosity as to the nature and origin of things; yet in it are distinctly discriminated and emphasized those very exterior conditions of human development to which, under the name of "the environment," modern philosophy attributes the moulding of all history. But it as carefully records the experimental proof that the *environment is not omnipotent*, as Mr. Buckle seems to teach; that it does not create nor compel progress, but only supplies conditions therefor. It thus not only confirms, by anticipation, the truths, but also fore-reads and rebukes the errors, of to-day.

So, then, it appears that in "the childhood of the world," when anatomic science was as yet unthought of, some eye was keen enough, and some hand skilful enough, to lay open, without a single false stroke, the whole bony structure which underlies and gives shape to human history; and that, while the idea of history was itself yet foreign to the race, some sagacious influence prompted the recording of that demonstration, as likely to have significance to those far-off generations "upon whom the ends of the world are come." If, according to the canon of historic criticism, the record of that which, at the particular date, normally "ought not to have been," involves a demand of faith in the supernatural, then clearly, upon proof of the antiquity of the Pentateuch, its self-evidencing penetration below and beyond the line of current human experience, as well as its unique and marvellous accuracy of prevision, marks it as supernaturally wrought out.

c. *The genetic Key.* — The complex mysteries of life find their centre, as the etymology of the word *nature* itself may hint, in birth; and birth is itself a mystery. That there is a certain continuity and uniformity in hereditary laws is clear. Had there been nothing more, there could have been no progress, but monotonous persistence only. But there *is* something more. Beside the constant, there is also an eccentric and incalculable element. In thick darkness, behind the sacred veil, the fluent life-elements are moulded into specific form, and quickened with a specific impulse under brooding wings. Thus comes every babe into life, — as Sir Arthur Helps well says, "a new creature, such as the world never saw before." The life, unfolding its variant tendencies under law we may study, but those tendencies themselves had already been determined in the germ, and the causes that produced them are, as Mr. Darwin confesses, "very obscure."

Nevertheless, into this "obscurity" all our lines of exploration run back; all problems cluster round and resolve themselves into that of "origin." The mystery of the plant, which lies open in the flower, was perfect already in the seed. In Nature and Scripture alike, Revelation lies hid in Genesis.

Genesis, accordingly, is not only the initial, but the continuous and central idea of the Sacred Record. The minuteness of detail with which an incidental and seemingly trivial occurrence is related in the 30th chapter of Genesis may here be in many ways suggestive. It may interest us but little to know that Jacob outwitted the crafty Laban, but we cannot fail to be struck with the novelty and shrewdness of his method. For we perceive that he recognized the law of "persistence of type," of "variation through the obscure action of external causes," of "persistence of varieties," and of "selection of the fittest," and turned them all to account. May not the recent treatise on the "Variation of Animals under Domestication" have been the unconscious fruit of a seed dropping from this ancient tree into a receptive soil?

In any case, the early pre-eminence assigned to birth, as the hiding-place of power and the gateway of the future, is manifest. Through that gateway hope looks onward in the first promise, for "the *seed* of the woman shall bruise the serpent's head," — and through it in response to that hope the Incarnate Son comes into the world, — through the new birth men enter the spiritual life here, — and the final death-agony is itself the birth-throe through which they enter into life beyond.

For this, again, is an element in the mystery; that birth holds life and death together in solution. It is not only a channel for the flow of continuous lines of force, it is also an abyss in which their flow is arrested and they are for the moment lost. Every child is a Benoni for whose sake the mother drifts under the arches of death's portals. The Mosaic economy "waxeth old, and is ready to vanish away," that the Gospel may be born. Thus all historic epochs have the features of a birth. Out of a dissolving race a new life emerges in Noah. Out of bleeding Egypt, through a Red Sea, Israel is born into a national existence. Out of the crumbling elements of the "kingdoms of this world" comes the new "kingdom within." We recognize the pertinence of the figure when we call the great epoch of modern history the *Renaissance*.

But birth implies not the extinction, but only the disintegration of the old; whose elements persist in the new life, though transformed. The "new man" of Christianity is neither Greek nor Jew, nor an original creation; but "out of twain one new man" is born. The progressive Greek had no point of departure; he "knew not God." The conservative Jew had a right point of departure, but he would not depart. Paul, by birth a Jew, by culture a Greek, when "born from above," was such a "new man;" in whom "strength and beauty" were blent into holiness.

There is a wide margin of mystery, but no caprice, in the ongoing of the life forces through birth. Local winds and currents are immeasurable, but the tidal wave is one. The "westward course of empire" is unmistakable. In the shaping of that course we now see how significant were the east and west vertebral lines of mountain structure; the stepping-stones across the Ægean to tempt the less adventurous Greeks to their marvellous land; the hiding of the new world until the old race — born out of Asia into Europe, and out of Europe, mingling the Saxon and Norman "twain," into near Britain — should have "strength to bring forth" a new life resolute enough to project itself across the greater sea; and the meeting here of a transverse mountain chain along which, as a barricade, the hindered flood of "peoples, nations, and tongues," flowing northward and southward, might mingle into one. That these river-banks of terrestrial configuration had a predestining force upon the progress of the race, we see; but were the river-banks themselves so wise in self forming, or was their form itself predestined? After the study of Humboldt, Ritter, and Guyot, does it seem so unreasonable to declare of the nations, with Paul, that God "hath *determined* the times before appointed, and the bounds of their habitation"?

If the structure of the earth reveal thus a pre-determinant drift; if the world of life show a "struggle" upward, "guided wittingly," by "natural selection," the "whole creation groaning and travailing in pain together until now" toward a final birth; if human history disclose a "stream of tendency" which uniformly "makes for righteousness," — then it is no longer hard to pronounce the Bible word, speaking of all this as "foreordained." The bluffs may be miles apart, between which the untrammelled river meanders at will, but they are there, and they cannot be overpassed. The sacrifice of Christ was a thing "before determined to *be done*," but Herod and Pilate and the rest freely determined *by whom* it should be done.

Under the scope of this law, even the subtile freedom of the birth forces is restrained. Even now, approximately, the "shadow" foretells "the coming events." By the light of our imperfect knowledge we can "prophesy in part." Could we see deeper in, we could see farther on. For *prophecy* is but *history recorded.*

Fitly, the Bible record closes with the prophetic Apocalypse, — the record of "things which *must* shortly come to pass," — showing how the future lies open in the past and present, when unsealed. As the flower is born out of root and stalk, completing and explaining it; as it gathers into its hidden looms the gnarled outlines, the stubborn fibres, the dull hues, weaves them anew into an ethereal beauty of texture, form, and color, and from acid juices distils into the air celestial perfumes; so the Apocalypse hangs upon the Scripture history, drawing the substance thereof into itself, but all transfigured and illuminated with the "glory to be revealed."

Dean Trench has reminded us, in his discussion of the "Epistles to the Seven Churches," how the order of their promised rewards hints at a historic sweep of vision from Eden, with its "tree of life," to the final consummation, and a seat beside the Victor "on his throne."

The vision itself begins with the seven-sealed scroll, already "written within and without," but as yet unopened. It opens inwardly, for the inward is the onward, of vision. As seal after seal is broken, the inner secrets of history are unfolded in their genetic order; the key to the "springing and germinant fulfilment of prophecy" is found. Egypt and Sodom live again; "the two witnesses," Moses and Elijah, do "indeed come again"; the Beast and the

False Prophet crush and delude wherever power and craft rule; and Babylon, "that great city," will trade as of old in all merchandise, and in the "souls of men," until she shall be cast like a "millstone into the sea."

But this seemingly chaotic flood has a silent onward drift. Over the formless void, as at the beginning, the Spirit broods. The first Genesis is revealed in the second. Out of the cry of anguish, the thunder of tempest, the crash of battle, emerge the chiming of harps, the radiance of glad faces, the vision of peace; out of confused and changing figures the clear outlines of the city "that lieth four square;" out of the womb of earth's midnight is born heaven's everlasting day. For He knows the "thoughts that He thinks towards us," that they are "thoughts of peace and not of evil, to give us an *expected end*."

X.

THE THEISTIC BASIS OF EVOLUTION.

By REV. JOHN COTTON SMITH, D.D.

X.

THE THEISTIC BASIS OF EVOLUTION.

By REV. JOHN COTTON SMITH, D.D.

IN considering the subject of "The Theistic Basis of Evolution," I shall endeavor to establish this proposition, — that supposing the law of evolution to be a universal law, including in its operation all the phenomena of the universe, we have in it an immense gain to Theism, and an argument stronger than any which has yet been used that the phenomenal universe, in all its minutest details, rests upon an invisible power, and is the manifestation of that conscious Intelligence and Will which we call God.

Had I known, when I selected this subject, that one so pre-eminently able and distinguished as Dr. McCosh was to lecture in this course upon substantially the same subject, I should have abandoned the undertaking, and left the field to the exclusive possession of one whom I so highly honor, and to whom I am glad to acknowledge myself as so greatly indebted. As it is, I am led to feel less regret at the coincidence of the subjects discussed, inasmuch as while I heartily concur in the general drift of Dr. McCosh's lecture, there are some points which, I think, should be more decidedly expressed.

In the consideration, then, of our subject, we are first to ask what the universality and all-comprehensiveness of the Law of Evolution involves. This can only be determined by following the history of phenomena, as we may be able to construct it from the materials which come under human observation, and in accordance with the conditions under which human opinion is formed.

Setting aside, then, for the present, all inquiry as to the origin of phenomena, or as to any power by which the changes of phenomena are produced, or as to any object which phenomena with their successive changes may be designed to accomplish, we are simply to consider, as far as we can, the phenomena of the universe as they successively appear, on the supposition of a universal evolution. Whether there was a time when the perceptible emerged from the imperceptible, or the perceptible has always existed, is not now to be considered. However that may be, there has been a period in time when the phenomenal is found to have existed, probably in a universally extended homogeneous mass, in a state of motion. Throughout this mass there is found to be a tendency to contraction or integration around various centres. There is, also, found to be a process by which differentiation in the mass is established, so that what was homogeneous becomes more or less heterogeneous. The universally diffused mass is broken up into ro-

THE THEISTIC BASIS OF EVOLUTION. 289

tating spheres. These spheres in the process of contraction or integration throw off smaller spheres, which, retaining the direction of their motion, revolve around the sphere from which they have been thrown.

In following the further progress of this evolution, which has thus resulted in the sidereal system, we are to confine ourselves to our own globe, which must be supposed to be in some sense typical of other worlds, and which furnishes us with all the necessary elements of the problem.

Taking the earth, then, at the time when it was thrown off from the gradually cooling mass, the same general process goes on. There is continued contraction and integration, and wider distinctions and differences of structure are established. With the gradual cooling of the earth a crust is formed, and the precipitation of vast masses of vapor, in the form of water, takes place. The dry land and the seas appear. Step by step, without any break in the continuous chain, each phenomenon linked with preceding phenomena, vast changes occur in the structure of the globe, resulting in its diversified surface and manifold conditions.

At last out of the inorganic, it may be at various points and at various times, in forms scarcely distinguishable from those which have preceded, the germs of the organic world appear. The process has at last resulted in the manifestation of life.

Out of the earth, without any break in the continuity of the process, the vegetal kingdom has come forth. The process of integration and differentiation goes on until the earth is covered with multitudinous forms of trees and plants and flowers. But in this plant life we find almost imperceptible gradations by which the transition to animal life is made. There is a widely extended area of life where it is exceedingly difficult to determine whether the forms belong to the vegetal or animal world. In the course of time, however, the distinctions of the animal world become more and more pronounced, and a similar process of integration and differentiation results in the various forms of animal life.

On the long line of animal development there is at last a persistent approach in the order of Primates to the genus Man. By imperceptible advance a stage in the evolution is reached; where the characteristics are for a time indeterminate, but finally, through progenitors of whom, perhaps, there are no traces now, there has come to be Man upon the earth.

Still the process goes on. The low and brutal aspects of primitive human life gradually disappear. Society comes to exist, and tends to more and more complex forms. Religious ideas clothe themselves in religious systems. Moral distinctions come to be more and more clearly defined, and through almost imperceptible gradations of progress the marvellous achievements of the highest civilization have been reached.

Careful study of the phenomenal world has led to the discovery of certain laws which serve to render in some degree comprehensible the nature and method of this process. Such laws are those of the persistence of force, of the persistence of the same relations among forces, of the continuity of motion in the direction of least resistance, of the evolution of the heterogeneous from the homogeneous, of the continuous redistribution of matter and motion, of heredity, of natural selection, and of the survival of the fittest. These are simply statements of some of the conditions of the process, and of the methods by which it is carried on.

This is as broad a statement of the law of evolution as can be made, for it recognizes no break in the invariable continuity from the first moment of time until now, and includes every minutest change which has taken place in the phenomenal universe.

Supposing this, then, to be the true history of the phenomenal world, we are to see what bearing it has upon our belief in a personal God.

Does the universality of the law of evolution, supposing it to be established, place Theism at any disadvantage, so that it will be any the less sure a conviction of the mind that God exists? That is the question first to be considered. We have, then, simply to compare two processes in nature; one in which the law of evolution, while it is almost universal in its operation, has been on certain occasions, now admitted to be very few, interrupted, and a new order of phenomena, not growing out of any previously existing, has been introduced. Such occasions are supposed, by those who regard this interrupted process as the true order of nature, to have been at least two, — the first appearance of life in general, and then the first appearance of human life. The other process is the one which we have been considering, in which all phenomena are linked with preceding phenomena, so that the effect upon the mind is that of a perpetual rolling forth of phenomena from that which already exists.

In comparing these two processes there is one thing first of all to be considered. When we speak of evolution, it by no means necessarily follows that all we find in any particular phenomenon was involved in its antecedent phenomenon, and that therefore the whole universe was actually involved in the phenomena with which the process of evolution began. While this is the apparent relation which antecedent have to succeeding phenomena, no one can say that there is not some power on the invisible side of nature which adds the elements of difference or advance at every step in the development. But suppose that the process of evolution must be regarded as involving the whole development in the phenomena with which the evolution begins. Is there anything in this idea which need to disturb a believer in a personal God? If it is a necessary conception of a process of evolution that all its stages shall be involved in the initial step, then the difficulty, if it be one, attends the partial and interrupted processes of evolution, the existence of which no one can deny, as well as a process supposed to be uninterrupted and universal. It is certainly just as conceivable that God, for I am now reasoning with Theists, should have involved the whole process in its first beginnings, as to have involved partial evolutions and developments in the phenomena from which they have sprung. If evolution must be conceived of as a necessary involving of the whole process in the first step with which it starts, then all the stages in the evolution of the inorganic world were involved in the conditions under which that evolution began. If this is the true idea of evolution, then all plants and animals were involved in the very earliest phenomena of plant or animal life; nay, all the marvellous developments of humanity slumbered potentially in the first man. But if this can be conceived, where is the difficulty in supposing that a power which could thus involve such vast series of development in the phenomena from which they spring, could endow the primitive elements from which nature is built up, with a potency which should secure the orderly development of the stupendous processes of the universe; and thus God stand behind a universal evolution? And surely if it is wonderful, and an argument for the existence of an Infinite Power, that there should be these long lines of evolution in which the whole development was involved in the beginning of the series, then is it much more wonderful, and constitutes a much stronger argument for a Divine Power, that not merely partial series of development, but that the whole vast evolution lay potentially in the original germs, out of which it has been brought forth.

We are not, however, shut up to this conception of evolution. It is conceivable that the elements of difference and advance have not been involved in preceding phenomena, but have been added at each minutest stage of the development. Taking this view, then, we may unhesitatingly affirm that it is a more wonderful exercise of wisdom and power to have carried on this process uninterruptedly, from first to last, than to have interrupted it from time to time; as if it were necessary to draw upon some new and reserved force for the advancing stages of the progress.

So far, then, as the question lies between a partial and a universal evolution, the gain for Theism is very great on the hypothesis that the evolution is continuous, and all-comprehending. But this, it must be admitted, only partially meets the case. The advocates of the hypothesis of immediate and isolated creation in certain cases may reply; the question is not merely between universal and partial evolution, but between universal evolution and partial systems of evolution, with the addition of certain acts of immediate creation.

Is there, then, any gain for Theism in the hypothesis of immediate creation in the introduction of life or of man into the system of nature? This is a question also, be it remembered, between Theists, who differ only as to the bearing of two almost parallel hypotheses upon the subject of the existence and agency of God.

It may be said, then, in the first place, what every Theist will be compelled to acknowledge, that in every step in a process of evolution — and that there are processes of evolution no Theist now will undertake to deny — there is involved the same creative power as could be involved in any act of immediate and isolated creation. The phenomenon has come to exist. The power which has caused its existence is the same, no matter whether it is exercised in one single act or distributed through a series of acts. A child is born into the world. It is the product of a process of evolution. Is it any the less a product of creative power? Would it be any more a creation if a pile of dust had, without any intervening process, been suddenly changed into its form and substance? Are we not all creatures of God? and would not the first man be as much a creature of God, supposing him to have been born of progenitors less than human, as we who are born, so far as our recent pedigree is concerned, of human ancestry? Would it make him any more a creature of God, if from a lump of clay, without any apparent intervention, he had suddenly become a full-grown man? The same power must be admitted to be somewhere back of the act, whether it occurs in a process of development, or as the result of an immediate isolated exercise of power.

I do not urge at this point the higher dignity and rationality (if I may use the word) of a process of evolution by which all phenomena are linked together in an orderly development. There is, however, I may be permitted to say, something exceedingly crude in the hypothesis of an interrupted process of development, as if God needed to display himself by arresting the orderly sequence of phenomena and beginning, as it were, anew; or as if God were remedying defects which he had discovered in his method, and were starting once more with the benefit of acquired experience. I do not mean to imply that the advocates of immediate and isolated acts of creation thus conceive of God, but they unconsciously render the creative agency of God liable to be so represented. When pressed with the proposition, which no argument can possibly refute, that God is just as necessary to every step in a process of evolution as he is to any act of immediate creation, they sometimes display an impatience, perhaps not unnatural, at having the existence and agency of God established by any other method to the exclusion of the favorite one, to which they have become accustomed. It almost seems at times as if they wanted to have Theism established in their own way or not at all.

During the late war Mr. Seward was in the habit of telling a story which illustrated the unreasonableness of certain opponents of slavery, who did not wish to have it abolished unless it could be done in the way which they thought best. The story is not without its application to the present case. Two men who were intimate friends had the one a son, and the other a daughter, and it had been a cherished purpose with the fathers that a matrimonial alliance should crown the friendship of the families. When intimating, however, to the children that the whole matter of their settlement for life had been duly arranged, there was an unfortunate omission to state what the proposed arrangement was. The young people having become attached to each other, and supposing that the intentions of their fathers were inconsistent with their own inclinations, were clandestinely married. On learning this fact, one of the fathers rushed to his friend to offer his congratulations, but found him, to his surprise, in a towering indignation. "Are you not satisfied, now that you have had your own way?" "No," said he, "I'm not satisfied merely to have my own way. I want to have my own way in my own way."

The question as to which view of the agency of God in nature is most in accordance with the representations of the Bible is, of course, a separate question. It may be well, however, to say a word as to the account which is given of the process of creation in the Book of Genesis. There is nothing in it which does not describe equally well an uninterrupted process of evolution, in which there are periods strongly marked by certain characteristics, such as the six periods called days, as a process of evolution broken in upon by a discontinuance and resumption of an established order of phenomena. The word בָּרָא which is translated "create," does not necessarily, perhaps not at all, involve the idea of immediate creation. It means, for the most part at least, to shape and to form. But even if it involved immediate creation, it would not answer the purpose of those who reject the hypothesis of continuous evolution. It is used but three times in the first chapter of Genesis, — once in connection with the heavens and the earth, once in connection with great whales, and once in connection with man. It is not used in connection with the first introduction of life upon the earth, and in the case of man it does not mean an absolutely new creation, for it is declared that he was created out of the dust of the earth. The whole account is a marvellous illustration of what we find so constantly in Scripture, — the description of natural phenomena according to their appearance, a description which is always necessarily true, and is always readily adjustable to any scientific discoveries which may be made. How the author of the Book of Genesis could have described so accurately the appearance of natural phenomena thousands of ages after they occurred, and thousands of years before the character and order of the phenomena were discovered by scientific investigation, it is for those who reject the idea of inspiration to decide. No apprehension could be more unreasonable than that the authority of the Bible is in danger of being overthrown by any scientific hypotheses, be they true or false. They cannot be used successfully against the claims of the Scriptures as a Divine revelation. There was a striking device among the Huguenots, I think, representing men with hammers, striking upon an anvil. Other men were standing by with fresh hammers to take the place of those that were broken. "Pound away, you rebels," was the motto; "your hammers break, the anvil of God's word stands."

The point which we have thus far reached seems, then, to be this, that the hypothesis of a universal

and all-comprehending process of evolution is a gain
for Theism, if it can be established. It brings the
agency of God in nature into harmony with all the
higher conceptions to which the best philosophy has
given rise. It removes the embarrassments which are
sure to attend any effort to make an act of special and
immediate creation cognizable by the mind, and it
invests the whole relation of God to the phenomenal
universe with new dignity and grandeur. It has been
claimed by some of the disciples of positive science
that the enlarged knowledge of nature which each
generation gains is gradually displacing the idea of
any personal agency in the world of nature. Let me
tell you what it is really doing. It is displacing what
I call untheistic conceptions of nature, which substituted the agency of inferior supernatural powers in
the place of the agency of God. Under its influence
the "fair humanities," as Coleridge calls them, of the
old religion have vanished. The supernatural beings
in forests, in valleys, by the sides of streams, — the
fairies of mediæval superstition, the great angels of the
spheres of whom Kepler dreamed, are known no more.
What has come in their place? Are we surrounded
by a mere unideal, phenomenal universe, which has
grown out of no thought, no all-comprehending plan?
No, a thousand times no! For if there is this universal, all-comprehending law of evolution, then there
is a stupendous plan of the universe, and the great
Power which sways the world touches nature at
every moment of time and at every point in space.
The progress of science is banishing the false super-

natural, but only that "God may" to us "be all in all."

It is something, then, to be hailed with joy, if it shall be found that science has made this contribution to a more rational conception of the universe in which a nobler Theism is necessarily involved. We are not disposed to sit down quietly under the verdict that it is still unproven. We rejoice to be moved forward by the impulse of a grand anticipation, and we yield ourselves to the enthusiasm which forecasts this great vindication of the highest rational relation of God to nature and man.

We are prepared, then, for a consideration, in general, of the grounds on which an acceptance of evolution as a universal law is anticipated. As we have already followed the probable history of phenomena on the hypothesis of universal evolution, we can now notice certain facts which seem strongly to indicate the truth of this hypothesis. In the sidereal system, for instance, as Mr. Herbert Spencer has pointed out, we have actually at the present time within our field of observation the various stages in its development to which I have already referred. The process of integration of which I have spoken would of course be more or less rapid according to the size of the spheres into which the original mass was broken. It is not unlikely that there are instances in which the whole cycle of changes has been passed through, and where the integration has been followed by a dispersion and diffusion of matter until it has returned to its original homogeneous condition. Such seems to have been the case with certain nebulæ where matter now exists in a gaseous form, constituting star-dust, or the material out of which stars are again to be made. Then there are other vast masses of matter where the process of integration seems to be far advanced. The spheres have been drawn closely together. Their proximity has given rise to anomalous systems such as that of binary stars. The aggregation of the mass is indicated also by the vast solitudes in the heavens from which it has retreated in upon itself. Spheres in the same system are in·different stages of their progress. Our globe, for instance, being so much smaller than Jupiter, is in a much more advanced state of integration. The moon being so much smaller, the process of integration in it is already so much the more complete. We have, therefore, probably within our own view, accessible to the scrutiny of the telescope and spectroscope, all the various stages of sidereal evolution.

When we strive to follow the steps of the development from the inorganic to the organic, we are to remember what Dr. McCosh has so ably pointed out, that the minuteness of the changes involved does not account for the introduction of any new principle. Unless life was by some power put originally into the series from which it is at last evolved, or is added to it when it first appears, we should have no life in the series at all. But the point to be noticed here is, that there are indications that when life first appeared on the earth there was no apparent break in the continuity of phenomena, but a simple movement by gradations, which could hardly be perceived, to the various phenomena of life. It makes the transition more comprehensible to remember that the matter constituting the living world is identical with that which forms the inorganic world. All the forces of the living world are probably identical with the forces of the inorganic world, or are convertible into them. Organic nature is built up all the time out of inorganic nature, and returns into inorganic nature again. One who is familiar with crystalline formation, with its delicate shoots branching out on either side from a central axis, would not be conscious of any disturbance of an established order in the appearance of plants in the midst of what had hitherto been inorganic nature.

If we turn from this point to one that has been treated with very great clearness and ability by Mr. John Fiske, we shall find most striking corroborations of the hypothesis of universal evolution. The view which Mr. Fiske presents is that of the oneness of all life at its base. It starts, no matter on what line of development it may be, from the same point. Taking, then, a point of origin, there is, according to Mr. Fiske, a divergence in diverse directions of vegetal and animal life, the more widely varying as they are further removed from the original point of divergence. Then, take in connection with this Professor Asa Gray's exceedingly interesting and valuable work on the "Relations of Religion and Science," where he shows that recent discoveries have completely bridged over the chasm which was formerly supposed to exist between animal and vegetable life. If we take into account also the wonderfully interesting work of Mr. Darwin on plants, in which the rudiments of purpose and volition in plant life are clearly shown to exist, we shall be likely to be deeply impressed with the unity and generic connection of all life.

If we turn then to Mr Darwin's marvellously complete and exhaustive consideration of the subject of the Descent of Man, it will be found to be a very strong argument for the hypothesis of universal evolution, or at least for the derivation of man from the animal life by which he was preceded. To say nothing else, it seems impossible to account for traces in man of the lower animal development, if not on this supposition. When we find rudimentary organs in man which have their counterpart as useful and necessary organs in lower animals, it is difficult to doubt the transmission by heredity of these abortive organs to man. But more than this, how marvellous is the revelation which is made to us in human embryology! The human child before birth passes through all the characteristic aspects of a lower animal life. It seems to bear the marks of its origin at every step of its development until birth. There is no meaning in the presence of these aspects unless they are traces of an actual development which has been passed through. And when we find that the same fact presents itself in lower animal life, where its significance is by common consent recognized, we hesitate at least to refuse to recognize its significance in the case of man.

A remarkable confirmation of this view is to be found

in the discovery by Professor Marsh of the various stages by which the horse as he now exists has been developed from an animal with five toes. This most significant discovery is now so well known, and its bearing so well understood, that I need not dwell longer upon it.

As it is no part of my purpose to construct an argument in behalf of the universality of the law of evolution, but only to point out some of the prominent indications that it will come to be recognized as a universal law, I do not feel called upon to consider the difficulties and objections which are urged against it, though I feel confident that, were there time so to do, the conclusion already reached would be found to be only the more strongly established.

There is a wonderful passage in Coleridge's "Aids to Reflection," which can hardly be considered as less than a prophecy of the discovery of this great law: "Every rank of creatures, as it ascends in the scale of creation, leaves death behind it or under it. The metal, at its height of being, seems a mute prophecy of the coming vegetation, into a mimic semblance of which it crystallizes. The blossom and flower, the acme of vegetable life, divide into correspondent organs with reciprocal functions, and by instinctive motions and approximations seems impatient of that fixure by which it is differenced in kind from the flower-shaped Psyche that flutters with free wing above it. And wonderfully, in the insect realm, doth the irritability, the proper seat of instinct, while yet the nascent sensibility is subordinated thereto, —

most wonderfully, I say, does the muscular life in the insect, and the musco-arterial in the bird, imitate and typically rehearse the adaptive understanding, yes, and the moral affections and charities of man. Let us carry ourselves back in spirit to the mysterious week, the teeming work-days of the Creator, as they rose in vision before the inspired historian of the generations of the heavens and of the earth, in the day that the Lord God made the earth and the heavens. And who that hath watched their way with an understanding heart could, as the vision evolving still advanced toward him, contemplate the loyal and filial bee; the home-building, wedded and divorceless swallow; and, above all, the manifoldly intelligent ant tribes, with their commonwealths and confederacies, their warriors and miners, the husband-folk that fold in their tiny flocks on the honeyed leaf, and the virgin sisters, with the holy instincts of maternal love, detached and in selfless purity, — and not say to himself, Behold the shadow of approaching humanity, the sun rising from behind in the kindling morning of creation. Thus all lower natures find their highest good in semblances and seekings of that which is higher and better. All things strive to ascend, and ascend in their striving."

But now we are brought to a point where the purpose and direction of the argument are to be changed. The argument so far has been addressed for the most part to Theists, and has had for its object to reconcile them to certain supposed principles and facts in nature, and to show that these principles and facts, if established, can only add to the firmness of that conclusion by which we hold fast to the being of a personal God. The considerations thus presented must avail with Theists, for they rest upon principles which all Theists admit. Now, however, we find ourselves confronted with the difficulties of those who have come to understand clearly the generic unity of the phenomenal universe, have embraced it all in one stupendous, all-comprehending law, but go no further, and fail to recognize the conscious intelligence and will on which all phenomena necessarily rest. When the Theist accepts the universal evolution, he supplies at once the theistic basis in thought. But for those who see only the phenomena linked together in this process of universal development, a new line of argument is necessary by which the theistic basis of the evolution may be established.

We have a point to start from in the distinct affirmations of one who would undoubtedly dissent from the conclusions I shall draw as to the theistic basis of evolution. Mr. Herbert Spencer, for I refer to him, says: "By the persistence of force we really mean the persistence of some power which transcends our knowledge and conception. The manifestations, as occurring either in ourselves or outside of us, do not persist; but that which persists is the unknown Cause of these manifestations. In other words, asserting the persistence of force is but another mode of asserting an unconditioned Reality, without beginning or end."

Here we find ourselves in the presence of that Agnosticism, which is supposed to be by many the final attitude which the human mind is to assume in regard to that Power which the Theist calls God. The whole realm in which this Power resides, this theory claims, is necessarily the Unknowable.

Now I undertake to say that the universality of evolution, if it is established, is pre-eminently calculated to overthrow the agnostic position. It is vain, indeed, even at the point where we already stand, to talk about the Unknowable. When Mr. Spencer tells us that the Unknowable is a Force which persists as a permanent reality, without beginning and without end, and that the phenomenal universe is only a manifestation of this eternal Reality, he gives us some most important items of knowledge about that which he calls the Unknown. But looking at the matter in the light of evolution, what is clearer than that we must ascribe Unity to that Power. It is everywhere the same. It must always be described by the same terms. It works throughout the universe by the same methods, and accomplishes the same ends. It binds all phenomena into one stupendous system, which can be conceived of by the mind instructed by familiarity with processes of evolution only as a unit, — its various parts related to each other and to the whole by one vast operation and one universal idea. On the supposition of an all-embracing evolution, no phenomena can possibly escape this unifying process of the mind. The unity of the whole, as contemplated by the mind, is absolutely complete. We have, then, as a result of a strictly scientific process the first great attribute of God : " Thy God is One God."

There is another conclusion to which we are irresistibly led, and that is, that the process over which this Power presides is the consummation of a vast design, and the outcome of a plan in which every phenomenon is so linked with all other phenomena that it must have been contemplated from the first. I know very well the ridicule with which the idea of design in nature is treated by the disciples of the agnostic school. And oftentimes abundant occasion is given for this ridicule by those who undertake to interpret the designs which they suppose they have discovered in the natural world. In the life of Heinrich Heine is an account of his interview with a citizen of Goslar, who undertook to entertain him by remarks on the proofs of purpose in nature. The trees, this individual said, were green because green was good for the eyes. To which Heine replied, "No doubt," and added that "God had created cattle because meat-broth was a strengthening diet for man; that he had made donkeys that they might serve for human comparison, and that he had created man that he might eat meat-broth and not be a donkey." "So long," Heine continues, "as this citizen was with me all nature lost its magic; as soon as he was gone the trees began again to speak, the sunbeams to be tuneful, the meadow flowerets to dance, and the blue heaven to embrace the green earth. Yes, I knew better. God has created man to adore the splendor of the world. In the Bible, the memoirs of God, it is expressly stated that he created man for his praise and glory."

But while men may be sadly mistaken in their efforts to interpret the designs of the power in nature which this school calls the Unknowable, the existence of design is established by a strictly scientific process. Prof. Bowen, Dr. Peabody, and the Bishop of Carlisle have of late rendered very valuable service by the application of mathematics to the establishing of moral truth. It is an accepted principle in the "logic of chance," that if a certain proportion out of a given number of phenomena contribute to a certain end, that the probabilities, mathematically expressed, that the end was designed are so great that it would be unreasonable to doubt. Even suppose nature to be a congeries of disjointed systems, each one traceable to an independent origin, still the evidence of design, by this method, would be overwhelming. But if all phenomena, linked together as they are supposed to be, on the hypothesis of universal evolution, are found to contribute to an orderly and advancing progress, then the probabilities in favor of design, as against the probability of a fortuitous concourse of phenomena contributing to a certain end, could be expressed only by a numerical statement, the figures of which could not be contained on the whole surface of the globe.

The authors of the "Rejected Addresses," in their commemoration of the rebuilding of Drury Lane Theatre, very cleverly satirized the doctrine of Lucretius that the world came to be by chance. Applying the principle of chance to the building up of this structure, they say: —

"From floating elements in chaos hurled,
Self-formed of atoms, sprang the infant world.
No great First Cause inspired the happy plot,
But all was matter, — and no matter what, —
Atoms attracted by some law occult,
Settling in spheres, — this globe was the result.
I sing how casual bricks, in airy climb,
Encountered casual cow-hair, casual lime ;
How rafters, borne through wondering clouds elate,
Kissed in their slope blue elemental slate,
Clasped solid beams in chance-directed fury,
And gave to birth our renovated Drury."

If, however, in spite of the stupendous unreasonableness of such a position, even from a strictly scientific point of view, any one should cling to the monstrous absurdity that all things may have come to be as they are by chance, then is there at least an equal possibility that chance may have given us a moral law, a supernatural system, miracles, redemption, eternal life. If, then, this inscrutable power, as it is called, has the attribute of unity, and works with design according to a plan excluding chance, all of which is scientifically established, there would seem to be little need of considering the question whether mind may not be a mere attribute of matter, — a mere material development. For, to say nothing of the impossibility of proving that there is any such thing as we call matter, while it is unquestionable that there is what we call mind, there is no little reason for supposing that mind and what we call matter are inseparably united, to be conceived of under one idea. So that mind necessarily underlies the material universe.

But one of the most significant facts in this whole controversy is yet to be considered. This agnostic position, so far as it is atheistic in its tendency, is broken down by its own advocates. There is nothing more remarkable than this in the whole history of philosophy.

The men to whom I shall refer are Professor Huxley, Schopenhauer, and Hartmann. We find these philosophers, who either assert our ignorance of God, or deny his existence altogether, talking about forces and a universal force, — and when they have searched phenomena through and through, they admit that there is a mysterious force beneath which eludes their grasp. Then Professor Huxley gives us the basis of a belief in a personal God when, baffled in his investigation of the inner mysteries of nature, he says: "If I were compelled to choose, I do not know whether I should express the facts of nature in terms of matter or terms of spirit." So that, after all, this whole system of materialism which has so much disquieted some, and been so enthusiastically defended by others, may have been dealing all the time with an immaterial and ideal universe resting in and existing only in the Divine mind.

But this admission of the utter baselessness possibly of the whole materialistic system is not all. It leaves us the reasonableness of the supposition that there is a universal spirit which either penetrates all nature or is nature itself. But now see how the other philosophers build up for us the argument in behalf of a personal God. A personal God must have will. Well, but Schopenhauer says that all force is will. He goes further and says that all matter is force, and that therefore matter is known to us only as will. There is, then, one all-pervading will; what seem to be causes in nature are only the occasions for the manifestation of the universal will. But then this infinite will is not a personal God, for a personal God must have intelligence as well as will.

Then comes Hartmann and says that there is not only a universal will into which all phenomena are resolved, but that it is an intelligent, though unconscious, will. This thinking and willing power lays out the plan of the universe, wills it to be such as it is, and carries all things on to their accomplishment. This universal power is like a God in a trance. Here Hartmann leaves us. But see the admissions which have been wrung from these deniers of a personal God. First, that everything, after all, may be spirit, thought, ideas, mind. Then that there is, at any rate, a universal *will*; and then, finally, that this universal will is infinitely intelligent, and adapts all means to all ends. We need now simply to add consciousness and we have a personal God. Add then love and goodness, and we have our Creator and heavenly Father.

Now this infinite, intelligent will without consciousness I call an imperfect and abnormal God. There is not enough of God in it to satisfy the necessities of reason. There is too much to render it possible to reconcile it with a denial of a personal God. Is it not reasonable, for that is the line of inquiry we are now pursuing, that if there is a. God at all it should be a normal God, with consciousness and affections, as well as intelligence and will?

An infinite, intelligent will without consciousness I hold to be an impossible conception. Having the intelligent will, the consciousness must in all reason be granted, and then come in all the demands of the soul, in the midst of the sins and sorrows of the world, which will find satisfaction nowhere but in the conviction of the existence of a personal God, with will, intelligence, and consciousness, infinitely wise and holy and good, in whom we live and move and have our being.

There is a wonderfully profound suggestion made by Professor Bowen, that the theory of evolution is the philosophy of Hegel applied to the world of material phenomena. Hegel's philosophy is a gigantic system in which all conceptions are necessarily evolved from thought. It is the higher ideal sphere of evolution. It gives us, its adherents claim, God, the incarnation, the verities of the Christian faith. Whether this be so or not, it can hardly be doubted that the new aspects in which the universe is presented by the principle of universal evolution will lead to a higher philosophy of God. If I dared to make any suggestion as to the drift of that philosophy, I should say it would be in the direction of the breaking down of the distinction between nature and spirit, and the illustration of St. Paul's wonderful declaration that God is all in all. This reconciliation of Pantheism with the personality of God on the one hand, and the independence in some sense of his creatures on the other, is the great problem for the Theism of the future. I should say that the theory, so emphatically condemned by the Vatican Council, of the evolution of the universe from the being of God, furnished the best possible starting-point for future investigation.

In the mean time, if we would hold fast to what is best in life, to the sources of noble enthusiasms, of grand and majestic works of art, of the sublimest poetry, of heroism, of pure morals, of saintly life, God as manifested in Jesus Christ must be enthroned in the adoring homage and love of all hearts.

> " Mourn not for them that mourn
> For sin's keen arrow with its rankling smart,
> God's hand will bind again what He hath torn,
>   He heals the broken heart.
>   But weep for him whose eye
> Sees in the midnight skies a starry dome
> Thick sown with worlds that whirl and hurry by,
>   Yet give the heart no home ;
>   Who marks through earth and space
> A strange dumb pageant pass before a vacant shrine,
> And feels within his inmost soul a place
>   Unfilled by the divine."

In the indescribably glorious revelation which this stupendous evolution makes to us of God, we can say with a new meaning and a deeper significance : —

" Thou, Lord, in the beginning hast laid the foundation of the earth, and the heavens are the works of thine hands. They shall perish, but thou remainest, and they all shall wax old as doth a garment, and as a vesture shalt thou fold them up and they shall be changed; but thou art the same, and thy years shall not fail."

www.ingramcontent.com/pod-product-compliance
Lightning Source LLC
Chambersburg PA
CBHW032044220426
43664CB00008B/849